"The weirdest and most curiously fascinating trial in the history of modern jurisprudence."
—*Philadelphia Record*

On November 28, 1928, at one minute past midnight, in a sparsely settled area of York County, Pennsylvania, Nelson Rehmeyer, self-proclaimed witch, was bludgeoned to death. Two days later his body was discovered and the murderers apprehended.

In their confessions, the accused left no doubt that their belief in witchcraft had led to the murder. They stated flatly that Rehmeyer had hexed them and that they were justified in killing him when he refused to give up a lock of hair and his copy of the witches' bible, needed to remove the curse.

In these pages, Arthur H. Lewis tells the whole fascinating story of Rehmeyer's murder and the ensuing trial. And he presents us with startling evidence that witchcraft is being practiced, even today, throughout the Pennsylvania Dutch country.

HEX
was originally published by Trident Press.

Other books by Arthur H. Lewis

La Belle Otero
Lament for the Molly Maguires

Published by Pocket Books

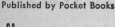 *Are there paperbound books you want
but cannot find in your retail stores?*

You can get any title in print in:
Pocket Book editions • Pocket *Cardinal* editions • Permabook editions or Washington Square Press editions. Simply send retail price, local sales tax, if any, plus 15¢ to cover mailing and handling costs for each book wanted to:
MAIL SERVICE DEPARTMENT
    POCKET BOOKS • A Division of Simon & Schuster, Inc.
    1 West 39th Street • New York, New York 10018
    Please send check or money order. We cannot be responsible for cash.
    Catalogue sent free on request.

Titles in these series are also available at discounts in quantity lots for industrial or sales-promotional use. For details write our Special Projects Agency: The Benjamin Company, Inc., 485 Madison Avenue, New York, N.Y. 10022.

HEX

ARTHUR H. LEWIS

PUBLISHED BY POCKET BOOKS NEW YORK

HEX

Trident edition published February, 1969
Pocket Book edition published May, 1970

This *Pocket Book* edition includes every word
contained in the original, higher-priced edition. It is printed
from brand-new plates made from completely reset, clear, easy-to-read
type. *Pocket Book* editions are published by Pocket Books, a division
of Simon & Schuster, Inc., 630 Fifth Avenue, New York, N.Y. 10020.
Trademarks registered in the United States and other countries.

Standard Book Number: 671—77156—6.
Library of Congress Catalog Card Number: 69—14545.
Copyright, ©, 1969, by Arthur H. Lewis. All rights reserved.

Printed in the U.S.A.

For my mother

Acknowledgments

IN GATHERING MATERIAL FOR THIS BOOK I HAD the help and cooperation of many people and wish to express my gratitude to them. I am particularly indebted to Charles H. Ness, of the Pennsylvania State University Libraries who gave me the idea for writing this book and to William T. Wallace, of York, who opened all paths for me in the hex belt; to Florence Collis, Renée Marke and Arthur L. Redstone for their editorial help; to the publishers and staff members of the *York Gazette and Daily,* the *York Dispatch,* the *Philadelphia Evening Bulletin,* the *Philadelphia Inquirer,* and the Reading Public Library; to Roger R. Angle, *York Gazette and Daily;* Mrs. Gertrude Apfelbaum, former publisher, Jim Thorpe (Pa.) *Times-Herald;* H. Michael Barnhart; Thomas Barrett, City Editor, Shenandoah (Pa.) *Evening Herald;* Mrs. Helen Bechtel; Mary and Knowles Blanchard; Mr. Justice Herbert B. Cohen, Supreme Court, Commonwealth of Pennsylvania; Joseph H. Davies, Associate Editor, Mahanoy City (Pa.) *Record-American;* Arthur W. Geiselman, Jr., *Baltimore Evening Sun;* Paul J. Gernert, Chairman, Pennsylvania Board of Pardons; Judge (Ret.) Harvey A. Gross; Earl Helfrick; Col. (Ret.) Wayne Homan; Dr. J. A. Hunt, former president, York County Medical Society; Harry P. Kissinger; William J. Krencewicz, Esq.; Herbert B. Krone; Herbert Lee; Bernard L. Lemisch, Esq.; Mrs. Mariska MacFarland; L. F. McCullough; Carlisle Mitzell, *York Gazette and Daily;* Rev. Charles M. Mitzell; McKinley C. Olsen, City Editor, *York Gazette and Daily;* Mrs. Leah W. Paules, First Deputy, Clerk of Court's Office, York County; Walter Partymiller, *York Gazette and Daily;* Louis F. Rauco, Newspaper Dept., Library of the Commonwealth of Pennsylvania; John F. Rauhauser, Jr., District Attorney, York County; Wayde P. Seidensticker, Esq.; Miss Ellen Shaffer; Herbert Davis and members of the staff of the Free Library of Philadelphia; Miss Katherine Abigail Shorey, Librarian; Miss Romaine Spangler and members of the staff of the Martin Memorial Library, York; Mrs. Anna Snelbecker, *York Dispatch;* Judge (Retired) Ray P. Sherwood; Curtis A. Thomas, former reporter, *York Dispatch* and *Harrisburg Patriot;* Walter W. VanBaman, Esq.; John Waltmeyer, County Editor, *York Dispatch;* and Dr. Baruch Weitzel, Professor of Religion, Dropsie College, Philadelphia, Pa.

HEX

1

THE JUDGE TURNED SIGHTLESS EYES IN MY DIrection, pulled on his meerschaum, then sank into the chair that Mrs. Sherwood said was tailored to fit her husband's lean, six-foot four-inch frame. He took a half-dozen leisurely puffs while I patiently watched the smoke curl out of floor-to-ceiling windows and sweep into a garden filled with York County's famed white roses.

Curt Thomas, who used to cover the courthouse for the *York Dispatch* and the *Harrisburg Patriot,* had forewarned me not to hurry the Judge or interrupt him with questions. So for three hours I hardly uttered a word while my host, in a voice that strongly belied his ninety-two years (and in a manner far more gracious than I'd been led to expect), reminisced about America's most notorious witchcraft trials since Salem.

Despite what today appears to be overwhelming evidence to the contrary, retired Judge Ray P. Sherwood is convinced justice was delivered in his Court of Oyer and Terminer in January of 1929. It was then that a self-confessed witch and two teen-age accomplices were found guilty of murdering another witch because he refused to surrender a lock of his hair and his working copy of the hexer's bible, John George Homan's *The Long Lost Friend.*

A study of the testimony clearly reveals the agonies of

the "hexed" and their sick compulsion to rid themselves of spells cast upon them by using the one unfailing method learned almost at the cradle. Yet Judge Sherwood, whose opinion is far from unique in York County, is still unwilling to accept the face-saving farce that this was a simple case of murder for profit. The profit?—ninety-seven pennies.

His Honor's point of view, in contrast to that held by disenchanted members of the working press who covered the trials, is shared by the first jury's foreman and two of the three defense lawyers. The third attorney, now Mr. Justice Herbert B. Cohen of the Pennsylvania State Supreme Court, begs to dissent.

Judge Sherwood is convinced a change of venue (admittedly none was asked for) was not necessary. This, despite a county-wide pre-trial atmosphere of hate for the three prisoners who exposed the Pennsylvania Dutch and their curiously medieval mores to an amused world. Actually, what the "People" wanted more than anything else was to end the trials swiftly so that the "furrin" press would go home and stop trapping unwary "Dumb Dutchmen" into silly but quotable answers to loaded questions.

The Judge challenges neither the abilities nor the wisdom of defense counsel, who accepted with unseemly alacrity—perhaps even with relief—the harsh verdicts, swiftly rendered, and made only token efforts to secure new trials, although even a cursory reading of the records reveals countless errors and unfair charges to the juries.

At last Judge Sherwood concluded his flow of recollections, then answered my queries with grave courtesy. When I, too, had finished he smiled slightly as still another memory took possession of him.

"If you're looking for a villain [I wasn't], forget about witches, 'hexerei,' potions and incantation manuals. You're not likely to find them in York. At one time I don't doubt we had quite a few powwowers in the wilds of the county but I would assume they went out of business years ago."

He chuckled. "I'm Scotch-Irish, myself. But I suppose everybody old enough to have lived among the Pennsylvania Dutch in bygone days had some contact with one of those well-meaning people—perhaps his parents took him to a powwower to have a wart removed.

"No, the real villain in the piece was Mr. Dudley Nichols, a newspaperman who covered the murder for the *New York World*.

"He was an excellent writer, I do admit, but he used vitriol instead of ink. Called us stupid clods and twentieth-century anachronisms, bound by fifteenth-century superstitions. He laid it on thick before, during and after the trials. It was he who led the pack in public abuse of the community. I can be amused now but at that time I assure you I was not."

He turned grim, but only for a moment. Then his expression lightened and he went on.

"I granted severances. Blymire, the first defendant, a self-proclaimed 'witch,' was scheduled for trial Monday, January 8, 1929. On the Sunday afternoon before, I was standing at the bar of the Lafayette Club—you know the one just off the Square on Market Street. It's a private organization, you know.

"York was filled with newspapermen from all over the country, in addition to a couple of foreign correspondents who were here to dissect us. We'd extended guest privileges to a few of these gentlemen, one of whom was Mr. Nichols. I recall quite vividly his pre-trial story that Sunday morning. It was one of his best, or worst, depending upon your point of view. It was about superstitions, ours in particular.

"At the moment I speak of, Mr. Nichols was offering a pack of cigarettes to his companions, one of whom was Mr. John McCullough of the *Philadelphia Inquirer,* and the other a representative of the *New York Times* whose name evades me at the moment. Each of the two accepted a cigarette.

"I probably wouldn't have noticed Nichols' next action if he had not extracted some of those long, blue- and red-tipped kitchen matches from his pocket. First, he lit Mr. McCullough's cigarette, next that of the *Time's* man. Then he blew out the match, struck a fresh one and lit his own.

"At this precise juncture, I caught Mr. Nichols' eye

3

and held it for a second. At least he had the decency to blush."

I laughed and was about to make a couple of confessions of my own. Instead I thanked the Judge for his kindness and drove back to my hotel. What I'd thought of revealing was my own youthful experience with a powwower.

Since early childhood I'd been troubled with a wart that grew to huge proportions on the fourth finger of my right hand, exactly at the knuckle. By the time I reached high school, it was so large it kept getting in my way, bumping into my violin bow, the sleeves of my shirts and jackets, the handlebar of my bicycle and assorted basketballs, baseballs and footballs.

My mother tried home remedies; our family physician attempted electrolysis; his son used a Remington .22 at close range. I might add that had John Reilly, Jr., not been such a poor marksman and missed me completely I would have lost the parasitic growth only because it no longer would have had a finger to feed upon.

I even attempted my own pharmacodynamics, ranging from sudden, furious bites to the use of nitric acid. This last was the most effective of all, temporarily at any rate. However, I discovered that constant application of that highly potent chemical kept exposing increasingly larger portions of bone and tissue.

Finally, during my senior year in high school, I was freed of my wart forever; I naturally say that with fingers crossed. In my home town of Mahanoy City, where a fairly large proportion of the polyglot population is of Pennsylvania Dutch origin, lived an elderly powwower named Lena Quinn. Pennsylvania Dutch herself, she acquired her Irish surname through marriage.

No member of my family had ever felt called upon to seek Lena's services. We relied more rather than less upon the skills of John M. Reilly, M.D., for disorders of the body, as we did upon my mother, who organized the local chapter of the Delphian Society, for vagaries of the spirit. As a matter of fact, my grandmother, although of German extraction, was something of an iconoclast and braved the devil himself by once calling Mrs. Quinn a "faker." My father, born on a farm near the Carpathian Mountains where vampires flourished, was understandably less skeptical.

Lena was a tolerant woman who did not allow the quarrel between my grandmother and herself to extend beyond their generation. Consequently she greeted me at Triers' Corner one autumn evening in 1922 with as much cordiality as she extended to my best friend, Joseph X. Kaier. Triers' Corner, with its antiquated tailor shop inside and a couple of hard benches outside, was an informal but highly respectable meeting place for the town's elders.

It had been a bad day for my wart and consequently for me. I'd attempted surgery with a red-hot pair of plumbers' pliers but the only results were a completely ruined glove and horribly painful second-degree burns. Lena took a quick glance at the wart, then averted her eyes. I didn't blame her; the growth, now a furiously angry crimson, resembled the headlight of a miniature locomotive.

"What did you do to your hand?" she asked, almost in horror.

I answered in full.

"Would you like to get rid of that wart?"

I assured her I'd be eternally grateful for whatever she could do, even if it was only the reduction of my wart to a size I could live with.

She nodded understandingly and took me to one side where we would not be overheard.

"Go over to Tulin's [a local poultry dealer] and get a pair of fresh chicken feet. Roast them over the coals and rub the drippings on your wart. Then bury them under the eaves of your house. When the chicken feet rot, so will your wart."

She then took my disfigured right hand and placed it tightly against her left palm. Next she bent down, blew her breath on the wart, then whispered some unintelligible incantation. She said "Jesus" three times, made the sign of the cross and dismissed me.

My friend Joe, a devout Roman Catholic, burst out laughing when I repeated Lena's instructions. Nevertheless, he went with me to Tulin's the following morning. I'd have gone there at once except that I knew the store was closed for the day.

Joe was my lookout man while I sneaked into our kitchen and toasted chicken feet over the coals, letting fat pour on my offending wart. I ran into an immediate problem when I discovered our house had no visible eaves, whereupon Joe kindly volunteered the use of his, which had. So, a half-hour later, with my friend performing the proper obsequies, we buried the feet in Kaiers' back garden.

Two weeks later my wart disappeared, apparently forever (nearly half a century later, my fingers are still crossed). This, however, was not the end of my adventure into the occult. About a month afterward, Joe, with a sheepish grin on his face, pointed to the fourth finger of his left hand where blossomed a smaller edition of "my" old wart.

I attended Joe's wake, held the evening after his death in February, 1959. There, on the fourth finger of his left hand, was the wart.

A second confession I'd thought of making to Judge Sherwood was that in my pocket I carried not only a copy of *The Long Lost Friend* I'd bought in York that morning but also a "Himmels-brief," guaranteed to protect the home against fire and pestilence. This had been given to me by a witch who practices both branches of his profession—"white" and "black" magic—less than a ten-minute walk from the Sherwood residence.

"White" magic, parenthetically, consists only of healing and, as they say in the area, is "chust for good." "Black" magic, on the contrary, is an evocation of the devil or the placement of a hex, a witch's curse, on some unsuspecting victim.

This practitioner of occult science, Erwin B. Emig, operates an office on one of York's main residential streets. Every evening, from seven until ten o'clock, he treats the real and imagined illnesses of patients who come from as far away as two hundred miles, although the majority of them live within a twenty-mile radius of

6

the city. He also exorcises spells from the hexed and, if properly rewarded, can be persuaded to cast a few reputedly effective counter-charms of his own. His only physical equipment for the miraculous successes he claims to have accomplished these past sixty years consists of two enormous family Bibles, a miscellaneous book or two and a highly polished oval stone about the size of a pullet egg.

Mr. Emig is by no means the sole survivor of a dying profession. For two months I visited a score or more of witches, powwowers, hexers and other dealers in black and white magic all over York, Lancaster, Dauphin, Schuylkill, Carbon and other counties where the Pennsylvania Dutch influence is strong. I'm sure I merely touched the surface.

I spent hours with a lady of ninety-four, a practicing powwower for the past seventy-nine years, whose clients, many ailing, kneel before her on the first and sixteenth of each month. She cures wildfire (erysipelas), stops blood, removes warts, heals third-degree burns quickly and painlessly and reverses the process of "opnema," the "wasting away." Herself a one-time victim of a hex that almost destroyed her, Mrs. Leah Frank refuses to practice black arts although she knows that the part of southern York County where she lives abounds in witches who prey on neighboring farmers.

There is a fifty-two-year-old Lancaster County gunsmith named Clair Frank (no kin to Mrs. Leah) whose life is protected by five invisible Indian guides, given or loaned to him by St. Peter one memorable night in 1939. When danger or disease threatens the well-being of this practitioner's patients, the quintet and their leader render them similar, albeit temporary, services.

Should a problem in hexerei seem unsolvable or a disease too severe even for the combined efforts of the gunsmith and his redskins, help is close at hand. His oldest son is the possessor of fifteen ectoplasmic Algonquins.

"Professor" Howard C. Resh of Hanover, Pennsylvania, practices his brand of powwowing, hexerei and faith healing in the dingy, Bible-laden parlor of his Victorian

7

monstrosity on the city's main business street. He openly advertises his profession on a three- by five-foot shingle hanging from his front porch, clearly visible from the highway below.

In Nesquehoning, Carbon County, Pennsylvania, there is a middle-aged powwower who uses holy water exclusively for her cures. Near Allentown, a fourteen-year-old girl who only recently discovered her powers is so busy with patients her high school studies are being neglected.

There is no doubt that the majority of these powwowers, faith healers, hexers, witches or *brauchers*—whatever they choose to call themselves or are labeled by clients— are sincere. They truly believe their supernatural gifts have been granted them by the Almighty through Christ's healing hands. The Bible is their *materia medica,* and, as did the ancient Jews in the cabala, they believe every word and symbol has a hidden meaning.

Most of these practitioners, and their patients as well, are convinced not only of the inherent ability of their favorite witch to heal or to remove a hex, but also of his power to cast a spell of his own should he be so motivated. Few necromancers will discuss this latter branch of their discipline; fewer still will admit counseling a client to resort to violence when all else fails.

Yet, in the Keystone State's Pennsylvania Dutch counties, there have been many murders directly attributable to sorcerers. One of the better known of these homicides was the 1934 slaying of Mrs. Susan Mummey, the "Witch of Ringtown Valley," while the most famous of all was that of Nelson D. Rehmeyer of Rehmeyer's Hollow, bludgeoned to death in 1928 at one minute past midnight beneath a full November moon.

2

AMONG THE MANY NECROMANCERS SCATTERED throughout rural and urban York County in the mid-twenties (one authority estimates their number to be in excess of a thousand), it would be difficult to find a more wretched, frustrated failure than John H. Blymire.

Quite a few experts stoutly maintain that the mystic powers of necromancy can be given by, taught to or inherited only from a member of the opposite sex. Thus, state these theorists, if a warlock (this classical name for a male witch is practically unknown in Pennsylvania Dutch territory) dies without female issue, his powers die with him.

A potent refutation of this principle is the family Blymire. John H. was a fourth-generation witch. Under normal circumstances this phenomenon of birth should have given him health, the fear of his family, the admiration of his patients and the respect of his colleagues. His cures and hexes should have been effective, and his large clientele should have included a high percentage of referrals from less powerful witches.

Instead, Blymire was sickly; his wife divorced him; his patients deserted him; his colleagues laughed at him; and, as for his curative powers, he had trouble "stopping blood," a *sine qua non* for even the most ineffectual of powwowers.

Blymire's ancestors, who came from the Palatinate, settled in Pennsylvania about 1799 on a farm at Hallam, in the east-central part of York County; there they have remained for almost one hundred seventy-five years. John's great, great grandfather was the first to arrive in the New World. Little is known about him; even his Christian name has been forgotten.

His son Jacob was born on the farm on November 17, 1819, the day and perhaps even the hour when Pennsylvania's most famous witch, "Mountain Mary," died in her tiny apple orchard in Oley Hills, Bucks County. Many, including his son Andrew, claim Jacob, who had a strange fondness for owls, was the spiritual legatee of "Die Berg Maria's" occult powers, which in turn were passed on to two more generations of Blymires. As subsequent events proved, they never got as far as John; or if they did, their efficacy by that time had become greatly diminished.

"Mountain Mary," wrote Frank Brown in the spring, 1966, issue of *Pennsylvania Folklore,* "frequently related that an owl came and drank out of her milk pail every evening when she was milking. She could not prevent the bird from getting near the pail except by catching it, since it was so tame that it couldn't be scared away.

"So one night she caught the owl and burned its feet slightly, holding it over the fire. The next morning a neighboring woman, whom she took to be the witch, couldn't put on her shoes on account of burned feet."

Andrew Blymire, born at Hallam in 1838, still alert and a practicing witch ninety-one years later, recalled his father vividly.

"He was the seventh son of a seventh son," this nonagenarian told an Associated Press reporter. Fortunately for posterity that otherwise unidentified member of the working press must have understood Pennsylvania Dutch, old Andrew Blymire's sole means of communication, since this ancient could neither read nor write and never mastered more than a few words of English.

"My father was a great healer; he could perform miracles. He had the power, maybe from 'Die Berg Maria.' He always had a pet owl that could talk. No matter how sick a body was he could cure him. Wunst when I was a little boy a neighbor came into our house screaming with the wildfire that was spread all over his body.

"*I* know how to relieve the wildfire, too, but not near so fast as my father could. In two minutes it was gone and the neighbor went home completely better and it never came back to bother him."

The reporter asked Blymire if he could describe the cure. The old man shrugged his shoulders.

"Very easy," he said. "Make the sign of the cross three times over every part of the wildfire with your hand. Then repeat, three times:

> Wildfire and the dragon, flew over a wagon
> The wildfire abated and the dragon skeated.

A painless, bloodless, non-surgical yet certain cure for hernia, one the famous Viennese surgeon Dr. Adolph Lorenz might have envied, was a specialty of the Blymires from Jacob through Emanuel.

"We used the 'egg treatment,' " Andrew told the reporter, but he refused to elaborate. However, this unfailing remedy for hernia was described by Robert I. Graham in the *Pennsylvania Dutchman* of April 1, 1951.

"The patient would get an egg from the nest of a black hen and then not speak to anyone. . . . When the patient brought the egg back to the [witch] doctor's office, the doctor would rub the egg across the ruptured area three times and then put the egg in an oven and close the door. When the white and the yolk of this egg are completely evaporated, the rupture of the patient would be gone."

The ability to cure was not the only power Andrew ascribed to his father and to himself and his son as well.

"If a man's cow dried up," recalled Andrew, "if his crops failed, if his wife could have no more babies, if his children got the liver complaint or the wasting away, my father knew right away who put the hex on. My father could take it off and put a strong one himself on the man who deserved it, whenever he wanted to.

"And all the time his pet owl that was pretty near a

hundred years old sat on his shoulder. I can hex the same and so can Emanuel. They come from all over to see us when they have troubles."

"What about your grandson John?" the reporter asked.

The old man sighed deeply before answering.

"Ach! Poor John. Maybe onct he could and maybe onct again he can now that the witch is dead."

John was born in a frame house his grandfather had built. It was on the same land his great grandfather farmed although, because each generation of Blymires left a smaller inheritance than it received, at John's birth little more than a truck patch remained from an original grant of three hundred twenty acres.

As a small child, John certainly must have been aware of his occult power. However, he was given little chance to use it because both his father and grandfather were active in their chosen field and had citizens from all over the city and county of York among their clients.

Completely ruled by superstition, this was a strange household in which John was born and raised. Yet his upbringing was hardly unique in that predominantly Pennsylvania Dutch section of the Keystone State.

"At least half of the 60,000 residents of the City of York believe in witchcraft," County Coroner L. U. Zech told Lockwood Phillips in the *New York Evening World,* January 2, 1929.

"And, as for the county's urban population of 90,000," he went on, "they not only believe in witchcraft but guide the minutest details of their lives by it."

The Coroner's opinions were substantiated by the *Pittsburgh Post-Gazette's* Ray Sprigle, later a Pulitzer Prize winner.

"No one who has not visited . . . Lancaster and York Counties," wrote Sprigle, "talked to physicians and county officials, listened to the conversation of the people in the streets and stores, can conceive of the grip that witchcraft and sorcery have in these communities.

"Officials in York will assure you that there are powwow doctors operating here whose fathers and grandfathers were powwow doctors."

Little, if anything, was ever done spontaneously in the

Blymire home. Nearly every movement each member of the family made, from John's aged great grandfather Andrew to his youngest sister Katrina, who died of "sickness in the head" at the age of eleven, was guided by rigid rules laid down in *The Long Lost Friend* and other vulgates.

One should neither plant nor construct anything on Ascension Day; otherwise the crops will fail and the buildings burn or be struck by lightning. Vinegar barrels must be stirred on the first Friday before the new moon. A baby should be carried to the attic as soon after birth as possible so it will grow up with a "high mind."

"A blossom on a fruit tree out of time is an omen of death," wrote John R. Mumaw, a collector of Pennsylvania Dutch folklore. "And a bird fluttering at the window after nightfall is an omen of death. It is a bad omen to fall sick on Sunday. If celery shoots seed the first year, it is a sign that someone in the family will die.

"The striking of the clock at the hour of twelve, while the family is seated at the table, is an omen of death. If, when one is churning butter, the butter fat will not gather, drive a nail into the floor at each leg of the churn. In that way the enchantment is destroyed and you will soon have butter. One takes a calf out of the stable backward so the cow will not get homesick for it.

> *Raya, raya drupa*
> *De boova mus m'r glupa.*

"This is a charm used to call for rain. The words are repeated while knocking together stones held in the hand."

Each month had certain "unlucky" days, when families were cautioned to remain close to their own firesides; if not they would be struck by some misfortune. For example, on June 17, one should neither work nor travel. October 6 was a bad time to start a lawsuit; August 20, the worst day of the year to become betrothed; and December 11, the most awful day to marry.

Sometime during each of John's mother's many pregnancies (she bore five girls and two boys and had at least

13

as many stillbirths and miscarriages), Emanuel tied a "Himmels-brief" around his wife's neck with a three-looped string. There it remained until after delivery. Translated from the German, the lengthy Himmels-brief reads in part:

"The blood of Jesus Christ, who is both God and man, protect me N. N. from all kinds of weapons and shields, guns and ammunition, long or short swords . . . or anything like them that have been fashioned since the birth of Christ. . . .

"Jesus Christ, protect me N. N. from all bad conspiracies from behind; . . . magic, traps or snares, and all kinds of enemies, both visible and invisible. . . .

"May the only true God protect me N. N. through the terrible suffering and dying and through the rose-colored blood which was on the cross. . . .

"Blood and power keep your strength, as Christ kept His, when He was martyred. With His holy five wounds you are connected and bound. All powers and strength must disappear before me as the men have disappeared who bound the hands of the Lord Christ to the cross. In the name of God, the Father, the Son, and the Holy Ghost. . . .

"Give strength to my right hand so that when I come into a strange land, no enemy or magician may harm or disturb me. + + +

"X X Z

"X. S. E. X. K. A. G. M. A. H. O.

"N. G. S. K. ss K Geistes

"Any woman in confinement, if she places this letter about her neck, will be delivered without danger."

John, who'd been seeing "visions" since the age of four, was less than seven years old when he "tried for" his first sickness. Grandfather Andrew, then about sixty-five, was experiencing difficulty passing water.

"My father killed an old hog," John told Dr. N. S. Yawger, psychiatrist at Eastern State Penitentiary. "Then he removed its bladder and burned it.

"After the ashes cooled, he told me to scrape them up with a spoon and feed them to Grandpa. I did and he swallowed them. Then I touched Grandpa's stomach all around where it hurt him and made the sign of the cross. After this I said the Lord's Prayer three times.

"When I got finished Grandpa stood up and passed his water easy. He didn't have no trouble with his bladder again."

John's first attempt at powwowing must be labeled a complete success. Old Andrew died in 1933 at the age of ninety-five without, it seems, ever having had any reason to consult a urologist.

Except for John, none of the Blymire siblings ever claimed occult powers or the ability to try for illnesses. An older sister, Helga, once had "visions" but nothing ever came of them and she died in a York County mental institution.

John was almost eight years old before he went to school and then it was only because of the intervention of truant officers, who had difficulty persuading Emanuel and his wife that a formal education for their children was not only important but compulsory.

John attended the same one-room rural schoolhouse where his sisters and brother went for brief, interrupted periods in their lives. His education could not have exceeded five eight-month terms broken frequently by his own sickness, the sicknesses of those for whom he was beginning to powwow or the necessity of performing household chores.

John's teacher, who saw him through his doubtful progression from first to fourth grade, had some recollections of her charge.

"He was not a very impressive little boy," Mrs. Olga Fochs told a reporter for the Philadelphia *Record,* "and not much different from some of his brothers and sisters, although I remember a couple of them better than I do John.

"He was a homely child with a long, pointy nose, and the other children made fun of him. I think he was too awkward to play games with his classmates, and usually sat around watching them at recess. They'd all heard about his 'supernatural' gifts and I think they were a little bit afraid of him. I know I was when he used to sit and stare. But I'm sure he meant no harm to me or to

15

anyone. At heart I think he must have been good and kind, just an unfortunate victim of his environment and upbringing.

"When I taught we had no Binet-Simon I.Q. tests, at least in my area, so I had no real way of measuring his intelligence. But I'd guess he was what we called 'slow normal,' perhaps *very* slow normal."

John was not what his impassioned lawyer labeled "feeble-minded." However, prison psychologists who later measured Blymire's intelligence quotient placed it in an area ranging between 78 and 85, a condition they term "dull normal."

Except for the fact that he was several inches shorter, John bore a striking physical resemblance to his father, who, wrote Ken Mack in the Philadelphia *Record,* "was as strange a figure as ever took oath as a witness in a Pennsylvania courtroom. Tall and emaciated, he had the look of some prehistoric bird."

Barely able to read and write, John left school at thirteen and got a job in a York cigar factory. His work record was spotty, interrupted by frequent absences to cure for illnesses incurred by neighbors, friends of the family and fellow employees. The latter, not averse to using John's services when a more experienced powwower was unavailable, regarded him with an admixture of fear and scorn.

Apparently John's cures were effective and long-lasting. One is remembered some fifty-eight years later by Albert Wagner, now a resident of a nursing home outside of Pittsburgh, Pennsylvania, but in 1911, Blymire's fellow employee at the factory.

"I had a terrible wheal in my right eye," recalled Wagner. "It never got no better and it used to pain me all the time so bad I couldn't sleep. I went to lots of healers but none of 'em could do nothin' and I gave 'em lots of money.

"This funny-looking kid John Blymire was workin' next to me. I heard his family did powwowin' and that they was pretty good but I didn't know 'em or where they was livin', and I'd heard John done some hisself.

"Well, one day when the pain got very bad, at

lunchtime, I says, 'John, do you think your papa or grandpop could cure my eye?' He looked at me and says, 'I can do it myself.' He was pretty young and I didn't exactly want to take a chanct but I guess I was desperate, so I asked him what I should do."

Wagner said Blymire glanced at the wheal before giving out instructions.

"He told me to bring in a dirty supper plate to work the next mornin'," Wagner continued. "I done what he said. I handed the plate to John and he put the side I et on against the sore eye and held it there a couple minutes.

"He kept on sayin' somethin' soft to hisself, kind of under his breath so I couldn't understand what it was. Then he took the plate away, stomped it to pieces, made the sign of the cross three times on my eye and told me I'd be better the next day.

"By God! Sure enough he was right. I slept good that night, the first time in months. When I woke up the next morning the wheal was gone altogether and I never had none again me whole life."

John's reputation for healing spread throughout the cigar factory and its environs. Like his fellow practitioners, he asked no fee and accepted with gratitude whatever was given to him. Frequently he was paid nothing for his services, nor was he compensated for earnings he lost because his pay was based on "piecework." All this must have been of considerable annoyance to members of York County's medical association, who were unable to compete with John and his colleagues quantitatively, qualitatively or pricewise.

In a household less accustomed to instant cures and black magic, the fifteen-year-old John might have become an egotist. Instead, he was rather humble and took for granted his powers to heal and, later, to punish.

3

TECHNICALLY SPEAKING, THE BLYMIRES WERE Lutherans, but except for weddings and funerals they rarely attended services at St. John's, the small church which served local farmers of that Christian denomination. Even though a large family Bible was to be seen in the Blymire parlor and a half-dozen pictures of Christ adorned the walls, their true Holy Writ, as in hundreds of other Pennsylvania Dutch households, was John George Homan's *The Long Lost Friend*.

Homan was born in Germany about 1775. On October 2, 1802, he and his wife, Anna Catherine, and one or possibly two of their children, arrived in Philadelphia on the sailing ship *Tom*.

"Anna Catherine," wrote Wilbur H. Oda in a publication of the Berks County Historical Society, "was indentured to Samuel Newbold, a farmer who lived in Burlington County, New Jersey. Homan (spelled variously as Hohmann, Homann and Hohman) bound himself as a servant to Adam Frankenfiehl . . . of Springfield Township, Bucks County, Pennsylvania.

"He was to serve there for three years and six months and to receive customary freedom, suits and twenty dollars in exchange for payment of his passage, which amounted to eighty-four dollars."

Homan and Anna Catherine served their individual

18

masters faithfully and upon their release from bondage joined each other to set up a household, first near Easton and finally, about 1811, in District Township near Reading.

A devout Roman Catholic, of whom there were comparatively few in Pennsylvania at the turn of the nineteenth century, Homan was a great believer in faith healing and the laying on of hands. He based his doctrine on the Fiftieth Psalm: "Call Me in the day of trouble. I shall deliver thee; thou shalt glorify Me."

Although he provided the pharmacopoeia and methodology for future generations of powwowers, Homan claimed he, himself, was no hexer. He announced this, according to Oda, in an 1816 broadside that stated, "When you buy a book from Homan, you never receive a Hexbook," as self-deluding a proclamation as can be imagined.

Homan's first appearance as an author took place about 1805 when he had someone run off a few hundred copies of a ballad he wrote. Despite the fact that his royalties amounted to less than a quarter of printing costs, Homan, like so many of his predecessors and successors, discovered seeing his name in print was a heady beverage. From that moment on he decided he would attempt to support his family on the precarious earnings of an author.

It is more than likely that Homan, in order to supplement what must have been a meager income indeed, resorted to less inspirational forms of creativity, including farming and perhaps even practicing what he preached in *The Long Lost Friend*.

As a farmer he was a failure (his five acres were sold out by the sheriff in 1825) and as a necromancer and visionary he could hardly be considered an overwhelming success. According to the Reading (Pennsylvania) *Adler* of January 28, 1823, Homan couldn't even find his own lost dog.

"On the night of January 5," he complained in a paid advertisement, "my little dog was either stolen or ran away. He was of grayish color, white around the neck, medium-sized with a stub tail. Around his neck was a

19

ribbon with a yellow ring. Whoever gives the undersigned any news of this little dog will receive a suitable reward for his trouble. By John George Homan."

The first edition of *The Long Lost Friend (Der Lang Verbogene Freund)* rolled off the presses at Reading, Pennsylvania, in 1819. While it was not an immediate success and never provided financial security for its author-editor, its success was a lasting one. An estimated one hundred fifty separate editions of this book (one as recent as 1958), totaling perhaps a half-million copies in all, have been published in the last century and a half. The eighty-four-page volume can be found wherever superstition prevails—meaning, of course, in most of the civilized world.

The book is a mishmash of original material, ancient Egyptian medicine, German Folklore, sorcery, gypsy magic, palliatives from the British Isles, "wisdom" from the Hebrew cabala and the transcendentalism of Albert Magnus, plus one highly recommended formula, the well-known Sator palindrome:

```
S A T O R
A R E P O
T E N E T
O P E R A
R O T A S
```

John Blymire told his prison psychiatrist he did not remember when he first acquired his own copy of *The Long Lost Friend,* he thought when he was fifteen or sixteen years of age. Had he heeded the admonition clearly stated on the last page of this slim volume, the dreadful misfortunes that dogged him the rest of his life probably would never have taken place.

On page eighty-four, Homan says with the utmost clarity:

"Whoever carries this book with him, is safe from all his enemies, visible or invisible: and whoever has this book with him cannot die without the holy corpse of Jesus Christ, nor drown in any water, nor burn up in any fire, nor can any unjust sentence be passed upon him. So help me."

Although neither reading nor any other mental exercise came easily to John H. Blymire, he still managed to memorize many lines in *The Long Lost Friend*. As a consequence, by the age of sixteen he was able to cope with almost any unusual situation.

He could cure a bite from the most dangerous snakes in the area—rattlers and copperheads—merely by touching the victim's wound with his fingertips, making the sign of the cross three times and muttering the following verse:

> God has created all things and they were good;
> Thou only, serpent, art damned.
> Cursed be thou and thy sting.
> Zing, zing, zing!

To replenish a man's sexual powers John's simple (and certainly pleasurable) prescription was a shot of rye whiskey with a dash of bitters, to be taken every morning. Patients opposed to alcoholic beverages in any form were given a dismal alternative—tea brewed from the acorns of a white oak and drunk without sugar or milk.

The high point in John's life came when he remembered, at the right time, the exact manner in which Homan provided the true believer with complete immunity against mad dogs. The event occurred in the summer of 1912 when Blymire was about seventeen and had been working in the cigar factory a little more than a year.

It was then, according to Amos King, who died a few months ago in a Chester, Pennsylvania, nursing home, that a mad dog ran through the street directly in front of a cigar factory where he and Blymire wrapped cigars.

"It happened just as the men were leavin' work for the day," the eighty-eight-year-old King said. "I didn't know Blymire at all. Only afterward I found out he was a powwower and maybe a witch.

"Well, this day I'm tellin' you about, it was very hot. Around five o'clock quittin' time, we was pilin' out of the door to go home. I lived in York then.

21

"All of a sudden somebody yells out, 'Mad dog! Mad dog!' and I looks up and sees a big brown collie tearin' down the sidewalk with froth comin' out of his mouth. He was headed straight for me and some fellows I was with.

"We all scrambled around, scared to death, and tried to push our way back in the factory to get out of his way. But we couldn't do nothin'; the other men were comin' out blockin' the door in. There must have been four, five hundred workin' inside and only one double door out so it was jammed."

King sucked on the "stogie" he was chewing, gathered a mouthful of brown saliva and aimed at a brass cuspidor within inches of my foot and at least four feet from his. After a sharp ping signaled a direct hit, King continued.

"We was sweatin' and pushin' and shovin' and some of us was screamin' with fear when a scrawny boy runs out right in front of the mad dog. Somebody shouts out who it is. I know now it was Blymire but I didn't know then.

"Well this skinny kid stands there blockin' the dog's path and the collie stops dead in his tracks although the foam was still comin' out of his mouth and he was howlin' crazy-like. Blymire looks the dog right in the eye and whispers somethin' to him. ['Dog hold thy nose to the ground. God has made me and thee, hound!' according to Homan.]

"Even though we all got very quiet all of a sudden so you could almost hear a pin drop, the only thing we could hear was the dog pantin'. Then John makes the sign of the cross over the collie's head.

"What happened next we couldn't believe our eyes. This here big dog stops frothin' at the mouth. Before we know it, John's pattin' his head and the dog's lickin' his hand. Then Blymire walks down the street and the dog follows, waggin' his tail like he belonged to him. I tell you, the next day we all of us knew who John H. Blymire was."

But John's triumph was short-lived. Soon after, somebody put a "hex" on him.

"A stronger power than I had got hold of me; tormented me almost every day of my life from then on," he later told counsel. "I couldn't eat; I couldn't sleep; my skin was getting too loose on me and I had the opnema. I couldn't take away anybody's hex no more and I couldn't put none on."

Blymire grew morose and while he still powwowed and was able to retain some of his clients, he had lost much of his enthusiasm and all of his confidence, a sad state of affairs for anyone; for a faith healer it was disastrous.

For the next fifteen years, until he cried out in triumph, "I killed the witch!" John's life was to become a zigzag flight from one necromancer to another all over York, Lancaster, Dauphin and Berks Counties in an increasingly frantic effort to find out who had put the hex on him.

Neither his father, who had considerable success tracking down powwowers guilty of casting spells on clients, nor old Andrew, who was even more adept at witch hunting, seemed able to help. They tried every known method, including the "Tetregammate Angen, Jesus Mazarenus, Rex Judeorum," an extremely powerful antidote, one Homan practically guarantees to dissipate the most puissant of hexes.

Each morning before he left home and each evening when he returned from York, John genuflected beneath a highly colored lithograph of Christ on Calvary, in the presence of his father and grandfather, and repeated the following:

"Like unto the cup and the wine, and the holy supper, our dear Lord Jesus Christ gave unto His dear disciples on Maundy Thursday, may the Lord Jesus guard me in daytime, and at night, that no dog may bite me, no wild beast tear me to pieces, no tree fall on me, no water rise against me, no fire-arms injure me, no weapons, no steel, no iron, cut me, no fire burn me, no false sentence fall upon me, no false tongue injure me, no rogue enrage me, and that no fiends, no witchcraft and enchantment can harm me. Amen."

But despite John's diligence and the close cooperation of father and grandfather, this nostrum failed and the hex remained. His appetite was gone and he could not sleep; he continued to lose weight and became so nervous that he jumped in fright at every unexpected sound. One

23

night, shortly after the kitchen clock had struck twelve, John heard a barn owl hoot seven consecutive times. Familiar with the legend of old Jacob Blymire, that seventh son of a seventh son, John was convinced it was the ghost of his great grandfather, buried only a few hundred yards away, who had put the hex on him.

Although John, of all people, should have realized logistics mean little to a witch and nothing to a ghost, he determined to place distance between himself and the family cemetery. Consequently, more in sorrow than in anger, he left home and took a furnished room in the 2700 block of Prospect Avenue.

For a few months longer, Blymire was able to keep his job at the cigar factory and, despite his lack of self-confidence, to maintain a sizable practice, with clients coming to him during and after work or at his living quarters.

John's erstwhile Prospect Avenue landlady has been dead for many years but her daughter, Mrs. Alice Klinedinst, then a teen-ager, remembers Blymire well and recalls the large number of patients who climbed to the lodger's third-floor-back room, there to be powwowed.

"He was a funny, scary little fellow when he lived with us," Mrs. Klinedinst recalled. "Real jittery. If you said anything suddenly behind him when he didn't know you were there, he'd start to twitch so bad you'd think he had the St. Vitus's dance. Until Mom made us stop, my brother and I used to creep up in back of John and slam our books to the ground. He'd jump so high he'd pretty near hit the ceiling.

"Then, the people who used to come to him for pow-wowing, traipsed up and down the stairs at all hours. They said he was a good one, though, and once, when I got sick in the night with awful pains in my stomach, Mom called him. He came right down and tried for me. The terrible ache I had left right away; I fell asleep soon and I was all better by morning.

"He cured for a neighbor's little girl who had the liver complaint and was hexed besides, they say. Well, John healed her and took off the curse. And one time he took off my brother's warts just by touching them with his fingertips, saying something to himself and making the sign of the cross three times."

Mrs. Klinedinst reflected for a moment.

"No," she concluded, "I can't say anything bad about John. Poor fellow, he was very kind and until he got into that awful trouble, you'd think he wouldn't hurt a fly. Some people around here say you really couldn't blame him. Not that I believe in all that stuff about witches and so on, but sometimes a person can have a run of hard luck and you just don't know who to blame."

Blymire quit the factory during the winter of 1913, shortly before his eighteenth birthday. By that time he'd moved from Prospect Avenue and had been in and out of several other rooming houses. He eked out a bare living as a janitor in a York hotel, busboy in a number of local restaurants and assistant to the sexton of a large Presbyterian church. He had just enough money to pay his modest rent, clothe himself in the clean, neat levis he constantly wore and supply himself with the little food he had to buy when he was not working in a place that dispensed it.

He had a few dollars left over every week to pay for the "free offering—give what you want" demanded by witches whose help he sought. When local necromancers failed him, he wandered farther afield. About 1915 or 1916 (Blymire never was too sure of any fixed dates), he traveled to Oley, a village outside of Reading, where he consulted a necromancer he remembered as "Professor Gentzler." The Professor extracted as much as five hundred dollars from young Blymire over a period of six months. He himself was a promising disciple of Berks County's most notorious witch, the late "Doctor" Joseph B. Hageman, who was exposed by the crusading Philadelphia *North American* as an avaricious faker who grew rich preying upon the superstitions of the poor and the ignorant.

4

"THERE IS A WITCH DOCTOR, A BRAGER [SIC], A powwow man, who has a thinly disguised, remunerative practice under the very nose of the Reading authorities," wrote Alice Rix in the *North American,* May 22, 1900. "His name and address are in the Reading Directory— Doctor Joseph B. Hageman, 839 Elm Street—and his waiting room is rarely empty. He sells powders, potions, forbiddings, blessings and charms.

"A gross, grizzled, dirty, old man, huge of head and face and jowl and hanging chin, with the monstrous body, long, thick arms, and short, thick legs of the bear; with big, fat, greasy hands like suet puddings boiled in bags; with squat, square feet; with a mouth open over a single row of brown and broken teeth; with bright, blue, questioning, kindly, smiling eyes—two spots of innocent blue upon a field of filth, forget-me-nots dropped on a dirty heap."

As the *North American* pointed out in that and subsequent issues, Hageman's methodology was typical of the *braucher*—the powwower—of his era. It was the same treatment applied to poor, deluded John H. Blymire by "Professor Gentzler," and is no different from the treatment still used today throughout Pennsylvania's "witch belt," as any interested observer can discover for himself.

Immediately upon the appearance of the *North American* on Reading's streets, the enraged Doctor Hageman brought an action for libel against merchant prince John Wanamaker's powerful newspaper. Hundreds of the *braucher's* patients rushed to his defense and those who were not illiterate penned furious "Letters to the Editor."

Not until March 7, 1903, was the oft-postponed trial begun in Philadelphia's Common Pleas Court No. 1 before Judge McCarthy. Witnesses by the score, all eager to testify in the plaintiff's behalf, jammed the City Hall's fourth-floor corridors.

Stories of miraculous cures and examples of the doctor's ability not only to heal his patients but also to protect them and their families from the machinations of the devil, were related under oath. A Reading alderman swore he was cured of "bad" blood by the regular use of a Dr. Hageman prescription he'd been taking for twenty-five years. Subsequent chemical analysis proved the prescription to consist of 110-proof cherry-flavored grain alcohol.

A farmer's wife averred that the charms she bought from the doctor at five dollars apiece (a replacement was essential every six months) were perfect for stopping the "hysterics" of her two-year-old daughter. A four-by-four-inch piece of burlap over which Hageman had made the sign of the cross three times, sold at a bargain price of $1.75. Placed under the pillow of a Bechtelsville grocery clerk each night, it permanently dispelled a flock of nocturnal witches who'd been flying unmolested in and out of this patient's closed bedroom windows for six years.

Hageman's special Himmels-briefs were sold by the hundreds, at prices ranging from one to twenty-five dollars, depending upon what the traffic would bear. When fire or lightning destroyed the homes where the Himmels-briefs had been hung in every room, the owners sadly admitted, again under oath, that it was their lack of faith rather than the doctor's lack of expertise that had caused the catastrophes.

On the sixth day of the proceedings, Hageman's case fell apart and was dismissed "with prejudice," so it could never be tried again in Philadelphia's courts. Defense counsel forced the plaintiff to admit that he had lied to his own attorneys about scholastic achievements he never possessed and that he actually was practicing medicine without a license, a fact he most vehemently denied at first.

The *North American,* having accomplished its mission to protect the gullible Berks County folk from the wiles of a cunning powwower, now had more column space than ever to promote its own brands of faith healing.

"DEAFNESS CURED," screamed a *North American* advertisement set in twenty-four-point type. " 'Actine' restored my hearing completely after all other remedies failed," testified the Reverend W. H. Moss of Joshua, Texas.

"Child Weakness," whatever *that* meant, "is not a matter of a day but of a steady common sense treatment." This particular "common sense treatment," given without benefit of a physician, consisted of daily doses of Scott's Emulsion at "fifty cents the generous size bottle."

Another paid Texas testimonial appeared in the columns of the *North American.* "My sister contracted a bad cold and became very weak," confided Mr. L. W. Miller, from the town of Dexter in the Lone Star State. "Her physician pronounced the disease CONSUMPTION and said that she could not recover, but a friend recommended *Jayne's Expectorant.* This gave immediate relief and eventually CURED HER."

"Cann's Kidney Cure" permanently relieved Fred J. Rice, a Bethlehem plumber, of "gravel." "Grove's Quinine Tablets" were certified to cure all liver ailments, and this benefactor of mankind also "positively healed stubborn stomach pains." No need for subscribers to the *North American* to rely on Himmels-briefs. Regular users of "California Fig Syrup—Two Dollars a bottle," were "Guaranteed happy homes, good health, and all blessings." What more could a man ask from any patent medicine?

An embittered Hageman, robbed of his dignity and, for the first time, under the close scrutiny of an awakened Berks County medical association, shut up shop forthwith. His dismayed but still loyal patients were forced to seek help elsewhere for their ailments—physical, pathological or demoniacal.

The chief beneficiary of Dr. Hageman's retirement was his star pupil and intern, Professor Gentzler, who informed young John H. Blymire it would take both time and money to determine which witch had been able to place such a powerful hex on a fellow necromancer.

Blymire had little money and not much time, but until he finally lost faith in Professor Gentzler, he commuted a distance of about eighty miles between York and Oley at least twice and often three times a week for a period of more than six months.

There was no direct transportation between York and the little Berks County village where the Professor practiced. When poor, behexed John Blymire had the funds he rode the Pennsylvania Railroad to Harrisburg, changed there for Reading coaches, then walked or hitchhiked a distance of fourteen miles to Professor Gentzler's office. Sometimes he traveled on inter-urban trolleys, walking from the end of one branch to the beginning of another; more often, he hitchhiked the entire way.

"It used to take me around ten or twelve hours to go there and get back to York," Blymire said. "Sometimes, when it snowed hard, it took longer. Couple times I had to sleep in a barn someplace it was drifting too much for anything to get through and then I didn't get home for twenty-four hours."

That, of course, gave John limited time for work, sleep or fun, but by holding night jobs with understanding employers who knew how stubborn a hex could be, Blymire managed to exist. He was then in his nineteenth year and weighed less than a hundred pounds. Winter and summer his head was covered with a battered straw hat, and the long, shiny, black coat and levis he wore hung about him like a scarecrow. His prominent nose seemed to extend farther and farther into the air as his pale cheeks grew thinner and thinner.

The few people who remember John from those days say that a description of him given years later by Ken Mack, staff correspondent for the Philadelphia *Record,* would have been accurate a decade earlier.

"With clothing that fits his scrawny body illy," wrote Mack, "a prominent Adam's apple that bobs in and out every time he swallows and a nose out of proportion to the rest of his face, poor Blymire looks like a sad circus clown or perhaps a comic valentine."

First, Professor Gentzler tried the procedures recognized by most necromancers as effective cures for the hex. He used Himmels-briefs, and when these did not bring forth the desired results, he brought into action Homan's special formula for the relief of particularly difficult cases.

"Christ's cross and Christ's crown, Christ Jesus' colored blood, be thou every hour good," Gentzler had his patient repeat after him every day for two weeks. "God, the Father, is before me; God, the Son, is beside me; God, the Holy Ghost, is behind me. Whoever now is stronger than these three persons may come, by day or night, to attack me."

This, too, failed and, almost as a last resort, the Professor strongly recommended the use of dove's blood, an expensive but highly effective witch's elixir. Taken internally, three drops at a time, twice daily (whether before or after meals could not be learned), it was supposed to bring lasting results.

However, John's hex remained. His anxieties grew, his head ached constantly, his nerves became more and more frayed and other maladies, real and imagined, struck him. He finally concluded that all the Professor's efforts had come to naught. The Professor, on the other hand, averred that John merely had lost faith. In any event, John sought help elsewhere.

At the time, he was living on South Pershing Street, York, in a rooming house operated by Joseph Halloway and his wife Daisy. Blymire had stayed in a succession of rooming houses all over the city, remaining in each until he was asked to leave because of his own eccentric behavior or until he, himself, tried to outguess his unknown hexer by changing his address.

The Halloways had a plump, pretty, seventeen-year-old daughter named Lilly, and John began "keeping company" with her almost from the first moment he set down

30

a battered carpetbag in his landlord's third-floor-rear bedroom. Lilly was the first girl he'd ever squired although, as subsequent events proved, he was not unaware of the facts of life.

With or without the blessings of the bride's parents (nobody remembers or cares), and certainly without much of a dowry, since the Halloways were poor people, Lilly and John were married in 1917 by a local Justice of the Peace.

No one knows the exact day of the ceremony or, as a matter of fact, much about the marriage itself. About all those who were involved and are still living recall is that the newlyweds continued to make their home at the Halloways; that three children were born; and that two of these died shortly after birth, while the third, a girl, survived at least long enough to see her father in the dock.

For perhaps three or four months after his entrance into the state of matrimony, John Blymire believed that he either had outwitted his as yet unrevealed hexer or, after five years of punishment, had earned that witch's absolution.

His headaches and other ailments vanished, his nerves grew strong and he was able to sleep. He got a steady job in a planing mill, and his powwowing, never completely abandoned even during the worst periods of hexerei, seemed to regain its potency. Patients who'd gone elsewhere since John's troubles returned to him for treatment and cure.

For the first time in years John was relatively content. During this brief period of freedom from persecution he actually made attempts, within the limits of his intelligence, to understand something of the blind forces controlling his destiny.

He would have found it difficult, if not impossible, to comprehend abstract doctrines or philosophies. Nevertheless, he was curious about the reasons behind his ability to comfort and heal. It might be noted here that there never has been any doubt in the minds of even the most orthodox members of the medical profession that "faith

31

healing"—frequently by the use of placebos—has cured many a patient of both real and imagined diseases.

An elderly York County general practitioner, whose name Blymire dimly recalled as "Schetzline," apparently took an interest in the youth, loaned him a few simplified medical texts and tried to explain something of the mysteries of the human mind. John could not remember how he met the doctor nor did he recall much of their actual conversations.

"When I said to Dr. Schetzline that a witch had been after me for a long time, he didn't laugh," John told his prison psychologist. "He told me that if a man believed something was true then it *was* true; that it was all in the mind. Then he explained how a sick person wants to be told he would get better and that was as good for patients as most of the prescriptions he gave out.

"I believed then that he was wrong about the witch that was persecuting me. I *know'd* it wasn't just in my mind. I listened to him anyways and I read a couple medical books he gave me. I didn't understand much they said but there was pictures about the human body and I learned what it looked like inside.

"He even examined me and said I might be suffering with the 'melancholy' and that I had a nervous disease he would try to cure. I didn't believe him but I said I'd let him try for me. He gave me medicine and I think maybe it helped some. I don't know. But after a little while I stopped taking it.

"I liked the doctor; he told me from the time he was a little boy he always wanted to heal. That was the same with me; that's all I ever wanted to do."

Unfortunately, John's contact with this enlightened, sympathetic physician was brief. Whether the doctor lost interest in Blymire or perhaps died is a matter of conjecture. Had their relationship continued, it is conceivable that Blymire might have been induced to rationalize his phobia, that Nelson D. Rehmeyer would have lived to a ripe old age in Rehmeyer's Hollow, and that the tragedy affecting so many people could have been averted.

Strong indications that John's witch had resumed his vendetta came with the sudden death of the Blymires' first child, a boy who lived less than five weeks. Lilly gave birth to another son prematurely. This infant survived for only three days.

Then John's nervousness returned. He no longer was able to sleep, his headaches came back and he developed a tic in his right cheek. He lost his job and his patients abandoned him. The hunt was on. This time he determined it would never cease until he had the name and address of the devil in human form bent on ruining his life.

5

BY 1920 BLYMIRE HAD CONSULTED A SCORE OR more of the most powerful witches in the area. One of these was Rufus Murray, a Negro necromancer who blended hexerei, voodooism and the cabala to make an excellent living out of the potpourri.

The Murrays were an old York family who had settled in the county shortly after the Revolution and who had lived on the wrong side of the tracks for at least four generations. Rufus, "called" to the profession from a hotel shoeshine parlor when in his late teens, had an enviable record of cures and was known to drive off the most stubborn of spells.

"You're bewitched. There's no question about it," Murray told Blymire after their seventh or eighth consultation at ten dollars each. "And it'll get worse before it gets better."

Murray's ace in the hole against particularly difficult cases of witchcraft was the so-called *Sixth and Seventh Books of Moses*. These are a distorted hodgepodge of Old Testament wisdom, the Talmud and the cabala, the latter an occult philosophy long since discarded.

"There is no such thing as a 'Sixth' and 'Seventh' Book

of Moses," stated Dr. Baruch Weitzel, a Professor of Religion at Philadelphia's Dropsie College and an authority on both the Old and New Testaments.

"Moses' Books were the *'Chumash,'* a Hebrew word meaning 'five.' Some authorities who ought to know better attribute those additional Books to others. They say the 'Sixth Book' is Joshua's, and the 'Seventh,' 'The Book of Judges.' But it's all ridiculous; they never existed."

Dr. Weitzel smiled and continued.

"If you're seeking references to sorcerers and witches in the Bible, you'll find at least one, all right. It's in Exodus, 22:17—*'Mechashefa Lo Techayeh'*—meaning literally, 'The witch shall not live.' "

The first problem Murray had to solve was quantitative rather than qualitative. If a single witch was in pursuit of his client, then a simple amulet, consisting of herbs wrapped in specially prepared parchment inscribed with a few Biblical verses, should suffice to dispel Blymire's hex. If, however, there were several demons involved, then a far more complicated procedure had to be followed; naturally, Murray's fees would then be proportionately higher.

There was no set price per demon, but before Blymire terminated the Negro's services, he was paying that necromancer eighteen dollars a week. Since five evil spirits (or *'Schedim,'* the Hebrew word for ghosts) were involved, this came to $3.60 per witch, a not unreasonable fee in view of the severe mental strain both doctor and patient were forced to endure.

Following instructions from Rabbi Acah bar Jacob, as noted in the Lewis de Claremont edition of *The Sixth and Seventh Books of Moses,* Murray warned his client to "stay out of direct sunlight, remain inside the house when the moon is full, hold your ears at the sound of a bell and *never* listen to the crowing of a cock." Obviously these admonitions put limitations on John's freedom of movement; in fact the final order cost him his job on a chicken farm.

As Murray's estimate of the number of witches grew, so did the amulet until, at final count, it must have been the size of a small grapefruit. Stuffed with hundreds of

34

verses from the Old Testament, it could have weighed as much as ten pounds.

Unfortunately, the wisdom of the ancient Hebrews proved ineffectual; the hex remained as destructive as ever. Blymire lost faith in Murray and, as the *New York Times* later reported, "Blymire began consultations with a Pennsylvania Dutch powwower named Sam Schmuck."

This last necromancer was no help. While his diagnosis was accurate—Blymire was hexed, all right—and his prognosis sound—it would get worse before it got better— Schmuck failed dismally to effect a cure because he could not discover the identity of the hexer.

Since the involuntary retirement of Reading's Professor Hageman, the most feared witch in the Keystone State's hex belt was another short, squat Pennsylvania Dutchman named Andrew C. Lenhart. For thirty years this sorcerer practiced his profession openly, unmolested by members of the medical profession, the York County Bureau of Health or York's Department of Public Safety.

"A hell of a lot of people including the cops were scared to death of Lenhart," Curt Thomas, former reporter for the *York Dispatch,* recalled. "They used to say that if this fat, ugly, little Dutchman put a spell on you, nobody, not even the devil himself, could remove it."

A shingle, hung on the porch of his home on Prospect Street near the intersection of Girard Avenue, York, announced to all that Doctor Lenhart was the recipient of special powers granted to him "by the Almighty, through Jesus Christ, Our Lord, His Son."

"If there ever was a more perverted use of religion," Thomas went on, "I wouldn't know where to find it. The big trouble with patients coming to consult Lenhart was that he'd never let them quit on their own. If they stopped coming he'd send word he'd no longer be responsible for what happened when they didn't return for 'treatments.' Most of them got the hint. The son-of-a-bitch got well-heeled on these poor, superstitious, ignorant yokels.

"And I'll tell you something else. Sometimes they followed his advice even when he indicated violence was the only way to beat a hex."

While authorities may have suspected Lenhart's counsel was behind a number of York County's unsolved uxoricides, they couldn't gather enough evidence to indict the Professor.

"Witnesses would be afraid to take the stand in court for fear that if they testified it was the Professor who advised them, he'd put a spell on them," Thomas recalled.

He thought for a moment, then continued.

"I can tell you about one murder, though, where there's no doubt the direct cause was Lenhart. He advised a poor, sick, troubled soul she'd have to do something about her husband if she wanted to get better, and she did, all right—she murdered him. It happened some six or seven years before they got Rehmeyer. The man was a fellow named Erwin Heagy. Lived near Abbotstown, 'bout twelve miles west of the city."

The Heagy slaying took place March 24, 1922.

"Erwin Samuel Heagy, forty-one years old, was shot and killed early yesterday morning by his wife, Sallie Jane (Blevenour) Heagy, while he lay in bed at their home a short distance north of the Lincoln Highway on the road leading to the protectory . . . ," declared the *York Gazette*.

"That the 'witches' led her to commit the act is the wail of the woman as she moans and weeps in a cell of the insane ward at the County Almshouse. . . . She is reported to have consulted local 'witch' doctors to try to take away the 'spell' from which she believed herself to be suffering.

"Powder marks and other evidence led the Coroner to believe that the man was asleep when the wife crept quietly into the bedroom and then fired the fatal shot. The report of the gun was the first indication that William Blevenour, Mrs. Heagy's brother, asleep in an adjoining room, perceived that something was wrong. Jumping from bed he ran to the Heagys' room. He found Mrs. Heagy clutching the revolver and her husband holding her by the wrist. . . . The man died . . . five minutes after the shot was fired."

The forty-two-year-old Mrs. Heagy was arrested. However, instead of confining her to a prison cell, District Attorney Walter VanBaman, later to defend one of the Rehmeyer murderers, showed more understanding than his successor and placed the woman under observation in a mental ward of the County Almshouse.

Dr. Lenhart was the next to last in a series of pow-wowers Mrs. Heagy had been consulting for ten years in a desperate effort to rid herself of a spell. In her confession, Mrs. Heagy told Mr. VanBaman that the final payment made to the Professor was ten dollars, a "free-will offering," made less than a month before the murder.

"He told me to beware of the man closer to me than anybody else. He couldn't have meant nobody but my husband, Erwin."

In addition to the only slightly veiled Delphic response to his patient's direct question—"Who put the hex on me?"—the Professor gave Mrs. Heagy a specially written Himmels-brief in which the name of the party of the first part was spelled out.

"Trotter head, Erwin Heagy. Forbid thee my house and premises. I, Erwin Heagy, forbid thee my horse and cow stable, forbid my bedstead that thou mayest not breathe upon me. Breathe into some other house until thou hast ascended every hill, until thou hast counted every fence post, until thou hast crossed every water, and thus dear day may come into my house. In the name of the Father, Son and Holy Ghost. Amen."

This gibberish was closed with three crosses and three dots placed alternately. Lenhart gave orders that his message was to be placed between a curtain and a paper covering the transom leading to the Heagys' yard. There it was found by the sheriff after the murder.

Unfortunately for all concerned, the Professor's spectral message never reached the witch for whom it was intended, the one Mrs. Heagy believed her husband had hired. The spell remained as potent as ever, causing its victim loss of sleep, weight and a general interest in life.

She complained to Lenhart and threatened to take her business elsewhere. As a matter of fact, unknown to the Professor, she had already consulted "Madame Florence," a necromancer whose shingle hung a few doors away from Dr. Lenhart's. This witch told her new client with far more truth than anyone could have then imagined, "There'll be a big change in your household before the March moon wanes."

The Professor was furious. Every time he saw his former patient pass by on her way to Madame Florence, Lenhart cast his bright blue eyes in Mrs. Heagy's direction, gave the sign of the cross three times, puckered fat lips and spat.

"When this happened," Mrs. Heagy told the sheriff, "I'd get a terrible pain in my stomach and shake all over."

On April 6, 1922, Mrs. Heagy ended all her earthly suffering by committing suicide in the Almshouse cell where she had been confined. Three days later she was buried by the side of her late husband in the cemetery of St. John's Lutheran Church, in Paradise (Pennsylvania).

As for Dr. Lenhart, unmolested by anyone, least of all by the York authorities, he continued to practice at his Linden Street office, no doubt busier than ever because of the favorable press notices he had received from his activities with the Heagys.

One of the Professor's newest clients was John Blymire. After a score of treatments at ten dollars each, Lenhart, although unable to claim complete success, could at least report great progress.

"The person who put the hex on you, John," he warned, "is somebody *very* close."

So John Blymire returned home and began to eye his wife, Lilly, with considerable suspicion. In turn, Lilly, with good reason, regarded her husband with considerable fear.

"I'm afraid of John," she told her father. "I think he's going to kill me."

Joseph Halloway did what he could to protect his daughter. Although a professed nonbeliever in witchcraft, he had been more than tolerant of his son-in-law's peculiar practices. He tried to reason with Blymire and convince him Lilly meant him no harm.

Halloway found it impossible to communicate with Blymire and came away from their brief interview certain that Lilly's fears were justified. This was early in June of 1923. Halloway then consulted a lawyer, who discussed the problem with Judge N. Sargent Ross of the York County Court of Common Pleas. Upon advice of counsel, Blymire was taken into custody on a warrant sworn out by his father-in-law. His Honor ordered a mental examination of the prisoner and appointed two psychiatrists, Doctors R. Miller and F. V. McConkey, to make the examination.

Blymire made no attempt to deny or belittle his anxieties and freely admitted his belief in witchcraft. The pair of psychiatrists concurred in the opinion that their patient was suffering from "psychoneurosis, neurasthenic type."

But, as Judge Ross wryly remarked later to Herbert Allen of the Associated Press, "If I jailed everybody in the county holding similar delusions and having similar anxieties, I'd have a hell of a job finding enough citizens to fill a jury box."

Nevertheless, the Court ordered John Blymire's commitment to the State Mental Hospital at Harrisburg for treatment.

"While we honored such classification as a mental disease, strictly speaking Blymire's was a borderline condition," declared staff psychiatrist Richard Ridgeway, a Johns Hopkins man himself.

"With proper treatment Blymire's condition could have been cleared up although the tendency to psychoneurosis continues because it is an attitude of the mind," the physician testified.

With one psychiatrist for more than a thousand patients, John's treatment at the institution was limited indeed. "I see about three hundred patients a day," Dr. Ridgeway said. "Blymire was one of them."

Assuming that Dr. Ridgeway put in a ten-hour day with no time out for lunch and that every inmate was lined up ready for admission to his office the moment his predecessor left, the psychiatrist could have spent a maximum of two minutes with each patient. From these logistics even a layman might conclude this was hardly enough time to cure Blymire's or anybody else's deep-seated neurosis.

Forty-eight days later Blymire, his mental condition possibly better and certainly no worse than it had been prior to his incarceration, escaped from the institution by merely walking out the front door and hitching a ride to York, twenty-six miles south of the capital city.

Hospital officials, no doubt relieved at the thought of one less mouth to be fed and one less mind to be cured, made no attempt to capture the escapee. Nor did his wife, Lilly, or his father-in-law seem to care as long as John stayed away from the Halloway household. Actually, by this time Lilly had begun divorce proceedings.

Under the Pennsylvania law of that time, all John had to do to avoid recommitment was to stay out of trouble for a year. After that, Judge Ross's order became null and void and Blymire would be as free as his neurosis permitted.

Blymire resumed his hunt. Whenever he heard of a witch he had not seen before, one who specialized in pinpointing unknown hexers, Blymire called upon him. If in John's professional opinion the new necromancer offered hope, the visits continued.

One such practitioner was Professor Charles W. Rice, of Orange Street, York. This powwower specialized in the cure of blindness—his prescription was sea-monster tears at $2.50 per drop plus the usual incantations, the sign of the cross and a Himmels-brief. He also had a reputation for removing spells from mysterious hexers.

Until the daughter of one of Rice's clients grew weary of paying him some twenty dollars a week to powwow cataracts from her mother's eyes and had the hexer arrested on charges of practicing medicine without a license, this witch enjoyed a lucrative practice. Blymire added one hundred dollars to Dr. Rice's bank account before transferring his hopes elsewhere. Meanwhile, another York County hex murder brought Professor Lenhart back into the news.

Wearing a charm she had bought from that practitioner of black art, sixteen-year-old Gertrude Rudy of suburban York was murdered on Armistice Day, 1927. Her body, a bullet through the heart, was discovered on the Maryland and Pennsylvania Railroad tracks by a factory watchman, John Goodling. Coincidentally, Goodling, a few months afterward, became one of Blymire's landlords.

The Professor admitted that Miss Rudy had been a patient. But what physical or mental ailment he was curing for, he would not reveal, no doubt basing his refusal on the established principle of "privileged conversations between patient and physician." While several subsequent arrests were made over the years—even Blymire was later unjustly accused of having been involved with the girl—no one was ever brought to trial for the Rudy murder. To this day, it remains unsolved.

A mild flurry of anger against Lenhart followed. For a brief period of time it seemed as though the authorities would finally close in on him. Unfortunately, even the police feared the Professor, his evil eye, his incantations and his ability to cast spells on enemies. Consequently he was let alone long enough to become the putative instigator of another murder.

On July 10, 1928, less than five months before the unhappy John H. Blymire finally broke the hex that had haunted him half his life, twenty-year-old Mrs. Helen Eiker of Gettysburg, Pennsylvania, shot and killed her husband, Percy. She had been hexed, she told the police, "by someone very close to me and this was my only way out." Her adviser, she told District Attorney John P. Butt, was none other than Professor Lenhart.

"For a long time I suffered with chest pains," Mrs. Eiker informed Butt, "and the Professor said he could cure them only after the hex was removed. [Whether Lenhart ordered the hexer removed, as well, was not revealed.] I never saw the Professor, but on June 10, I wrote him what was the matter with me."

With unexpected consideration for his client's purse, the Professor informed Mrs. Eiker he could cure her just as easily by mail and thus save the money she might have spent on train fare to and from York. He said she needed the full powwow treatment and she sent him an $11.50 money order and told him to go ahead.

At a brief trial, Mrs. Eiker was convicted of murder in

41

the second degree. Her sentence was later reduced to manslaughter.

Lenhart carried on, passing out his murderous advice to poor, deluded citizens who accepted it without question. No one knows how much money this witch extracted from hypochondriacs and from patients whose real diseases should have been brought to the attention of reputable medical practitioners.

"I know what a curse the powwow man has been to people with cancer and other diseases that might have been checked or cured had they been placed in the hands of the nearest country doctor of legitimate training," wrote Cornelius Weygant, the brilliant Pennsylvania Dutch writer, in his *Red Hills Revisited*.

"I know of one trained physician who will treat patients either by the orthodox methods he learned in medical school or by such methods as his father, the powwow man, used. I could show you long lines of cars outside of the offices of powwow men. I could cite you the case of a man who gave up a lucrative business to go into hexerei, and who did better with it than he did with the original trade. . . .

"There are no more people following the strange ways of the powwow men than there are people who follow the practitioners of this cult or that 'ism' held beyond the pale by the physicians of recognized standing.

"A badly scared man or a doomed man will turn to anyone who gives him hope."

Now, even in bright sunlight on York's broad streets, Blymire had trouble catching his breath. He knew that his unnamed witch was stalking him closer than ever, ready to enact his final moment of destruction. On nights when the moon was full, Blymire could look out of his bedroom window and see a huge gray owl perched on his grandfather's shoulder, hooting harshly.

No answer came forth from this night bird's eternal question.

6

AMONG THE UNCOUNTED NUMBER OF POW-
wowers who had cured for Blymire was an elderly recluse
named Nelson D. Rehmeyer of Rehmeyer's Hollow, four
miles east of Shrewsbury and just north of the Maryland
border. This was not far from Hallam, where the Blymires lived.

The "Hollow," stretching for nearly two miles along
the Codorus River, is in a sparsely settled, deeply wooded
area of York County. So heavy is the foliage that in
whole sections of the Hollow, the sun doesn't penetrate
for months. The farm of Rehmeyer's nearest neighbor,
Spangler E. Hildenbrand, is almost half a mile away.

Access to the Hollow from the main highway, through
narrow, winding, dirt roads, was difficult at best and
there were days when the only motorized vehicles able to
make their way through were the old Model T's. When
melting snows and spring rains flooded the normally
swift-flowing Codorus, it was impossible to get either into
or out of Rehmeyer's farmhouse.

Even today, almost within sight of a four-lane, limited-
access expressway sweeping traffic from Harrisburg to the
nation's capital, Rehmeyer's Hollow is hard to reach.
Roads leading to this gloomy bit of Pennsylvania are
narrow, winding and often muddy and the foliage hang-

ing over the whole area remains dense. A musty scent of decaying flora and fauna hangs over everything and the casual visitor has an eery feeling that he has suddenly stepped into a bygone civilization.

Although it has new occupants, the farmhouse where Nelson Rehmeyer lived remains little changed from the days when John Blymire was a child. It is a two-story frame dwelling, crudely built, yet strong enough to withstand the severest of winter's storms. There are two rooms on each of the floors and a large, unpaved earthen cellar below, reached through a trapdoor in the front parlor. It was in this dim, candle-lit basement that Nelson D. Rehmeyer practiced witchcraft.

Rehmeyer was a powerfully built man; he weighed better than two hundred pounds and was well over six feet tall with correspondingly broad shoulders. His arms were long and his hands huge. Only his head was out of proportion, far too small for the thick, short neck upon which it rested.

The nose was prominent, mouth small, lips thin, and face covered with a salt-and-pepper stubble, matching the thick, rarely combed hair on his head. Deep-set eyes, penetrating and blue, and high cheekbones were evidence that somehow, somewhere, Rehmeyer's Pennsylvania Dutch ancestry must have been broken by a member of the Algonquin or Delaware tribes who once roamed this part of the Keystone State where the Rehmeyers first settled before the Revolution.

A *braucher,* powwow man, faith healer and hexer, he was known throughout the countryside as the "Witch of Rehmeyer's Hollow." Taciturn, moody, given to frequent visions, he was difficult to live with. His wife, who bore him two children, both girls, discovered this fact and finally left him. Their separation was not unfriendly nor was there ever any thought of divorce. They saw each other from time to time and when the girls were sick they were taken to their father to be cured for. Years after she left him, Cora Rehmeyer still called on her husband to powwow off a string of warts encircling her wrist.

The Rehmeyers and Blymires had known each other for years. John's mother, Agnes, an unobtrusive woman who had to cope with more than the usual family problems and rarely left her home, was a Sunday School classmate of Cora Rehmeyer.

From time to time, when the Blymire children were ill and neither their father nor grandfather seemed able to cure for them, they were taken to Rehmeyer's farm, there to be powwowed back to health. John was five years old when he paid his first visit to Nelson Rehmeyer. He had been suffering with opnema, the wasting away (actually malnutrition), and one winter's night he became so ill that his father bundled him up, borrowed a neighbor's horse and buggy and drove him through the drifting snow to the Witch of Rehmeyer's Hollow, eight miles away.

Emanuel beat on the farmhouse door until he aroused the sleeping Rehmeyer. Then, while Emanuel remained in the kitchen, the powwower picked up the screaming child and carried him down into the dark basement. A half-hour later the pair emerged through the trapdoor, John sleeping peacefully in the *braucher*'s arms.

"Make him pee in a pot before sunrise," Rehmeyer advised Emanuel. "Then boil an egg in his urine. Bore three small holes in it with a needle and carry it to an anthill made by big ants. John will be better as soon as the egg is et."

By spring the child had recovered. Once more, for another illness, he was taken to Rehmeyer to be cured for. When John was ten years old Rehmeyer hired him to dig potatoes. His pay of twenty-five cents a day was a welcome addition to the Blymires' budget. The family, by then, had little of their farm left except for a small vegetable patch. Emanuel was working as a basket weaver in nearby New Freedom.

To be even the part-time helper of a *braucher* with a reputation such as Rehmeyer possessed must have taken considerable courage for a boy taught from babyhood to fear witches and stay out of their way. How terrified he must have been to be alone in the gloomy farmhouse with this huge, silent man who could at will command the presence of Beelzebub, the very prince of devils. What dreams, what nightmares must have followed those dreadful days John spent in Rehmeyer's Hollow! It would be more than twenty years before John was to visit the *braucher* again.

Blymire continued the long, ceaseless pursuit of his still unknown hexer, a quest that was soon to end with success. In the summer of 1928, perhaps the most trying period in John's life, he was boarding at the home of Mrs. Myrtle Downey on Duke Street in the City of York.

"I felt terrible sorry for him," Blymire's landlady recalled. "He was acting very peculiar. He would talk to hisself, mumble, lock hisself in his room most of the time except when he did odd jobs somewhere or cured for a couple of people who thought he could help them.

"Maybe he did some good. I don't know. He was always saying he was bewitched and if he could find out who put a spell on him he'd be well and get his strength back."

Along a bend in the broad Susquehanna, almost at the midpoint between the red rose city of Lancaster and the white rose city of York, lies the village of Marietta. The best, most respected and most feared resident of this tiny Pennsylvania Dutch community in 1928 was Mrs. Nellie Noll. Not for nothing was this ancient crone, then in her nineties, known as both the "River Witch" and the "High Priestess of Marietta."

For over three-quarters of a century, Nellie Noll, whose ancestors founded the town where she was born and raised, practiced necromancy in all forms. The childless Widow Noll (her husband died on their honeymoon in 1854) could never have been over four feet, eight inches tall but when old age had shrunk her body she stood less than fifty inches high.

"Her bird-like face was deeply wrinkled, her nose hooked, her back humped, and her sparse white hair straggly," reported the Lancaster *Intelligencer,* "but her bright, blue eyes were sharp and piercing. When she looked directly at anyone it was as though the subject of her gaze was under a hypnotic spell."

Mrs. Noll, who had cured for four generations of Marietta's citizens, no longer accepted new patients. It was only because she felt deeply sorry for poor, troubled John Blymire that he was able to persuade her to take his case. A reference from a York colleague may have helped.

Strangely enough, Blymire had never before heard of Marietta's High Priestess. She was recommended to him by a York powwow woman, Mrs. Clara Horner, at whose office on Green Street John had been undergoing treatment.

"If Nellie Noll can't cure you, John," said Mrs. Horner, honest enough to admit her own failure with this patient, "I don't know who can. She don't take on no more cures but if you tell her I sent you maybe she will."

Mrs. Noll's fee was the usual—five dollars per treatment. During their initial session she told John he was bewitched, certainly no surprise to him. At the end of the second session the High Priestess assured John it was a man, not a woman (as John had once suspected to the discomfiture of his wife), who had put the spell on him. At their third session she was sure the hexer was old. At the fourth she informed her client that his nemesis lived not in York but in the country. After the fifth meeting she told Blymire that she was getting close and the hexer had known his victim since early childhood.

John had good reason to remember their sixth meeting.

"Mrs. Noll kept starin' and starin' at me for a long time and didn't say nothin'. I was quiet and didn't say nothin' either. Then all of a sudden she speaks out.

" 'I know who bewitched you, John,' she says, and my heart beat so fast I thought it would jump out of my body.

" 'Who is it?' I asks.

" 'He's an old gentleman from down in the country.'

"I says, '*What* old gentleman? There are lots of old gentlemen from down in the country.'

"She answers, 'Rehmeyer.'

"I says, '*What* Rehmeyer? There are lots of Rehmeyers down in the country.'

"She answers, '*Nelson* Rehmeyer.'

"I can't *believe* what she's tellin' me. I know'd Nelson Rehmeyer since I was a little kid and he know'd me, too. So I says, 'Are you sure, Mrs. Noll?' and she says, 'I'll prove it, John.' So I says, 'Go ahead and prove it, Mrs. Noll.' "

By way of proof the High Priestess instructed her client to take a dollar bill out of his pocket.

"I says all right," Blymire continued, "and took one out and started to hand it over to her.

" 'No,' she says, 'you hold it in your left hand.'

"I done that and she tells me to put it on my right palm with the picture face up and I done that too.

" 'Now,' she says, 'take a good look at the picture on the dollar bill.'

"I look down at the picture and look and look and look. And all of a sudden there's Nelson Rehmeyer's face staring right up at me out of my hand. It was just as though he was right in front of me. He had light gray hair and he was dressed in dark clothes. I could see him down to his waist and he had a white shirt on.

" 'By God!' I says. 'The old lady's right.' Now I know who behexed me all these years. I was sure what I had to do next but I wanted Mrs. Noll to tell me herself."

For John Blymire the long hard pull was nearly over. The last step—to break the spell—should be easy.

"I asked the old lady what I must do.

" 'Get the book or the hair,' she says, and I know'd what she meant but I asks anyways.

" 'What book?'

" '*The Long Lost Friend*,' she answers.

" 'What'll I do with it when I get it?'

" 'Burn it,' she says. 'Burn it good!'

" 'What if I can't find it?'

" 'Then get a lock of his hair and bury it between six and eight feet of earth. Do this and you'll never be hexed no more!' "

7

IN JOHN BLYMIRE'S TROUBLED EXISTENCE HE had found little time or inclination to make friends. Except for his wife, who had long since divorced him and married somebody else, the only person Blymire might honestly have called a friend was a fourteen-year-old boy named John Curry.

For young Curry, his chance meeting with the thirty-two-year-old powwower was the most tragic event in his life, one which was to haunt him all the rest of his days and to cast a shadow on his descendants.

Curry's father, William, was a hard-working farm mechanic. He was a kindly, decent man, and while his son's recollections of him are dim, he was able to recall going fishing with his father several times on the Susquehanna River.

When William Curry was mustered out of the service in 1919—he was a volunteer in the Army Engineers—he used his soldier's bonus to make a down payment on a house in Cardiff, Maryland, near the Pennsylvania border. Here he opened his own shop. Three months later he died of a heart attack; he was thirty years old, his son not quite six.

With only the small amount of cash she received when his tools were sold at auction, William's wife, Anna, was left nearly penniless. The mortgage was foreclosed and she and her son, John, moved in with a distant relative at Gatchelville, York County, Pennsylvania. Anna, a pretty woman of twenty-seven with no profession, trade or talents, remarried within a year.

Her new husband, Alexander MacLean, was a shiftless, ill-tempered drunk. He was rough enough to his wife and to the three children she bore him, but to his stepson, John, he was brutal. Anna, a weak, ineffectual woman, was afraid of him and seldom, if ever, intervened.

Years later, John spoke about his childhood to Herbert Lee, a York artist who got to know him well.

"My stepfather used to beat the hell out of me every time he had a couple of drinks, and that was every day," John said. "He hated me. I guess I reminded him of my own father. He had a trade—he was supposed to be a printer and maybe he did work a day or two a month—but my mother had to support all of us. Whatever the old man earned he spent on liquor.

49

"My mother worked in a mill or factory wherever we lived to keep the family going and I used to be afraid to come home from school. I'd hide someplace 'till I saw her come in. Not that she ever did much to stop the old man; she was scared to death of him, but I felt that if she wasn't around he'd kill me."

John thought for a moment.

"Then we used to move to some other town every couple of months; I guess we didn't pay the rent and we'd be kicked out. We were hungry half the time. I used to like school but we moved so often I never had the same teacher for more than one term. We lived all over the county—Felton, Winterstown, Gatchelville and then York.

"One night my stepfather hit me so hard my mother got afraid he was going to kill me. I was ten years old, that's all. The next day she said I'd better go away. So she took me down to a farm near Muddy Creek Forks in the lower end of the county and asked a friend of my father's, Frank Kolter, if he'd take care of me.

"I stayed with Mr. Kolter and his wife—they didn't have any kids of their own—for about a year. Then I came home."

John Curry attended school until he was thirteen years old and had completed eight grades. Miss Helen Goepert, one of his former teachers, recalled that young Curry was a bright, willing boy, eager to learn, but she added, "He was absent so many days that even though he tried hard he never could catch up with the rest of the class.

"He didn't have a chance. I knew he was having trouble at home but I didn't realize it was so bad. Maybe if we had known what was going on there and had done something about it things wouldn't have turned out the way they did."

She sighed regretfully. "It's too late now."

Despite what must have been a highly restricted diet, John Curry at thirteen was a husky, well-built, broad-shouldered youth. He was five feet, eight inches tall, weighed one hundred fifty pounds and appeared to be at least eighteen years old. About this time his stepfather stopped beating him and concentrated on his own daughters, John's half-sisters.

Young Curry made a break from home shortly after February 21, 1928, his thirteenth birthday. He enlisted in the United States Army and was sent to Fort Meade for basic training.

"I was happy," he recalled. "It was a good life. I only got about thirty dollars a month but I didn't need any cash at all so I sent the whole pay to Mom.

"But then somebody from York or someplace wrote a letter to the General. They investigated me, found out how old I really was and kicked me out of the service in three months. Oh man! If they'd only let me stay, my life would have been different."

When John returned to York he obtained his "working papers" and got a job in the Bobrow Cigar Factory. The MacLeans were then living at 136 East Princess Street. Alexander hadn't done a day's work in nearly three years and home conditions were deplorable. Except for a few cents a week "spending money," John turned his wages over to his mother. He had a dim recollection of once using the change his mother gave him to buy a sketch pad and crayons.

"I always liked to draw," he recalled, "and whenever I got my hands on a pencil I'd sketch something. There was a store near the factory that sold kids' school supplies and one day I bought a box of crayons and a pad and took them to the house. I drew a picture of my mother and she said it was pretty good.

"But there wasn't much chance to do anything in the house. It was so noisy and besides I didn't have anyplace to myself, so I didn't bother anymore."

Until he met John Blymire in June of 1928, there wasn't a single person John Curry could have called a friend.

"He sat next to me at work," Curry said later, "and we started to talk. I knew he was a powwow man but I didn't care. That stuff didn't mean a thing to me and he listened to me when I said something to him.

"He used to tell me some pretty wild stories, about people being behexed and how he could cure sickness and disease. And lots of men and women in the factory came to John to be tried for when they had something the matter with them. He did a good job on them, too.

"He could take off warts—I saw this happen many a time. So after a while I thought maybe he might know what he was talking about and there was something to all this hex stuff."

For the first few months of their brief acquaintance, the only time Curry saw Blymire was during factory hours. Then one day after work, the older man invited the youth to come to his furnished room.

Curry thought he went to Blymire's room only twice, but added, "He came to our house lots of times. My mother didn't object and my stepfather was too drunk to care."

This was a strange friendship between the troubled, bewitched Blymire and young, lonely John Curry. The familiar phrase "father image" comes to mind at once, although it would be difficult to imagine two men more unalike than John Blymire and William Curry. Yet Blymire apparently provided John Curry with something he needed desperately and, in turn, young Curry supplied the older man with an attentive and admiring listener.

It would have been far better for John Curry if conversations between himself and Blymire had been about sex; unfortunately, their chief topic was hex. This was several months before Mrs. Noll, the Witch of Marietta, revealed to Blymire the powwower who had put the spell on him. During this period, Blymire was still on his quest.

"Some nights we'd walk around York," Curry said, "and John would take me to places where he'd be curing for people. He didn't seem to mind if I watched him powwow. Then sometimes he'd tell me about himself—how sick he always was after he was sixteen or seventeen, how bad luck seemed to follow him everywhere he went and how he was trying to find out the name of the witch who'd hexed him.

"He asked me once if I ever thought somebody'd put a spell on me, because my luck wasn't good either. At first I laughed and then I thought to myself maybe this guy's got something."

Unquestionably his association with Blymire was a heady beverage for young Curry. It must have been flattering, indeed, to be taken into the older man's confidence; to witness, and perhaps even participate in, this *braucher's* "cures." He had found a friend who would listen to him and to his troubles. Despite the fact that powwowism, hexerei or other forms of witchcraft had no place in the MacLean household, he began to believe that there actually might be some mysterious power he could blame for the harsh life he had led for at least nine of his fourteen years.

There does not seem to be any other explanation for John Curry's involvement in the final episode of his brief relationship with John Blymire. It is far easier to comprehend why the youthful Wilbert G. Hess became the third member of John Blymire's murderous trio.

Milton J. Hess, Wilbert's father, was a York County farmer just as his father, grandfather and great grandfather had been. They were of the good, solid, churchgoing, God-fearing Pennsylvania Dutch stock—predominantly Lutheran, except for an occasional Amish, Mennonite or Dunkard. There were even a few scattered Presbyterians, Baptists and Methodists in the family, the latter denominations usually acquired through marriage.

The family probably originated in the Palatinate, but it would be as difficult for a genealogist to trace the ancestry of almost any York County "Hess" as it would be for him to follow the family line of a Greater London "Smith," a Glamorganshire "Morgan" or a Galway "Kelly," with or without the extra "e."

Milton J. Hess was married to a Glatfelter girl, Alice. It might be noted here that the one sure way a candidate can be certain of election in this area of the Keystone State is to secure the combined votes of all the Hesses and Glatfelters, unless, of course, his opponent is a Gross, a Stoltzfuss or a Hostetter.

Mrs. Hess's middle name was "Ouida," an indication that either her mother or her father was a devotee of Maria Louise de la Ramée, two of whose novels signed with that *nom de plume*—*Under Two Flags* and *Moths*—were American best sellers in the Civil War years. Whatever romanticism Alice Ouida Glatfelter Hess may have inherited from her parents was diverted into superstition. She, her husband and their five sons were among the most ardent believers of hexerei in all the county or perhaps even in the great Commonwealth of Pennsylvania.

They obeyed all the rules and regulations laid down by generations of local *brauchers;* on the walls in each of their nine rooms were framed Himmels-briefs in juxtaposition with pictures of Jesus. When Mrs. Hess was pregnant, every bit of camphor was carefully removed from the house and stored in the barn, there to remain until the morning following her delivery. At childbirth, a powwower, usually a male, accompanied the midwife in attendance.

When the children were about to cut their teeth, Milton made a preparation of boiled rabbit brains and rubbed it into the boys' gums to prevent pain and to insure durable, decay-free dentures. Wilbert, the third-born, developed whooping cough at the age of eight, and the cure was straight out of *The Long Lost Friend.*

The Hess family's favorite witch, whoever it was at the time, cut three bunches of hair from the crown of the head of a child inmate at the County Home, one who had never seen his father. Using unbleached thread, the hair was then sewn into an unbleached bag and hung around Wilbert's neck until the whooping cough was gone.

For many years Milton J. Hess was a successful farmer. His crops were plentiful, his hens laid the usual quota of eggs and his cows gave the prescribed quantity of milk. He tithed and paid his taxes without undue strain on the budget. There was ample food on the table, his sons went to school regularly—through tenth grade, at any rate—and in general, the family's health was excellent.

When Clayton, the oldest boy, married Edna Gross in 1926, Milton furnished most of the money and much of the labor to build a house adjacent to his own for the newly wedded couple. He also loaned Clayton enough cash to make the down payment on an automobile.

Although there was no need to supplement the family

income, Alice Ouida Hess operated a stand three days a week in the York Central Market. There, for "pin money," she sold the fancy vegetables, fruits and flowers she raised in her garden in back of the kitchen.

In the spring of 1926, for no apparent reason, disaster struck the Hess household.

"All at once," Hess testified, "my wheat and my corn was no good and my potatoes was rotten. My chickens was stole and what hens was left wouldn't lay. My cattle wouldn't eat and couldn't give no milk.

"My family and I was sufferin' somethin' wonderful!"

In addition to agricultural difficulties and problems in animal husbandry, there were physical ailments to cope with.

"I felt as though, all of a sudden, my flesh was being boiled continuously," Hess lamented. "I couldn't work; I couldn't rest. I was in a terrible predicament, and that just kept me so wonderful that I just had at last to be convinced that there was somethin' doin'. . . .

"My family was in terrible shape. I was so grieved that I just didn't know what to do anymore because when I seen my wife in the condition she was in and even the children, why, it was enough to set any man crazy."

Mrs. Hess felt the same way.

"My family was so wonderful," she later testified under oath, "I didn't know what to do, and I was so wonderful put out and down I couldn't do my own work; I didn't know how to do nothin'. I couldn't as much as make meals for my children no more or for my boy and his family. . . .

"I was gettin' that far that I didn't care if my children got anythin' to eat anymore or anythin' else anymore. I just couldn't follow. . . ."

Although nothing particularly "wonderful" was happening to the seventeen-year-old Wilbert, he, too, was caught up in the encircling problems. He worked alongside of his father every day on the farm and heard him complain constantly about crop failure and fiscal problems. Wilbert brooded when he saw his mother, to whom he was much attached, change from a cheerful, bustling housewife and teller of funny stories into a sad, silent woman, unwilling or perhaps even unable to communicate with him, his brothers or his father.

Conditions in the Hess household worsened. By the winter of 1927, income from the farm could no longer support the family. In the spring of 1928 Milton sold off most of his land until he was left with only fourteen acres and five perches. He got a part-time job in the York Y.M.C.A., then was hired full time as a truck driver for the Pennsylvania Tool Company at 202 North George Street, York. His wife's "pin money" stand at the Market now became an important item in the family budget.

Not for a single moment was there any doubt in the minds of Milton J., Alice Ouida or any other Hess what was the direct cause of the family's continuing misfortunes.

"We was bewitched," Milton testified.

Alice Ouida concurred. "Somebody put a hex on us. It was wonderful strong!"

All potential enemies the Hesses might have acquired in their lives (and no doubt a few friends and relatives as well) were discussed at family conferences. Even Edna Gross Hess, Clayton's bride, was asked to contribute her own suggestions on the chance—there were plenty of precedents to go on—that the Hess hex might have been a concealed part of her dowry.

For some time a neighbor, Ida J. Hess (no relative), was suspected because she and the Milton J. Hesses had had trouble several months before over a right-of-way between the two farm properties.

"The Mister thought maybe Ida had somethin' to do with our hex," Alice Ouida said. "She was so wonderful mean."

There had been no change for the better by June of 1928 when Milton J. Hess met John H. Blymire. The tool company's garage was in an alley in back of its North George Street entrance. Directly opposite the garage was the Widow Detwiler's boarding house, where Blymire was living in a third-floor-rear room.

The men usually would see each other in the morning when Hess backed his loaded truck out of the garage as Blymire left Detwiler's for whatever job he was holding down. Almost every evening they met again. At first, each man, deeply concerned with his own problems, merely nodded to the other. Later they began to speak and in a few weeks, Hess was pouring out his troubles to a most understanding, sympathetic listener.

While there is no evidence to support this premise, it is unlikely that John Blymire was the only *braucher* Milton Hess had consulted since his family's recent bewitchment. For all anyone knows, he might even have paid a few visits to the office of Professor Lenhart, who would remain in active practice for some time to come.

8

THE TESTIMONY OF SEVERAL TRIAL WITNESSES shows some confusion about an alias Blymire used when Milton J. Hess introduced him to his wife and sons. That Blymire was known to the rest of the Hess family as "John Albright" was proved beyond a reasonable doubt. It was also established that young Curry was called "John Russell" when Blymire took him to the Hess farm. The aliases, however and whenever used, were about as senseless as anything else in the preposterous Rehmeyer murder.

For years Blymire had been a familiar character in and around York. Consequently Hess, thoroughly oriented to local *brauchers,* must have recognized him at once. Besides, Blymire never had any reason to conceal his identity or profession. Even during his most unhappy time, he still sought new clients. So it hardly seems likely he would tell Hess his name was "John Albright."

However, during his son's trial, Milton never claimed he knew Blymire by any name other than his own, while the rest of the Hess family, including the defendant, Wilbert, testified they knew Blymire only as John Albright. So be it!

Hess and Blymire saw each other almost every day

throughout the summer of 1928 but only for ten or fifteen minutes at a time and always near the Pennsylvania Tool Company's garage. Some time before the Witch of Marietta brought to a successful conclusion her client's long search for his hexer, Blymire paid his first visit to what was left of the Hess farm. He came there at the request of Milton; John "Russell" Curry came along.

Blymire made a spot check—farm, house, barn and animals—all were in a deplorable condition. To a *braucher* with Blymire's experience it was obvious at once that some unknown witch had cast a spell on the Hess family. Things were so desperate in the household that even a novice must reach the same conclusion.

Blymire estimated that the total cost to remove the hex and reveal the hexer (and he guaranteed nothing) would be approximately forty dollars. Hess never questioned the price or the value of these services, nor did he make an attempt to reduce the fee. However, all he could scrape up was ten dollars; this he turned over to his new pow-wower, who accepted the sum on account.

While Curry trailed behind as an observer, Blymire, muttering incantations, slowly walked around the truck patch and chicken coop and then into the barn. When he stepped outside a half-hour later, he handed Hess a piece of paper, a Himmels-brief of his own concoction; he told his client to sign it and carry it with him at all times.

Back in his room, Blymire spent the next few days attempting to discover the name of the Hess hexer. He admitted failure the following week when he returned to the farm. Nor had the special Himmels-brief Hess had faithfully been carrying with him caused any appreciable change in the family fate or fortune.

Milton or some other member of his family suggested Ida J. Hess as the potential enemy. Blymire gave it considerable thought but said that he felt this neighbor had nothing to do with any spell cast on his client. The search went on.

It was about this time that Blymire's personal quest came to an end with Mrs. Noll's revelation of Nelson D. Rehmeyer. So Blymire, admitting if only to himself his inability to relieve the Hesses, humbly crossed the

Susquehanna River once more to seek counsel from the High Priestess.

In exchange for the same ten dollars Milton Hess had given to Blymire, Mrs. Noll furnished him with startling news. It was the Witch of Rehmeyer's Hollow who had put the hex on the Milton J. Hesses.

Presumably without extra compensation, the Witch of Marietta obligingly added John Curry's name to the rolls of those who had come under Nelson D. Rehmeyer's spell. From here on in, as Mrs. Noll had pointed out to Blymire once before, the solution to their mutual problems was possession of the book or the lock.

One evening early in November—the exact date never was established—Blymire, this time without Curry, went to the Hess farm to break the news; he had at last discovered that Nelson D. Rehmeyer was the witch who had hexed them all.

Both Milton and his wife were astonished.

"I never heard of him even wunst," Milton declared.

Blymire then explained who Rehmeyer was and gave the Hesses full details of the *braucher*'s background. When Milton asked whether Blymire was sure, the latter, as a clincher, informed his clients that it was the Witch of Marietta who had revealed Rehmeyer's name. They *had* heard of Mrs. Noll.

"Do you think maybe Ida Hess hired him to do it?" Alice asked, apparently unwilling to give an honorable discharge to the neighbor she disliked and had long suspected. Blymire shrugged his shoulders. Who hired the *braucher* was irrelevant; their objective was to break the spell, and Blymire and his clients all knew there was only one authorized method.

Milton, whose ten hard-to-come-by dollars were invested in the venture, was more practical than Alice. He asked Blymire to explain the procedure.

"First, I gotta get the upper hand over Rehmeyer's willpower," Blymire answered, "and then I'll let you know what's gotta be done next."

Apparently Blymire hoped to accomplish this initial stage of his mission by remote control, since what he did for the next ten days was sit in his room and think. On

59

the afternoon of Sunday, November 25, 1928, with John Curry present, Blymire confessed to Milton Hess that his mental dominance over the Witch of Rehmeyer's Hollow was incomplete. More direct action was necessary.

"It was pretty near dusk that Sunday," Clayton, Milton's oldest son, recalled. "We was all there—Mom, Pop, Edna [his wife], me and Wilbert. This was the first time Edna or me ever seen Blymire but we was told his name was John Albright.

"That Curry kid was there, too, but they told me and Edna *his* name was something else, Russell, they said. It didn't make no difference to us whatever they was called."

Formal introductions must have been confusing.

"The Mister [Milton J.] and us knew Blymire's right name," Alice recalled. "The Mister knew Curry's real name but I thought it was Russell. Edna, Clayton and Wilbert thought they was called John Albright and John Russell."

A conference was held in the kitchen, with little time wasted on social amenities. On hand were Milton J., Clayton, Blymire, Curry and Wilbert. Edna and her mother-in-law were in the dining room adjacent to the kitchen, in sight of the conferees but out of earshot. They knew the subject of the conclave. Transportation was the first problem and for twenty-four hours more the only one the Hesses were requested to solve.

"Blymire asked me if I'd take him and Curry down to the woods Monday night," Clayton testified. "I said if Pop wanted me to I will if Edna can come along with us. Pop said he wanted me to and Blymire says he can't see no objections to bringing Edna along so I said yes."

By "woods," Blymire was referring to the deep forest of hemlock, spruce and pine surrounding Rehmeyer's Hollow. Inside a small clearing was Rehmeyer's house, where Blymire had not been for more than twenty years.

Clayton advised the conferees they would have to wait until about 6:30 P.M. when he and his younger brother, Wilbert, returned home from work. Both men were employed at the Hess Lumber Yard in York, where Clayton was a foreman. The owners of the yard were distant relatives of the Milton J. Hess family.

Despite the fact that Blymire and his acolyte would have preferred to get a much earlier start so that they could arrive at the Hollow to face the witch in broad daylight, there was nothing they could do but acquiesce. Clayton owned the only car in the Hess family and neither Blymire nor Curry had access to any other. On November 26, 1928, the sun set at 4:21 P.M., so it would be pitch dark even before they began the trip.

The Hesses finished supper hurriedly that Monday evening, got into Clayton's ancient Dodge and started for York, twenty-five miles away. It was then a few minutes past seven. Milton was working late at the lumber yard and did not arrive at the farm until 10 P.M., long after the others were on their way.

In the car with Clayton, who was driving, were Wilbert, Alice and Edna. They went directly to the MacLean home on Princess Street where Blymire and Curry were waiting for them. Curry's mother was at church; his half-sisters were out and the *paterfamilias* was far too drunk to know or care who entered or left his house.

"After we pick up 'Albright' and the 'Russell' boy," Mrs. Hess said, "we drive down from York on the Susquehanna Trail. When we gets in front of Jake Markey's farm near us Wilbert says he don't feel so good and he wants out."

It never was fully determined whether Wilbert had a case of nerves or indigestion. However, in view of the meal he had bolted less than an hour before, historians are inclined to lean toward the latter theory. "For supper that night," Mrs. Hess recollected, "we had pork and mashed potatoes, sauerkraut, some leftover sausage, pickled hard-boiled eggs and shoofly pie."

Wilbert's mother continued. "So I ask Mr. Albright if it was all right to let him out and the powwow man says 'yes,' he didn't need Wilbert for nothin'. So we stop, let Wilbert out, and I tell him to go on right home.

"The powwow man was settin' up front with Clayton to tell him where to go but he didn't need directions 'till we get to Hametown. Me, Edna and young Russell was in the back. We didn't talk much; just sat quiet.

"At the Hametown church Albright says to Clayton, 'Here's where we turn off at.' Clayton says, 'Right or left?' and Albright answers, 'Right.' So we turn off in this here narrow dirt road and drive for a couple more miles. There's no cars on it but our'n. I know'd we wuz headin' for Hopewell but I didn't know exactly where.

"It was terrible dark; you couldn't see nothin'. Then it started to drizzle hard and Clayton's wipers wasn't workin' so good, so we had to keep stoppin' all the time so's we could get the windshield wiped off. That young boy, Russell, was very polite and he jumped out of the car every time to wipe it with a rag."

Clayton knew exactly where he was.

"We're in the woods at the edge of Rehmeyer's Hollow," he said. "I heard it was about two miles in from there to the clearin' where the old witch had his house. Albright says to me, 'Here's where we want out.' The kid says nothin'; I think maybe he's a little bit afraid thinkin' about where he's goin'.

"It's black as pitch and it's very scary. I wouldn't want to be out in these here woods by myself; you don't know what's goin' on in the Hollow. By now it's pourin'; you can hear the wind whistlin' through the trees and the Codorus rushin' by and I can't wait to turn around and go back. Albright lets me.

"He says, 'All right, Clayt,' and him and the kid step out the car. He says, 'Russell and me'll be back maybe Friday or Saturday. We'll have the book or we'll bury a lock of the old devil's hair by then and that'll take the spell offen your Mom and Pop. We'll see your Mom at the Market then.' "

With Curry bringing up the rear, Blymire trudged through the starless night along the gloomy road until the farmhouse was reached. There they were in for a bitter disappointment; the place was in total darkness. Blymire pounded on the door for five or ten minutes. After a while he gave up and they left.

"I figured maybe the devil was over at his wife's place. I know'd they didn't live together no more but I thought maybe she might know where he was. He still used to see her. Her place was outside the Hollow maybe a mile or a mile and a half away.

"There was a light in Mrs. Rehmeyer's and she opened the door for us. 'Where's the Mister?' I asks, and she says she don't know. 'Maybe the old devil cock's with Emma Glatfelter,' she says. 'That's who he's been layin' around with lately.' "

The hunters retraced their steps; they had been gone from Rehmeyer's house for about two hours and by then it was close to midnight.

"This time," Blymire continued, "there was a light on the second floor where the old witch used to sleep. I rapped on the door hard and after a while he comes down in his nightshirt. He's mean lookin', worse'n I ever remembered him. He's a big man, too, far bigger'n I ever thought. I don't know if he recognizes me—I ain't seen him in more'n twenty years—but anyways he opens the door and says, 'What do you fellows want?'

"I says, 'Can we come in?' and he says, 'Yes,' so we walk inside and he gives us a chair in the parlor. We sat down to talk."

Too close to his objective to beat around the bush, Blymire asked a leading question the moment he and Curry were seated in their host's parlor.

"Have you ever seen the book?"

Rehmeyer nodded; he knew exactly what his guest meant.

"Then I asks him if he has one," Blymire went on, "and he says, 'Yes.' "

The preliminaries over and the results satisfying to Blymire, conversation turned to other topics.

"We talked about farmin' and he told us he was down at the Glatfelters when we was at his house first and we chewed the fat about lots of other things 'till it got pretty late.

"I guess we must have brought up the subject of how I come out to see the old devil when I was a kid to have him cure for me and when I picked potatoes for him but I don't remember. John [Curry] didn't say nothin'. He oney kept listenin'."

Meanwhile, occupying part of Blymire's mind was the struggle to get control of Rehmeyer's willpower so that "Then the old devil would hand over the book or tell me where it was so I could get it myself and we could go home."

No one knows for how many hours past midnight the two conspirators sat talking to their host in his dim, candle-lit parlor and listening to the rain beat a sharp tattoo against the tin roof. Outside there was the swish of a cold November wind blowing through the pines, the spruce and the hemlocks, and the roar of the swollen Codorus sweeping through the Hollow.

How many times Blymire's eyes must have been drawn to the trapdoor beneath which lay the dank, gloomy cellar where Rehmeyer practiced black magic. Finally their host grew tired.

" 'I'm goin' up to bed,' the old witch tole me," Blymire said. " 'You fellows can sleep down here.' He climbed up the stairs and when he got to the top he blowed out the candle; we wuz left in the dark.

"Then he must have thought more of it and he called down, 'You kin have a candle if you want one,' but I says, 'No, never mind, we'd just as soon sleep in the dark.' So John pulls a couple chairs together to stretch out on and I stretched out on a couch in the kitchen."

Curry dropped off to sleep at once but Blymire had work to do and stayed awake. "I kept tryin' to control the old man's willpower but I couldn't seem to. His was stronger'n mine."

An hour or two before dawn, Blymire wakened his fellow conspirator for a whispered conference. "I can't win over that devil," he said; his companion then asked what the next step would be. Blymire pondered. Should they sneak upstairs and use physical force to overpower Rehmeyer and make him surrender the book or submit to the removal of a lock of his hair?

But Blymire was fully aware that his antagonist, who towered over each conspirator, possessed far more strength than the pair could possibly muster jointly. Against such a strong and wily foe a sneak attack appeared impossible.

"The witch might be up there awake and waitin'," Blymire said. "I believe he's too much for me and you to take him, John. We're gonna need help. Go back to sleep now and I'll tell you tomorrow what we'll do."

It seems likely that Rehmeyer, a cunning man who certainly knew what went on in his own bailiwick, had been told of Blymire's fixation and was aware of his midnight guests' intent. It is probable, too, that the old man was playing cat and mouse, laughing inwardly at the clumsy plotters.

Their host was on hand early. "He give us breakfast," Blymire said, "and then we tole him good-bye. Then me and John hitched a ride to York; I know'd what we was gonna do next."

There is some question about the sequence of the pair's next steps. At first Blymire told authorities it was on Tuesday, November 27, immediately following their arrival in York, that he and Curry went directly to Swartz's hardware store on South George Street to buy twenty-five feet of heavy rope.

However, Blymire later changed his story and told police he and his companion had made the purchase the preceding day, Monday, November 26. Curry, badly badgered by the District Attorney, corroborated Blymire's amended testimony. Unless District Attorney Herrmann felt he would strengthen his case by adding to the time for premeditation, there seemed little reason for him to make this point, since the purchase and ultimate use of the rope were never denied by either defendant.

In retrospect it appears more likely that the rope was bought on Tuesday only after Blymire's failure to gain control over Rehmeyer's will. Neither Clayton nor any other member of the Hess family recalls seeing the rope when they delivered Blymire and his young companion to the edge of the Hollow. It would not have been easy to conceal that much hemp.

"Curry had no money to buy the rope [nor much of an incentive, either], so I paid for it," Blymire testified. "At Swartz's, Curry reached for the rope but Mr. Swartz wouldn't hand it to him. He handed it to me and after I had it, Curry took the rope and we went up to their house and we cut it up into about fourteen foot-and-a-half lengths.

"At first I was gonna use tar rope but then I thought a little. 'No,' I told John, 'we won't take that kind of rope because that will cut his hands or feet.' "

(It is to be hoped the Witch of Rehmeyer's Hollow appreciated his murderers' thoughtfulness.)

"So I stayed with Johnny all day and then we goes out to Hess's farm again," Blymire recalled.

Late that afternoon the pair, carrying those fourteen lengths of heavy rope, hitched a ride to the Hess farm, there to await the arrival of Clayton and Wilbert. Clayton would supply the transportation and his younger brother the additional manpower Blymire needed to finish the job.

9

WHILE IT'S UNLIKELY THEY WOULD HAVE AP-proved of murder even as a last resort, Wilbert's mother, father and older brother not only were aware of Blymire's dogged determination to get the book or the lock, but approved of it as well. The Hesses were a closely knit family; when one suffered, all did, and Wilbert was a loyal son and brother. Under these circumstances his course of action that fatal night could not have been other than what it was. For two years Wilbert's mother and father had cried out tragically, "We're suffering something wonderful." Here, now, was a chance for their son to be a hero and make their home a happy one again.

It must have been quite a shock and a subsequent bitter disappointment for Alice Ouida Hess and Edna, her daughter-in-law, to see Blymire and young Curry walk through the gate and up to the house that Tuesday evening.

"When Clayton and us dumped them off Monday night, he said he wouldn't see us 'till Friday or Saturday and here they was back again sooner," Mrs. Hess complained. To her sorrow, she soon learned why: Their hex was still on.

The weather was chilly but clear and the pair of conspirators sat on the kitchen steps waiting. They said they weren't hungry; Mrs. Hess fed them anyway. About seven o'clock, Clayton and Wilbert came home.

"I give Edna and my boys their supper," Mrs. Hess said. "Then, while me and Clayton's wife redd up the table, they talked about what they was gonna do—get the hair or the book that night for sure.

"Blymire told Clayton they needed Wilbert bad to help. The Mister wasn't home so Clayton says it was all right with him for Wilbert to go if he wanted to. Wilbert says he'd ruther not but then he says, 'I'll go along for it for the good of us all.'"

Clayton claimed his younger brother made a further protest.

"Just before he got in the car he says, 'I don't think I want to go,' and Blymire says, 'Go along, Hessy. Nothin'll happen. I'll take care of you.'"

Clayton knew that his father already had approved of Blymire's de-hexing *modus operandi,* and that had he been home he would have allowed, perhaps even urged, Wilbert to join Blymire and Curry on the venture.

"Blymire explained to us what had to be done to get the book or the lock before that Sunday [November 25]," Milton testified, "and I made arrangements to get them there to Rehmeyer's."

As for Mrs. Hess, she not only gave Wilbert her consent to become part of the trio; she even handed him transportation money so that he would be in time for work the following morning, Wednesday, November 28.

When Wilbert asked his mother if she *really* wanted him to go to Rehmeyer's Hollow, she acquiesced, albeit reluctantly.

"I says, 'Well, if it is no other way to rid us of our trouble, why he can go along because nobody knows what I had on myself,'" Mrs. Hess testified. "He [Blymire] said it must be one out of my side, that I had to get rid of our trouble that way."

The fare from the bus stop nearest to Rehmeyer's Hollow into the City of York was a half-dollar.

"My mother told me it would be all right if I had to lose a day's work for something like this," Wilbert declared under oath, "but she gave me fifty cents to come back if I could. She didn't urge me to go with Blymire and Curry but she said it was O.K. I went for my father's and mother's benefit."

It was past ten-thirty that bright, moonlit night before Blymire, carrying fourteen lengths of rope, climbed into the Dodge and sat beside Clayton. The two boys, Wilbert and Curry, sat in the rear seat. Edna and her mother-in-law waved good-bye as the car pulled out of the driveway.

Inside the car there was almost complete silence as Clayton headed north on the Susquehanna Trail, now Route 111.

"The only thing was said," Clayton recalled, "was when I turned off the main road toward the Hollow. Blymire was tellin' me what had to be done before the night was gonna be over."

On this second trip to Rehmeyer's, Clayton took his passengers to within a mile of the house.

"I dropped them off and turned 'round right away and headed for home," Clayton testified.

With Blymire in the lead, the trio walked silently, single file, along the muddy road. Overhead a full Thanksgiving moon helped light their path. The time was now a short while before midnight and the witch's house was in complete darkness. Blymire strode onto the porch.

"I rapped on the door," he said, "and after a bit he opened his bedroom window and stuck his head out.

" 'What do you want?' he says, and I says, 'I want the book.' So then he lights a lamp and he comes down and opens the door and we all three walk in."

Although Rehmeyer certainly must have recognized his guests of the preceding night, until he opened the door to admit Blymire and Curry he might not have been aware of the husky Wilbert's presence. But even had he known he had three visitors whose intent Blymire clearly announced, chances are that Rehmeyer was so sure of his own powers he would not have denied them admittance.

Blymire, followed by Curry and Hess, pushed past Rehmeyer into the parlor they had vacated some eighteen hours before.

"As soon as we gets in the house," Blymire testified, "I says, 'Where's the book?' The old witch don't answer; he don't say nothin'."

Unfazed, perhaps even amused at the effrontery of a witch whose powers had long since waned and who was obviously a victim of someone's hexerei, Rehmeyer ignored his guests. He pulled a gray sweater from a hook and donned it, then picked up a nickel-plated flashlight. Then, to the consternation of the visitors, he brushed by them, went into the kitchen, opened the door and walked out of the house. Before his visitors could recover from their surprise he was back with an armful of wood.

"It's cold in here," he commented. "You can see your breath." Carefully he placed some kindling in the stove, put the rest on the floor beside it and rubbed his hands together to warm them. Without uttering a word he stood in front of the stove for several minutes, his back to Blymire, Hess and Curry.

There was no sound except for the rapid, frightened breaths of the visitors and the crackle of burning wood. Then, as a glow from the hot stove lid threw a pale red light into the corners of the darkened parlor, Rehmeyer, grinning enough to show two rows of long, uneven, yellow teeth, turned around.

"What's this about a book?" he asked Blymire. "Whose book do you mean?" knowing, of course, exactly what Blymire meant.

In a voice pitched high from fear and anger, Blymire replied.

"You know what I'm talkin' about, Rehmeyer. Where's it at?"

"I don't see no book," Rehmeyer answered, standing beside a table and still grinning. "Maybe it's in the paper rack or behind where you slept last night."

Blymire pulled the couch from the wall and pretended

to look behind and beneath it. But by then he'd had enough, and with a shrill cry he went into action.

"Blymire pushed the couch against Rehmeyer," Hess recalled, "grabbed him and made motions for me to do the same. I got hold of him and Curry grabbed him, too, and the three of us throwed him to the floor and held him there.

"Blymire shouted out, 'Tie his legs, John, so we can cut his hair!' "

Curry grabbed a length of the rope he'd concealed inside his shirt and attempted to tie the struggling Rehmeyer's legs.

"But the old man kicked hard and the rope flew out of my hands and he knocked me away," the fourteen-year-old conspirator said. "Then Rehmeyer yells out, 'Let me up and I'll give you the book.' So Hess and Blymire, who're sittin' on him, let him up. He stands in the middle of the floor, reaches in his pants and throws his pocketbook at Blymire. [The wallet was empty.]

"Blymire says, 'That's not the book I mean and you know it.' Then the old man goes for Blymire full force."

Except for slight and relatively unimportant discrepancies, each member of the trio told essentially the same story about the murder itself. After tossing his pocketbook at Blymire, who disregarded it, the older witch fought desperately, realizing for the first time that his life might be in danger despite his powerful physique and the quantities of Himmels-briefs he had on hand.

"I grabbed an old chair as the witch tried to jump me and I struck at him," Blymire admitted. "But I missed; the chair hit the ground and flew to pieces. Then Hessy and I grabbed him and at the same time threw him down and Curry jumped him again. I yelled for rope."

Curry handed Blymire one of the lengths of hemp, expecting that the latter would tie the victim's hands or legs. "Instead," Curry said, "he tied it around Rehmeyer's neck."

For several minutes longer the fight raged over the parlor floor, with Rehmeyer struggling hard but getting weaker all the time.

"He was lyin' on his right side," Blymire testified,

"When Curry walks out to the wood box and gets a block and hits Rehmeyer over the head twict. We wuz beatin' him at the same time. Curry hits him again with the block and the blood just rushed out. Then Curry dropped the block and walked 'round him."

Authorities never were able to determine who struck the fatal blow, but before the battle ended Rehmeyer was kicked in the head and stomach and his face battered almost beyond recognition.

"After a while," Blymire admitted, "he made a groan like you know, took a few deep breaths, and he was gone. I shook him and said, 'Oh my God! He's dead.'"

But his fellow conspirators claim what Blymire actually said was, "Thank God! The witch is dead."

10

WITH REHMEYER TO BE FEARED NO LONGER, the trio explored the house. Up and downstairs they searched every possible place where they thought he might have concealed the "book." They ransacked the kitchen and parlor; looked in back of the Himmels-briefs on every wall; reached into closets, on shelves, in drawers, through clothing and beneath the mattress to no avail. But they did not enter the only room where Blymire must have known it would be—that dark basement below the trapdoor where the witch's body lay prone.

Actually, as Blymire declared later, "It didn't make no difference anymore whether we found the book or cut off a lock of Rehmeyer's hair and buried it eight feet below the ground like Mrs. Noll tole me. The witch was dead; the spell was off. I couldn't be hexed no more."

In the bedroom they found a tin box containing a small amount of change. Whether there was as much as the $2.80 District Attorney Herrmann claimed or as little as ninety-seven pennies—Wilbert's estimate—does not seem to be of any particular importance. The motive for the murder of Nelson D. Rehmeyer certainly was not robbery.

Whatever amount of cash they found was divided equally. During the subsequent trials the Commonwealth attempted to prove this was a murder for profit; it made much of the fact that Hess, on the night of his arrest, claimed he was gypped. But fat, little Counselor Gross proved that the boy didn't even know what the word "gypped" meant.

The culprits then began what must go on record as a depressingly naïve attempt to conceal a murder. When the trio entered Rehmeyer's home, both Blymire and Curry were wearing coarse canvas gloves. However, during the ensuing struggle with their victim, they discarded them, so that their fingerprints could have been found practically anywhere. Hess's hands were bare.

Curry believed it would be no problem to conceal their identities.

"Throw some water around the floor," he said, "and we'll wash away our fingerprints."

Blymire, not at all sure such precautions were really necessary, nonetheless obeyed.

"I got two dippers of water out of the basin and threw them all over the floor," the older conspirator admitted. "While I was doin' this, Curry gets the rope over alongside the window and ties it around Rehmeyer's neck, not tight, and pulled him away.

"Then I pours the water alongside of Rehmeyer on that side. Hessy grads the mattress or chaff tick—I can't just say what it was—offen the couch and throws it on Rehmeyer; then Curry gets the lamp offen the table, takes off the top, takes off the burner, and takes the oil and puts it alongside of Rehmeyer."

Curry's (or Hess's) plan was clear now, even to the slow-thinking Blymire, who would certainly have preferred to walk out of Rehmeyer's Hollow, go home and start living again with nothing to fear. Nevertheless, he cooperated with his fellow conspirators.

"Curry says to me," Blymire testified, " 'John, have you got a match?' and I says, 'No, I don't smoke. It ain't

72

good for you and I don't have no matches neither.' I says, 'Hessy, have *you* got a match?' and Hessy starts to reach for one. But Curry says, 'I got one,' and strikes it, throws it down and it burns a little but it goes out.

"Curry gets another match and it starts to burn. Then Hessy went outside; I followed, and then Curry. We wuz in the house less'n a half-hour. Curry pulls the door shut. I don't know if he locks it. When we gets out on the porch, he says something about the key. We goes over the porch to the fence."

As they neared the barn Blymire unthinkingly looked over his left shoulder at the full November moon rising on top of the smoldering house. At that moment he saw something emerge from the closed door.

"My hair stood up on end," he said. "There was a shadow coming out of the house. It started toward me. 'My God!' I says to myself, 'The old witch ain't dead yet!' "

But Rehmeyer was as dead as he'd ever be; the shadow moved upward and into the night and Blymire breathed a sigh of relief.

"We starts to run away as hard as we can," Blymire recalled. "We run all the way through the Hollow and up the hill, and kept goin' pretty near to Hametown church. Then we slows down a bit to get our wind and starts toward Hessy's house. We figured we'd get Clayton to run John and me back to York so we could go to work."

It had been a long night; the cocks were crowing when the trio of murderers reached the Hess farm. Young Wilbert stepped onto the porch and rapped softly on the front windowpane. A few minutes later Mrs. Hess, still in her nightgown, opened the front door to face her dutiful son.

"My God! What's happened?" she cried out. "You're covered with blood."

At this Wilbert burst into tears and buried his face on his mother's shoulder.

"Oh, Mom," he sobbed, "I didn't want to do what I did but I had to. The witch is dead. Now I hope youse'll get better."

"It's all right, Wilbert," she answered. "Everythin's

gonna be all right. Don't you worry none. Go in the kitchen and wash yourself while I tell your father."

But before Mrs. Hess could call her husband she saw Blymire and Curry standing silently outside. She told them to come in and clean up and handed them fresh towels. Then she rapped hard on the party wall, arousing Clayton and his wife, Edna, and after this awakened her sleeping husband. It was almost 5:30 A.M. when all the participants were assembled in the kitchen to listen to Wilbert and the other two fill in the details.

At no time did any of the conferees have the slightest intention of notifying the police. With the exception of young Curry, who knew he had done wrong, they all considered this a justifiable homicide; the sooner it was forgotten, the better for everyone.

About seven o'clock that Wednesday morning, Clayton delivered a contented Blymire to his boarding house in the alley behind the Pennsylvania Tool Company's plant. Then he dropped Curry off at the Princess Street address. There was no sympathetic mother on hand to greet this fourteen-year-old when he got home. Mrs. MacLean had left for work an hour before, John's half-sisters were sound asleep and his stepfather was stretched out on the parlor floor in a drunken stupor, "snoring," as Curry said, "like he could wake the dead."

John went upstairs; tried to rest; gave up in a little while; left the house, and went to work.

The Hess family was able to enjoy its Thanksgiving turkey dinner in peace and quiet; Rehmeyer's murder was not discovered until early on the morning of Friday, November 30. The cry of a hungry farm animal led to the gruesome find.

So obvious was the murderers' trail that their apprehension, the discovery of Rehmeyer's body and the motive for the slaying were announced simultaneously in the *York Dispatch*. This newspaper broke the story on the morning of Friday, November 30, 1928.

"Belief in witchcraft led to the murder last Tuesday night of Nelson D. Rehmeyer, farmer, in his lonely home in the North Hopewell Township about four miles west of Shrewsbury. An effort to get a lock of the victim's hair as a charm to break a 'spell' believed to have been cast by a witch on the family of Milton J. Hess, R D 9, York Township, was the direct cause of the killing.

"John Blymire, aged 32 years, Chestnut and Pine Streets; John Curry, aged 14 years, 136 East Princess Street; Wilbert G. Hess, aged 18 years, York, R D 9, by their own confessions, made before the District Attorney, Amos W. Herrmann, did the killing. . . .

"The braying of an unfed mule about noon yesterday led Oscar Glatfelter to investigate and make the horrible discovery of Rehmeyer's battered and charred body. . . ."

Glatfelter, whose farm was about a mile and a half from the Hollow, was Rehmeyer's nearest neighbor to the north.

"I used to see the old man pass my place every day," he recalled, "but for a couple of days I missed him. On Thanksgiving, after we finished eating, some time after noon I passed his place when I heard the mule. It sounded hungry.

"I went inside the stable and found the animal hadn't been fed. Then I walked to the house. I rapped on the front door but nobody answered so I walked around to the kitchen door. It was closed but it wasn't locked. I walked inside and found Rehmeyer laying on the floor.

"Then I ran to Dave Vanover's [a nearby farmer] and him and his son Roland came back with me. Then we run over to Hildenbrand's [another neighbor, this one a mile and a half south of the Hollow]. He has a phone and we calls Dr. Gerry out in Shrewsbury and tells him to come quick. After that all of us run back to Rehmeyer's place to wait."

A half-hour later the Shrewsbury physician chugged up the Hollow in his Model T to Rehmeyer's farmhouse, where a score of neighboring farmers and their wives and children had assembled to enjoy the excitement not normally provided for the citizens of rural York County.

As for Dr. Gerry, that practitioner took one look at the body, knew the old man was beyond his or other mortal help and called the York County Coroner, L. U. Zech. The Coroner's physician, Dr. W. H. Shellhammer, ordered the body removed and an autopsy performed.

There was no question about the manner of the old witch's death.

"Blymire and Curry," the *York Gazette* continued, "were arrested shortly after midnight in York and readily admitted the killing. They implicated a third person who turned out to be Hess. The latter was taken into custody at his work in the Hess Lumber Yard, Grantley, between eight and nine this morning."

The first clue (and the only one necessary) to the identity of the killers came from the Widow Rehmeyer.

"This past Monday, November 26 [the night Blymire and Curry were their victim's overnight guests], two men came to my house after supper," Mrs. Rehmeyer told police. "It was around eight or nine o'clock. I don't remember exactly. They asked me if I knew where Mr. Rehmeyer could be found.

"I said I thought he was at his house; him and me hadn't been livin' together for seven or eight years. I'm keepin' our two daughters, Edna and Beatrice, on our old farm. Our place is a couple miles from the Hollow.

"I recognized one of the men as John Blymire, who used to live in the Valley. I didn't know who the other one was. The last time I seen the Mister was over a week ago. He was here then and tole me he was havin' trouble with the potato crop and that if he didn't sell it for a good price he'd have to go to the bank and draw money for the winter. I don't think he had much."

After their arrest, Blymire and Curry were taken to the York City Hall where each was questioned for hours by the District Attorney, Chief of Police Michel Schwint, Detective Ralph Keech, another arresting officer and a member of the prosecutor's staff. During this time, bystanders and working members of the press were able to wander in and out of the interrogation rooms at will.

Judged even by the loose standards of those halcyon days of police questioning forty years before the United States Supreme Court's decision in the matter of *Escobedo* v. *Illinois,* there is grave reason to doubt that the constitutional rights of any of the three prisoners were respected.

The *York Gazette* was on the street that afternoon

with both Blymire's and Curry's full confessions; Hess's came a few hours later. The wire services, A.P., U.P. and I.N.S., filed their separate stories. Before that Thanksgiving weekend was over, most of America and a considerable portion of the rest of the civilized world had been alerted to the fact that a practicing witch had been murdered in York County, Pennsylvania, in the year of our Lord, 1928.

Yet Mr. William Bolitho, the *New York World*'s famous correspondent, complained that coverage of what he labeled the "voodoo murder" was neither adequate nor astute.

"The so-called voodoo murder in Pennsylvania," carped Mr. Bolitho on December 6, 1928, "will not get the attention it deserves in America, I feel. I have already seen at least two other news stories which would have made the London *Times* come out in streamer headlines, and the Paris *Temps* use italics, which is the way it made up the news of the Armistice.

"Any European who is not psittacine, or parrot-minded, is struck with the sobriety of the American press and its deliberate waste of good sensation where it does not fit into a strictly conventional conception of melodrama. So this evocation of the spirits of the depths, the uprising into view of that gigantic, imperturbably sullen face which we call the devil in the banality of the times, the overtones of cruelty, terror and death, will hardly ever make the front page."

In spite of Mr. B.'s complaints, and to the extreme annoyance of the Lafayette Club and the York Chamber of Commerce, the hex murder did make the front pages of a respectable number of United States dailies during the ensuing weeks, although admittedly this Manhattan gentleman stirred his colleagues of the working press into greater and more imaginative efforts.

Mr. Pulitzer's star columnist continued to cavil:

"Yet even aesthetically the affair has its importance. What becomes of the elaboration of a wholly banal, wholly new America—the Babbitt warren—that European writers and native idealists have built up, and talked most Americans into believing themselves, when only an hour as the motor runs from Philadelphia [pretty fast driving, even in a Stutz or Marmon] genuine witches are killing each other at midnight with incantations 'round infernal fires.

"Here, at any rate, is antiquity as old and genuine and romantic as anything in Europe. . . . Witchcraft, and uncommonly orthodox witchcraft, is being practiced in blood and death only two blocks off Main Street by adepts in the pure tradition of terror and imagination of the stone age. . . .

"How easy it would be to put the whole affair in current jargon! Two highly introverted, intuitive farmers who have a superiority complex of power try to inhibit each other in a contest of witchcraft. Each by making deep attacks on the other's subconscious mind inflicts much damage. One is gradually pushed under. A terrible mood of depression and ruin is forced on him, that he calls by the old name of being bewitched.

"The only way to escape from ultimate destruction by this is to kill and bury his enemy symbolically by cutting off a lock of his hair and burying it eight feet deep. . . . With two friends and fellow sufferers he attempts to accomplish this. The other wizard resists, is killed; his body is burnt to make a ceremonial job of it. All perfectly straightforward for anyone who was brought up in a sensible nursery. When arrested the victorious warlock exclaims, as any psychoanalyst knows he ought to, 'Well, I'm kind of at ease now. Not bewitched any more.' "

Mr. Bolitho closes with a word of advice to members of the legal profession and the statute makers.

"That lawyers and law makers will have to turn their eye in the near future and try to make a jurisprudence which, whatever the name, will be substantially one of witchcraft and sorcery, is in the growing complications created by the authorized and unauthorized practice of psychoanalysis, the most modern of sciences.

"It is a pity that these practitioners of the most ancient art cannot profit by it."

The one who profited least of all was the late Nelson D. Rehmeyer, whose burial on the Sunday following his murder closed the most exciting Thanksgiving weekend

78

residents of southeastern York County had had for many generations.

"The funeral of the victim of the fiendish crime was held at two o'clock yesterday afternoon," reported the Hanover (Pennsylvania) *Record-Herald* of December 3, 1928. "Following brief services at the funeral home of John T. Wagner at Shrewsbury, the body was taken to St. John's Saddler's Church in Hopewell Township where concluding services were held.

"Borne by six neighbors, the mortal remains of Nelson D. Rehmeyer, battered and burned, were carried to the church cemetery on a hill beside the church where they found a last resting place.

"The services in Saddler's were in peaceful contrast to the violent crime that was enacted in that lonely little farmhouse not many miles away last Tuesday night. Long before the funeral cortege was scheduled to arrive a large crowd had gathered."

Saddler's, frequently spelled "Sadler's," a red brick building constructed about 1807 and named for a prominent North Hopewell Township family, is typical of the tiny churches that dot the area, hubs of wheels whose spokes reach out to a rim encompassing a dozen or so farms. In Saddler's churchyard, as in many other local burial grounds, are interred seven generations of parishioners.

"The little church, which seats about 150, slowly began to fill and when the funeral party arrived Funeral Director Wagner had to bring in a lot of portable chairs, and even then he could not accommodate those who attended the obsequies," commented the *Record-Herald*.

"Many ranged themselves on the aisle and along the rear walls as services progressed. On the grounds outside 125 automobiles were parked and there were quite a few horses and wagons.

"Miss Pauline Hess, the church organist, softly played the hymn, 'Take It to the Lord in Prayer,' as the casket was borne into the church by six neighbors of Mr. Rehmeyer, David Vanover, John Jones, Josiah Jones, Spangler Hildenbrand, James Nicholas and Fred

Rehmeyer. The widow and two children followed and were led sobbing to their pews near the front of the church. Then the choir sang 'Nearer My God to Thee.' "

The sermon was preached by the Reverend George E. Howersox, who served not only Saddler's but also several other small rural congregations from the "mother" church, Christ Lutheran of Shrewsbury. Pastor Howersox, with more *sangfroid* than one would expect considering the milieu in which most of his part-time communicants were born and raised, took this opportunity to berate the practice of necromancy.

"Reverend Howersox," continued the *Record-Herald,* "read the Scripture lesson from the 55th Chapter of Isaiah, which is a call to faith and repentance, 'Let the wicked forsake his way and the uprighteous man his thoughts,' and, 'Let him turn unto the Lord. . . .'

"Reverend Howersox prayed for enlightenment so 'that we might not practice evil arts and that we shall follow Him who said, "I am the Light of the world." ' "

The pastor added a word of concern for the trio whose actions were the direct cause of his appearance at Saddler's that Sunday.

"May they come to repentance and contrition for their deeds, and show them the Light," exhorted the minister.

Members of the York Chamber of Commerce were not the only citizens distressed by the notoriety their bailiwick had achieved as a result of Rehmeyer's murder. The Reverend Howersox shared these feelings.

"How dreadful," he commented, "that the murder has been spread in public print throughout the length and breadth of the land and has given this community ugly publicity that is surely not welcome. We can only pray that these outsiders who would publicly cast aspersions on our people and hold them up to ridicule will cease these bitter castigations, return to their own cities and ponder upon the similarity between their superstitions and ways and our own."

Alas! As future events proved, the Reverend Howersox's prayers went unheeded and no doubt unheard by those who needed them most; the worst was yet to come.

"The only note to jar the quiet, peaceful scene in the cemetery," concluded the *Record-Herald*, "was the activities of a battery of cameramen from York, Philadelphia, Baltimore and other places, recording the scene for their papers."

II

SPANGLER E. HILDENBRAND, REHMEYER'S NEAREST neighbor to the south, who had the added distinction not only of helping Oscar Glatfelter "turn over" the body but also of being a "bearer," vividly recalls the excitement the murder generated from the time the unfed mule brayed to the moment the third panel returned to the box and announced a verdict. It may also be recalled it was from Hildenbrand's telephone, the only one in the valley, that aid was summoned to Rehmeyer's Hollow.

"Man," he reflected, "you shoulda seen how them cars packed the roads when word got out. They came from Harrisburg, Philly, Pittsburgh, Baltimore, New Jersey, Ohio and so on and I know they came from England and France once the trial got under way.

"For weeks on end I could hardly get any work done day or night without some male or female reporter interruptin' me askin' to interview me. They kept takin' my picture and printin' what I said in newspapers everywhere all over the country. It got so I could hardly eat my meals without the front doorbell ringin' and there'd be another newspaper reporter outside wantin' to come in and talk to me and ask a lot of silly questions.

"They'd be snoopin' every place you could think of; crazy ones crawlin' in and out of holes and behind barns, dozens of 'em with their cameras takin' shots of people by day and powder flashes by night. It seems like there were hundreds of 'em prowlin' through the Hollow and 'round the old man's farm shoutin' their questions and writin' down the answers. We never had nothin' like it before or since.

"And in York, man! You shoulda been there. Cars with license tags from twenty different states; more strangers on the streets than durin' the Fair. Every hotel room taken and every restaurant jammed to the doors."

Hildenbrand, a heavyset, broad-shouldered farmer with red cheeks and clear gray eyes, who certainly must be in his early seventies but looks ten years younger, took off his striped cap, laid it on a fence post, scratched his thick gray hair and continued.

"And for what?" he asked rhetorically. "I never could understand why everybody in the world got so upset just because they murdered old man Rehmeyer. Sure, I knew the old witch but I never did believe they killed him because he hexed Blymire. I think they did it to get his gold. Time the gov'ment went off the gold standard and called it all in."

There would have been little point in reminding this otherwise clear-thinking farmer that in 1928 Calvin Coolidge was about to bequeath his legacy of prosperity to Mr. Hoover, Franklin Delano Roosevelt was four years away from the White House and there was no need to swell the coffers of Fort Knox.

In any event, if Rehmeyer had any gold to cache, he hid it so well it was not found by his murderers, his wife, his two daughters or the present occupants of his old house in the Hollow. For one who did business with His Satanic Majesty for profit, the witch died a comparatively poor man, especially in this prosperous farm country where estates of $100,000 or more are not uncommon.

"A modest estate of $1,500 is disposed of in the will of Nelson D. Rehmeyer, North Hopewell Township farmer . . ," stated the Hanover *Record-Herald* on December 12, 1928. "The will was probated yesterday in the office of Register of Wills Paul R. Schweitzer, and letters testamentary on the estate were granted to Edna Rehmeyer, daughter of the deceased. Amos W. Herrmann, District Attorney, appears as attorney for the executrix.

"Rehmeyer died possessed of personal property of the value of $500 and real estate of the value of $1,000. The man did not possess the great wealth neighbors credited him with having."

For one whose knowledge of the occult was so intimate and who was said to have trafficked with the devil, Rehmeyer wrote a singularly humble preamble.

"Knowing the uncertainty of life," he declared, "I do hereby will and bequeath . . . all of the land on the north side of the public road leading through my farm to my daughter Beatrice."

Land on the south side of the road went to his younger daughter, Edna. 'Their mother, Cora A.," Rehmeyer continued, "shall have the right to have her home on the farm as long as she lives or does not marry again. . . . In witness thereof, I, Nelson D. Rehmeyer, the testator, have this, my will set my hand and seal this 10th day of March, A.D., One Thousand Nine Hundred and Twenty-three. . . ."

Less than a week after the trio of murderers was apprehended, the Commonwealth of Pennsylvania took its first official steps to get the speedy trials of the three killers under way. Amos W. Herrmann represented the Commonwealth. Only the briefest biography of the District Attorney is needed. This lackluster member of the Bar was an honest but pedestrian lawyer and politician whose sole claim to fame was achieved from the lucky fluke of being prosecutor when Blymire, *et al.*, determined to get the book or the lock. Herrmann served one term in office—1926 to 1930—and then faded into obscurity. He died in 1948.

Judge Sherwood appointed counsel to represent Blymire and Curry, both of whom were paupers *de jure* as well as *de facto*. Hess's family, however, rallied financial support from its numerous branches scattered all through the lower end of the county and raised sufficient funds to hire Harvey A. Gross, by far the best criminal lawyer in the area.

A frequent complaint of York County members of the bar (particularly those who have lost cases to him) is that Harvey A. Gross must have at least one relative on every jury. Of course, a reasonably close relationship—nephew, niece, cousin, etc.—is a legitimate "challenge for cause." But to eliminate every prospective panelist simply because he is related by blood or marriage to Harvey A. would put an undue strain on the York County Jury Commission, a handicap taxpayers would not expect them to overcome.

Ancestors of Harvey A. Gross, all good solid Pennsylvania Dutchmen from the Palatinate, settled in York County on farms and in villages long before the Revolution. They fought in that war and in every American conflict since. Most of them and their numerous offspring remained within voting distance of what, for three days, was the capital of the United States.

"Harvey A.," as he is called frequently, or "Judge," a title he held for two ten-year terms in Orphan's Court, retiring from the bench the same year Judge Sherwood did, is a short, stocky man with a jutting jaw and slightly protruding incisors, physical characteristics giving him a striking resemblance to a miniature bulldog. Actually, his nickname during the many years he has been engaged in the practice of law in York County has been "Bulldog Gross." It might be added that this is the sobriquet he himself prefers best of all.

Ever since he turned seventy, nearly every reporter who has interviewed him says somewhere in the lead, "Even at three score and ten, Harvey A. Gross is alert, vigorous, healthy and still in active practice before the York County Bar." Two decades later this reporter can still make the statement and be as close to the truth as are most gentlemen of the press. However, it must be admitted that at ninety "Bulldog Gross" no longer tries jury cases; he acts mainly as a consultant, and is giving serious thought to complete retirement. A childless widower, he lives alone in the rambling old York townhouse where he brought his bride half a century ago. Mrs. Gross died in 1958.

The Judge was born and raised in Kralltown, a farming village in the southern end of the county.

"My father was a wagon maker and a damned good one just like his father and grandfather before him. But wagon making was only my father's avocation; his true love was teaching school. Salaries were so low in those

84

days he had to do something else to support his family. For four months he followed a trade that had been in our family for a couple of generations.

"Oh, yes. I almost forgot. He had a Civil War pension of four dollars a month; lost his leg at Antietam. My mother was a Quaker, a well-educated woman, too. All my early years I attended one-room schools and then I went to the State Teachers' College at Kutztown, only they called it the Normal School then. After I got my teacher's certificate, I attended Dickinson Law and graduated at eighteen, too young to be admitted to the Bar. So I had to wait three more years for that. Meanwhile I taught in the same little red schoolhouse I attended myself when I was a child."

Young Harvey A. Gross had no trouble finding clients. "I had more cousins, uncles and aunts in the county looking for advice, most of it free, than you could shake a stick at," he said. "They came to see me the minute I hung up my shingle."

In 1908, he served as Assistant District Attorney and the following year ran for that office on the Democratic ticket. He was defeated, he claims, by less than twenty votes. In 1913 he made another attempt and this time was elected by a huge plurality. He dropped out of active politics until 1938. Governor George H. Earle then appointed him to the Orphan's Court, a Bench on which he served well until 1957, when he decided not to run again.

Unlike their brothers-in-law in major cities, few members of the York County Bar restrict their practice to criminal law. Judge Gross was no exception, despite the fact that he represented far more exposed sinners than did most of his colleagues and with far more successes than failures.

He knows the law and he knows it well. Many of his acquittals were won because of his cold, methodical application of this basic knowledge and his merciless, systematic destruction of Commonwealth witnesses. There were times, however (his defense of Wilbert Hess is an example), when he forgot statutes and used histrionics and the hortative approach to extract tears of sympathy from the eyes of the twelve, and his own as well.

Long since retired members of the working press who once covered the York County Courts of Oyer and Terminer and saw the "Old Bulldog" in action at the height of his glory claim the chief reason for his great success was the empathy he was able to establish between the panel and himself.

"It was just as though he were saying to the twelve 'good men and true,' 'Look, fellows, you and I are nothing but Dumb Dutchmen,' and he'd put on the accent thick. 'Let's stick together and show those other guys how the Dumb Dutch do it,'" recalled Curt Thomas.

"That was fine," this reporter added, "until the opposition was able to pull the same act."

Judge Gross has two favorite stories about himself. The first concerns a client who insisted on pleading "not guilty" despite the fact that three highly reputable witnesses, including the owner, had seen him steal several cases of beer and load them in the trunk of a car.

"There wasn't any question about it," Bulldog Gross recalled, "and I knew damned well the D.A. wouldn't have any trouble proving the theft. I told my client he *must* plead guilty and throw himself on the mercy of the court. But he refused, so what could I do?

"I tried the case and I couldn't believe it when the jury came in with a verdict of 'not guilty.' The judge was furious and ordered the panel's names stricken from the list. The next morning the foreman met me on the street—his name coincidentally was Gross, too. I thanked him; he looked at me a bit sheepishly.

"'You know, Harve,' he said, 'that Gross feller you represented yesterday sure as hell stole the beer. But I told them eleven others on the jury that if we said he did, Harve Gross wouldn't like it, so we all decided to turn him loose.'"

The other tale the Bulldog enjoys retelling involves a remark his friend Clarence Darrow made to several other members of the Bar lunching in the Biltmore Hotel in New York, on January 12, 1929, a few hours before Gross was scheduled to address the Hess jury.

Commented Darrow, who'd followed the case closely and was bitter about the harsh decisions given Blymire and Curry, "There'll be a different verdict in the Hess case because there's a different kind of lawyer trying *this* one."

In age, tenacity and ethnic background there is great similarity between Bulldog Gross and Attorney Walter W. VanBaman, Curry's counsel. At ninety-one, this ruddy-cheeked, remarkably handsome lawyer is the active head of his own law firm, walks two miles to and from his office and home every day, has all his own teeth and a full crop of snow-white, wavy hair. In 1966 he celebrated the sixty-fifth anniversary of his admission to the Bar. It might be said here that Mr. VanBaman, like so many of his colleagues of that era, never attended law school; he merely "read for the law" in an attorney's office where he served an apprenticeship, then passed his "bars."

Mr. VanBaman, too, had a fling at politics, although he never achieved the Judgeship he once hoped for. In a stiff primary battle, he failed to get his party's nomination. However, in 1922 he ran for the office of District Attorney and beat his Republican opponent by a slim majority.

The practice of criminal law never did appeal to Mr. VanBaman despite (or possibly because of) his four years as District Attorney. So it was with considerable reluctance that he was persuaded to accept the thankless, time-consuming, unremunerative task of representing fourteen-year-old John Curry, whose story he never believed anyway. Even after forty years he remains unconvinced that witchcraft had anything to do with the case except in the minds of the working press and quite probably in that of his considerably younger friend, Mr. Justice Cohen, then only young Herb Cohen, just beginning the practice of law and in need of a few friends of importance.

Herbert B. Cohen's roots do not penetrate deeply into the fertile soil of York County. As a matter of fact, Mr. Cohen is a first-generation American. His parents were Eastern European Jews who emigrated to the United States shortly after the turn of the century. To the future Justice, this highly suspicious ancestry was an enormous handicap in an area where there were quite a few citizens who had never met a Jew and who, if they had, might not recognize him as such without the expected pair of horns.

Today, of course, in an age of professed enlightenment, the situation has changed for the better even in York County, where the presence of Jews is tolerated and possibly welcomed by the more liberal members of the local society. The one exception to progress is the Lafayette Club, inner sanctum of the Establishment. Here in this hex-ridden temple of prejudice on Market Street, there is no "tokenism," and rigid rules are never bent to permit the entry of a Hebrew or a Negro.

As for Jewish merchants, their shops do no better nor worse than those owned by Christians. But in medicine where Mr. Justice Cohen's older brother Milton is a respected practitioner, and in osteopathy, optometry and podiatry, Jews are not only well patronized but actually sought after, because, their Gentile patients reason, if a Jew can get through any of these disciplines, he's got to be good.

In the legal profession, where the disposal of a man's money—past, present or future—rather than the treatment of his physical ailments is the prime consideration, York County Christians are inclined to put their trust in fellow Christians in preference to Jewish advocates. In politics, however, there is a healthy respect, tinged with fear, for the Jew among the approximately 110,000 registered York County voters. This is due in a large measure to the astuteness of one man, Mr. Justice Herbert B. Cohen.

For years Mr. Cohen was the true, albeit offstage, leader of York County's Democratic Committee. This organization was once an impotent subsidiary of the Republican Party, existing on its patronage whenever the law required at least one appointive or elective member of the minority party to serve on a bureau or commission.

But Mr. C. would tolerate none of this servile coexistence so, as soon as he could, he tossed out the collaborationists, chose loyal young henchmen in their stead and methodically proceeded to oust the entrenched opposition. Within a few years his revitalized party took over

88

city and county offices and in 1934 it played a leading role in electing George H. Earle, the first Democratic governor Pennsylvania had in half a century.

Meanwhile, Mr. Cohen's fortunes rose with those of his party. A grateful constituency sent him to the State Legislature in Harrisburg where he soon became the party whip, and, in 1955, he was elected to the highest Commonwealth office a non-Christian ever held—Attorney General. Less than two years later another Democratic governor, George M. Leader, a friend, colleague and protégé of Mr. Cohen, appointed him to the State Supreme Court, a most enviable position for Jew or Gentile.

It should be stated parenthetically that Mr. Justice Cohen is an excellent, apolitical jurist, an honorable man. Never once in his long politico-legal career could he be legitimately accused of betraying anyone's trust to line his own pockets or of profiting personally at the People's expense except in the accepted Jacksonian principle of spoils to the victor.

Of course, these interesting milestones in Mr. Justice Cohen's career were passed long after this immature, inexperienced law school graduate was asked (a polite word for ordered) by the Court before whom he was a humble petitioner to undertake the defense of a murderer who needed a Clarence Darrow to draw a sporting chance. Mr. Darrow undoubtedly would have insisted upon more time to prepare a capital case of such importance and, after exploring community attitudes, would have demanded a change of venue.

But young Herb Cohen, who had a recent bride to support, no money or family connections and a practice only two years old, and who was in addition a member of a minority group, had to say "yes" even though he certainly realized the cards were stacked against him and his client, John H. Blymire.

"I needed this one like a hole in the head," Mr. Justice Cohen recalled. "I was twenty-seven years old; I'd just about gotten out of law school, passed my bars and started to practice, and I'd never tried a criminal case before and damned few civil ones either.

"I had three weeks to prepare the defense of a pauper

89

who not only admitted his guilt and signed a damaging confession but bragged about the murder and never once, in public or private, displayed the least bit of remorse, and the mood of the county was vengeful. Furthermore, I'd been warned there was to be no 'nonsense' about hexerei or witchcraft and that His Honor would frown deeply upon any attempt to view the crime as anything more than homicide in the commission of a felonious attempt to rob Nelson D. Rehmeyer.

"We were getting blasted with adverse publicity from all over the county. 'Get it over with, the faster the better,' were the unspoken orders of the day. So you see why I wasn't too happy about taking on this one."

There can be little doubt that the orders Mr. Cohen was asked to obey came from the confines of the Lafayette Club, which unquestionably issued similar instructions to the York Chamber of Commerce.

12

ON DECEMBER 5, THE TRIO OF MURDERERS WAS brought before a York Justice of the Peace.

"Six questions and as many answers from only one witness, Constable Ralph Keech, constituted the entire proceedings at the hearing before Alderman Walter F. Owen this morning in the case of John Blymire, Wilbert G. Hess and John C. Curry, charged with the murder of Nelson D. Rehmeyer," declared the *York Dispatch*.

"The hearing, from the first word to the last, consumed not more than three minutes. Just sufficient evidence was produced to establish the fact of Rehmeyer's death and that the three prisoners had a hand in it.

"Constable Keech was called to the stand and was sworn by the Alderman. District Attorney Herrmann put the questions."

The *Dispatch* continued: " 'Did you arrest John Blymire, John Curry and Wilbert G. Hess?' District Attorney Herrmann asked.

" 'I arrested John Blymire and Curry but not Hess.'

" 'Did any of them make any statements that would indicate they did or did not have a hand in the killing of Nelson Rehmeyer?'

" 'They all made statements that they took part in the slaying.'

" 'In your presence?'

" 'In my presence, yes, all three of them.'

" 'Did you see Nelson Rehmeyer?'

" 'I did.'

" 'Where?'

" 'At his home.'

" 'Was he dead or alive?'

" 'He was dead.'

" 'That's all,' concluded the District Attorney.

" 'Cross examine,' said Alderman Owen. 'What attorney wishes to question the witness first?'

"Harvey A. Gross for Wilbert G. Hess, Walter W. VanBaman for John Curry and Herbert B. Cohen for John Blymire said they would ask no questions and were satisfied that the hearing be concluded.

"Alderman Owen then recommitted the three prisoners to jail to await action of the January grand jury."

Had not Wilbert's mother been present to add a touch of drama, this preliminary hearing would have been a dull affair and a disappointment to newspapermen and photographers on hand who were drawn, at this early stage, from cities only as remote as Harrisburg, Gettysburg, Hanover, Lancaster, Lebanon and other Central Pennsylvania communities. Still in type and not to appear in the *New York World* until the morrow was Mr. Bolitho's call to arms.

"The only dramatic incident during the morning in the alderman's office," continued the *York Dispatch,* "was the appearance of Mr. and Mrs. Milton J. Hess, parents of one of the prisoners. They entered the room with Attorney Harvey A. Gross and Mrs. Hess appeared at the desk of the alderman. The latter apparently did not recognize her and curtly asked, 'Who is this woman?'

"Mrs. Hess, highly nervous because of worries she has suffered since the tragedy, broke into sobs and seemed to collapse. The alderman was about to tell her to take a place in his waiting room when Attorney Gross directed that she be seated on one of the other chairs provided for counsel. Mrs. Hess sat directly in front of her son. It was with great effort that she suppressed the convulsive sobs that shook her body and frequently there were low moans from her."

Counselor Gross, himself, was surprised at Mrs. Hess's display of emotion.

"She was a big, self-controlled, domineering woman and maybe a bit backward mentally. Poor Wilbert was tied to her apron strings."

The Bulldog smiled a bit at the memory. "And that's exactly what I showed 'em at the trial."

In the rear of Alderman Owen's minuscule courtroom sat Blymire's father, Emanuel, and his grandfather, old Andrew, to give him what comfort they thought he might need. But fourteen-year-old John Curry stood alone at the Bar. His mother was at work, his half-sisters at school and Alexander MacLean, shamed by all the notoriety his ungrateful stepson had caused, had disappeared from Princess Street, not to be seen for a month. However, he did return to his adopted city during the trials to cadge free drinks in local bars as a quasi-hero, shaking his head sadly and no doubt telling all who would listen that "if only John would have paid heed to his stepfather, he wouldn't have turned out so bad and disgraced me and his mother."

Obviously stung by local and regional editorials denouncing the prevalence of witches in York County, and perhaps dismayed by the realization that so many potential patients were being diverted to non-members, the York County Medical Society, on the day following Alderman Owen's hearing, promised to take direct action against those practitioners who scorned Hippocrates and chose the devil in his stead.

"Dr. P. A. Noll [hopefully unrelated to the Witch of Marietta], Secretary of the York County Medical Society, will have his organization consider a plan of immediate action . . . and propose that a committee be appointed to conduct an educational campaign to inform the public of the evils of witchcraft and its allied 'charms,'" stated the *York Dispatch*.

Asked by the press if his group would go beyond exhortation and take to the law to drive out regional practitioners of black and white arts, the medical man shrugged his shoulders.

"We tried that a couple of times and it didn't work out," he admitted. "Few months ago a fellow from Dallastown named Leber went to 'Professor' Lenhart here in York to be cured for the 'liver complaint.' That old quack said it would cost him two hundred dollars and Leber put up the cash. He belonged to a lodge that payed sick benefits, but when he went to claim them, the lodge officers told Brother Leber he'd first have to present a certificate from a qualified physician, not a powwower.

"So then the man was sent to Dr. Benjamin Hoover at Wrightsville. In filling out the patient's form, Dr. Hoover discovered that what previous treatment Leber had was from the notorious 'Professor' Lenhart.

"Of course Lenhart couldn't do a damned thing for him [whether Dr. Hoover did more is not a matter of record] and Leber wanted somebody to get his money back from the powwower."

When word of the affair reached Dr. Noll's ears, he advised his colleague at Wrightsville to have the patient sign an affidavit relating all the facts in the case. The Society, its counsel advised, could then proceed against Lenhart on charges of practicing medicine without a license.

"We were all set," Dr. Noll said. "This was one time we felt we had the 'Professor.' But when Leber was told he'd have to appear against the witch doctor, he backed down. 'I'm scared,' he said. 'If I do he'll put a spell on me.' What could we do? We dropped it; that's the way it's been all along.

"Maybe now that they have Blymire in custody," he reflected, "people will be willing to testify and we'll be able to do something positive."

With some naïveté, the Hanover *Record-Herald* took

cognizance of **Dr.** Noll's published hopes the following day. This newspaper is the spokesman for a modern city of 18,000 where witchcraft still flourishes on Main Street four decades later. In 1928, however, the *Record-Herald* was apparently taken aback to learn that necromancy was part of community mores, and it expressed the hope that since the proper authorities had now been alerted, black magic in York County would disappear forthwith.

"EXIT WITCHCRAFT," was the headline.

"Phenomenal as it may seem to have witchcraft come to light in this year of the march of progress, the fact remains that a good-sized circle of devotees to the art are to be found in and near York County.

"Realizing that they were largely responsible for the death of one man and seeing the possible damages and unhappiness that could further be visited on the county, the officials have become incensed and the work of arresting those who are teaching witchcraft has begun in earnest. It is the proper motive and will work a great effect on the communities where the 'powwow' doctors have been dominating men and women.

"There can be nothing good that comes from teaching that happiness will follow the death of any man and which incites one person to rid the world of the one who is casting a black spell over his life. Let the good work of the officials continue!"

Needled into action by the press, Governor John S. Fisher summoned Dr. Noll and officials of other county medical societies in the "afflicted" areas, then ordered his State Police Commissioner to take immediate action against the Commonwealth's legion of witches. The investigation got off to an inspired start; evidence against hexers began to pour in.

FIVE BABIES ALLOWED TO DIE IN COUNTY
WITHOUT MEDICAL ATTENTION, PROBE
BRINGS OUT
Attended Only by Powwower

were the page-one headlines of the Hanover *Record-Herald*. The story follows:

"Five small children who were 'treated' by powwow practitioners but for whom there was no medical attention, it was proven, are known to have died in York County in the last two years.

"But although Coroner Zech knew the hocus-pocus of Southern Pennsylvania's witchcraft survival had replaced the care of a physician, no report of this fact ever was made to the authorities who could have investigated the deaths.

"The startling admission that he had made no effort to bring about official action in these cases was made by the Coroner shortly after Dr. P. A. Noll declared scores of children die each year under the same circumstances."

Mr. Zech was frank enough.

" 'I remember these cases very distinctly,' the Coroner said, 'particularly three of them, and I knew there were five or more.

" 'In all cases the child had been found to be undernourished or suffering from a disease, and a powwow practitioner had been called in. The parents in each case admitted they had not provided any medical attention for the children. In most of the cases, if I remember correctly, broncho-pneumonia was the cause of death.'

"It was when the Coroner was asked for the names of the children who had died under those circumstances that he admitted failure to notify county officials of the fact that the 'powwow' superstition had entered the cases.

" 'In looking over my records,' he said, 'I find I did not mark the powwow cases. I only listed the cause of death. . . . There never has been a thorough investigation of the cases made. The usual practices of powwow believers had been employed in the cases of childhood.' "

The Rx ordered by the *braucher* in charge of at least one of the patients who died came directly from *The Long Lost Friend*.

" 'The powwow practitioner burned an egg tied in a piece of woolen string,' Coroner Zech said. 'This is the standard powwow "cure" for a cold.' His statement came as a climax to an army of facts brought out about the practices of powwow healers and witch doctors in York County," concluded the *Record-Herald*.

Obviously misunderstanding the announced purpose behind the Commonwealth's well-publicized investigation, one York housewife called upon the authorities to help her solve a problem of some immediacy.

"Mrs. Mary Lehman, wife of John Lehman, visited the office of Coroner L. U. Zech in the Rosenmiller Building this morning to inform him that someone had cast a 'spell' over her home," said the *York Dispatch* on December 6, 1928.

"The woman appeared in a highly nervous state and gave every evidence of being in fear of the 'spell.' The Lehmans—husband, wife and daughter, Fannie, 16 years old—live in a house on what is commonly called Gravel Hill. The house is one of a row of four situated on an elevation on the west side of North George Street, north of Jefferson Avenue.

"After she related her story of the 'spook' and how she saw him make motions with the hands, Coroner Zech tried to convince the woman that it was a creation of her imagination; that there are no such things as 'spooks' and 'spells.' He advised her to go home and rest. He assured her that if she would forget the whole thing everything would be all right."

Annoyed by the Coroner's soothsaying and with her hopes for state aid dashed by this nonbeliever's attitude, Mrs. Lehman ended the interview by informing the gentleman that he didn't know what he was talking about. "Every night a witch comes in front of my home and makes all sorts of signs at me. Then his face turns into an animal [the species was not identified] and he disappears."

Undaunted by Mrs. L.'s attitude, area physicians nonetheless continued their campaign to wipe out necromancy.

"The proposed crusade against the practice of witchcraft and its allied evil creeds in York County, to be recommended to the York County Medical Society by its secretary, Dr. P. A. Noll, is likely to be a forerunner of concerted action throughout the state," declared the *Dispatch* on December 10.

"Dr. Noll indicated that after the local medical society

takes definite steps in a movement which is gaining momentum here daily for the purpose of eradicating 'powwowism,' he will urge units of the State Medical Association to take similar actions.

"The movement will be pushed with such determination that it is hoped to have the state legislature take cognizance of it. The Commonwealth of Pennsylvania will assist in our investigation."

Proof that the Commonwealth's offer of assistance was no idle gesture came with a release from the governor's office, together with a one-column photograph, informing all that an undercover agent, using an alias, had come directly from Harrisburg to gather evidence of hexerei in York County.

"The full scope of activities of local voodoo doctors and 'powwowers' is being investigated by Charles N. Fry, a special investigator of the state board of medical education and licensure, since the recent witchcraft murder of Nelson D. Rehmeyer . . . and the subsequent exposure of the practice of the so-called 'black art' here," stated the *Dispatch* on December 10.

"The visit of the state inspector was veiled in secrecy; it was learned that he did not disclose his identity [despite the photograph and advance notice] to several persons upon whom he called to secure data against unlicensed practitioners with a view of prosecuting them.

"He called on Dr. P. A. Noll . . . to whom he revealed his identity and the object of his visit, but he visited local officials incognito. He stated that his department has been put on the *qui vive* by the revelations made in York County incidental to a murder and the unearthing [literally, one wonders?] of a number of deaths attributed to 'powwow' treatments.

"Agent Fry secured from various unrevealed sources the names of alleged 'powwow' doctors and other persons not physicians who give 'treatments' to sick people and charge money. . . ."

The only mystery about undercover agent Fry's visit to York County is why the governor's office made it a mystery. All this sleuth had to do to gather information was to walk the streets of York or any other community in the area and read the shingles affixed to hundreds of doors and front porches to find out who was practicing medicine without a license.

A few days later the much ballyhooed investigation came to an end that had been predicted by members of the working press.

"They'd been through it before a half-dozen times," recalled Herman A. Lowe of the *Philadelphia Inquirer,* who had been sent to York to do a story of the probe. "They told me it would fall apart; that we were wasting our time if we expected prosecutions.

"There was no trouble getting evidence. In about twenty-four hours I was treated for warts, bunions, gout, the liver complaint, Chinese rot, falling hair, falling teeth. You name it; I had it, and the witches had a cure for it. The deal cost the *Inquirer* forty dollars in fees to pay out an average of two bucks to every powwow artist who 'cured for' me.

"For a city-raised boy it was hard to believe such things existed in America. But the guys on the *Dispatch* and *Gazette* laughed at my innocence. 'It's a way of life up in this neck of the woods and it'll never change,' they claimed. I stayed around a couple more days to find out if they were right. They were."

The Hanover *Record-Herald,* bubbling over with optimism scarcely a week before, was the first to acknowledge that this investigation would go the way of all others.

"The members of that 'vicious circle of voodoo doctors' who prey upon the fears of the superstitious can breathe easier. There will be no prosecutions," said that paper on December 15.

"Deputy Superintendent of Public Instruction, Charles D. Koch, Harrisburg, acting secretary of the State Board, came to York yesterday. He was accompanied by Charles Fry, an inspector of the board, but their movements were veiled in deepest secrecy.

"Dr. Koch . . . went to the county courthouse, entered the District Attorney's office and held a conference with someone, but District Attorney Amos Herrmann, when later seen, was noncommunicative of his visit.

" 'What I may have done or planned to do while in York is my personal business and is of no concern to anyone else,' Dr. Koch declared.

" 'What did you do while in York?' he was asked by a representative of the *York Gazette*. 'I did nothing. I was down on personal business,' he said.

" 'Purely personal business and nothing connected with the powwow cases?' he was asked.

" 'That's right,' he said. 'I did see the District Attorney. But we are making no prosecutions now.' "

Herman Lowe, still baffled, asked a member of the *Dispatch* staff why the Deputy Superintendent refused to do anything and why he was so secretive.

"That's simple," was the reply. "If you think Koch's doctorate in education means anything when it comes to witchcraft you're wrong. He's *still* a Dutchman and he's *still* scared to death Lenhart or some other brager'll put a hex on him if he does anything to harm the trade. That's the *only* reason the probe will come to nothing.

"The reason for secrecy? I don't know. Unless Dr. Koch thinks he's kidding the witches, who he should know are omniscient."

A reporter from the Harrisburg Associated Press Bureau dug into Dr. Koch's bureau records and came up with the fact that York's famous Professor Lenhart had once taken a State Board examination for faith healing. He had done rather poorly, attaining a mark of 3.66 out of a possible 100. "An illiterate" was written at the bottom of the test paper.

The following day that newspaperman put the question to Pennsylvania's Acting Superintendent of Public Instruction. "Why," he asked, "are you permitting Lenhart to practice without a license?"

At this Dr. Koch turned around angrily and said, "That's none of your business."

Strangely enough the probe's final blow was struck by those who had the most to gain, financially at least, by its success.

"The York County Medical Society last night went on record as being willing to furnish information against 'powwow' and other quack doctors but if prosecutions are to be brought, they must come from state officials or the District Attorney's office," said the *York Dispatch* on December 21.

"The organization concluded that it was not the duty of the medical profession to bring action. This decision was reached after a report was presented by its health and public instruction committee, which has been investigating the activities of illegal practitioners."

This, then, was the atmosphere smothering York County's Courts of Oyer and Terminer as the witchcraft trials of John Blymire, John Curry and Wilbert Hess opened.

13

STRUCK SUDDENLY BY THE FACT THAT THEY were about to have a major production of international appeal within the confines of their beautiful but inefficient old courthouse, members of the Bench took it upon themselves to keep the anticipated crowds from becoming unruly and, at the same time, to prevent the trials from turning into a three-ring circus.

"Unusual public interest being manifested in the witchcraft murder cases to come before the January sessions court next week caused President Judge Henry Niles . . . to appear before the county commissioners today and advise that precautions be taken in the handling of crowds that will be attracted," said the *Harrisburg Patriot.*

"Arrangements were made at the conference for the employment of several tipstaves in addition to the extras who are on duty at the sessions of the several criminal courts.

"The officials planned to keep the courtrooms free as possible for the accommodation of jurors and witnesses and to prevent overcrowding by people whose only object is to have their curiosities satisfied. It was . . . decided by the county commissioners . . . to prohibit extending telegraph wires into the building.

"The taking of pictures within the temple of justice will also be banned by officials. In fact it was agreed to do everything necessary to keep the people . . . attracted by the trials [orderly] and permit the wheels of justice to function as smoothly as possible."

Professional handicappers had already worked out the prisoners' defense and predicted the verdicts several days before the first of the three trials began. Blymire would plead insanity and spend the rest of his days in a mental institution. Hess's defense was to be based on the family's belief in witchcraft and a loving, obedient son's understandable desire to remove the hex from his parents. The verdict? Five to ten years on a charge of manslaughter, and out in three.

About Curry there was no question in the minds of these prognosticators. Because of his extreme youth and unfortunate background he would throw himself on the mercy of the court and at worst be sent to an institution for juvenile delinquents, there to stay until he reached the age of twenty-one. Or so said the Philadelphia *Evening Public Ledger*.

Unfortunately, the dopesters did not take into consideration that in the York County Courts of Oyer and Terminer in January, 1929, there was no mercy and, for that matter, not much justice.

For its pre-trial story, the enterprising Lancaster *New Era* got the jump on regional competitors by dispatching a reporter to New York to interview a witchcraft expert, Mr. W. B. Seabrook, whose book, *The Magic Island*, was a 1929 best seller.

"The trial at York should afford the public an accidental glimpse of what is transpiring in many rural sections of the United States," Seabrook said in his Greenwich Village studio apartment. "I say accidental because had no murder resulted there would have been no publicity. The trial may tend to educate the general public to what witchcraft is, just as the trial at Dayton, Tennessee, brought about wide discussion of evolution.

101

"If it is brought out in the trial that whatever power a sorcerer may have does not come from God, the devil or any supernatural force, but only from things that can be explained by rational psychology, then you will have delivered the countryside from superstitions and fear.

"The trial, properly conducted and given wide publicity, might prove of real educational value for this country."

At the same time dopesters were making their book, the District Attorney was making his; being, in a sense, closer to the horse's mouth, he had a better chance of winning his bets than they had.

"The sole motive for the murder of Nelson D. Rehmeyer was robbery," Mr. Herrmann told the *Gazette and Daily*. "That is why the Commonwealth will demand the death penalty for all three killers. As for hexerei witchcraft and so on, that is so much hogwash and we'll have none of it in this courtroom."

Even at this point in the proceedings, with area coverage expanding and reporters flocking into York from all over the country, with A.P., U.P. and I.N.S. demanding and getting extra wires, with the telephone company pressed into installing scores of extra lines and with journalistic rumblings heard from far-off London, Paris and Berlin, local officials still hoped to keep the trials a kind of regional secret.

"Only those having business in the court will be admitted," declared the *Dispatch* on Friday, January 4, quoting the Bench. "The court is determined that there shall not be an army of feature writers, of news writers and others on hand to make the courtroom an arena of the spectacular."

Hopes of the Bench were dashed on Sunday, January 6, when Dudley Nichols let loose a syndicated tirade that rocked the Chamber of Commerce and the City and County of York and established a pattern of subjective journalism (if this is not a contradiction in terms) for others to follow during the course of all three trials.

"Here in York," wrote Mr. Nichols in the *New York World,* "witchcraft is still as implicitly believed as ever it was in Salem in the old days. People glance fearfully at

102

the full moon and imagine they see humped figures riding the birch broom across its yellow face. The black cat is one shape of the fiend, and headaches, backaches and other human ills are the hexes or spells of sorcerers. Barns and cowsheds bear strange chalked crosses to unhex the cattle and horses stalled within."

Perhaps, in the interest of science, I ought to point out that according to the best authorities, Mr. Nichols was wrong about the purpose of those many-colored signs seen all over the Pennsylvania Dutch country. In the words of the late Johnny Ott, a Lenhartsville artist who painted thousands of them over a period of forty years, they have no anti-hex value and are simply "chust for nice."

"Fathers and mothers of sick children," continued Mr. Nichols, "go about muttering conjurations. And the medicinemen or hex doctors, beyond doubt most of them wildly sincere in their practices, blow upon bedridden people or 'try' for them in various ways, as treating is called."

There was no escape from scorn for York County burghers. Close upon the heels of Mr. Nichols' publicly expressed contempt came a bitter editorial in J. David Stern's liberal Philadelphia *Record*.

"We proudly announced our independence of faith based on ignorance and beliefs which have their foundation in fear.

"And then comes some appalling occurrence such as the 'witchcraft' murder in York County, and all our pride, all our satisfied complacency, melt away. Such a tragedy is as disturbing as a thunderbolt striking close at hand on a sleepy summer afternoon. The ignorance and fears of the savages have not been uprooted by our boasted civilization. In some communities, we find, they still rule the thoughts and actions of large numbers of people.

"Such conditions seem impossible. But there is the charred body of Nelson Rehmeyer, and there are the confessions of the men who killed him, to prove that they are all too real.

"The men who have told of their parts in this terrible

103

crime are Americans, Americans of what we are accustomed to call 'good stock.' They have had all the advantages that America offers. . . . Yet all this failed to wipe out their belief in witchcraft, spells, incantations and strange rites that have no place in American civilization."

Within days other condemnatory editorials and news stories depicting the general horror of life in York County appeared in the press in all forty-eight states. For two weeks more there was to be little peace for residents of Pennsylvania's hex belt.

There was a measure of tranquility, however, for Blymire's two young collaborators.

"Hess and Curry," declared the *New York Times,* "on the eve of their trial professed their peace of mind as a result of their . . . conversion at an evangelistic service in the county jail, while Blymire has remained firm all along in his statement that now Rehmeyer is dead, he no longer feels bewitched."

Long before the sun rose over the lush farms, cities and villages on Monday, January 7, York County's narrow "Pinchot" roads and its broad highways were filled with every conceivable vehicle from mule carts to Pierce Arrows, their occupants drawn irresistibly to the courthouse.

"There," said the Philadelphia *Record,* "will be held the weirdest and most curiously fascinating murder trial in the history of modern jurisprudence."

14

ON A COLD, CLEAR JANUARY DAY, AT 9:30 A.M., John Curry was formally arraigned before Judge Henry O. Niles and a Grand Jury sitting in Courtroom Number One. A half-hour later a true bill of murder was returned against this fourteen-year-old. The Blymire and Hess arraignments followed in that order and with like consequences. At 10:35 the trio, handcuffed together, was brought into Judge Sherwood's Courtroom Number Two.

Number Two was and still is the smallest of the county's courtrooms, with just barely enough space to accommodate the judge, prosecutor, potential panelists, witnesses, defendants, counsel and others essential to the case on trial plus a press table for one or two local newspapermen. Since attendance at previous trials held here never had reached capacity, there had been no previous complaint about the room's size. However, the scores of newspapermen from all over the country who were clamoring for admittance bitterly assailed presiding Judge Niles's choice of Number Two, which was defended strongly and smugly by representatives of the city's dailies whose accustomed presence at the press table normally passed unnoticed.

"They [the 'furrin' press] had their troubles when they tried to have Judge Sherwood accord them greater privileges than the court had proposed, which were mainly to permit representatives of the accredited press associations, A.P., U.P. and I.N.S., and representatives of York newspapers within the railing before the bar of the court; all others had to find a place in the courtroom if there were any vacant chairs," stated the *Gazette and Daily*.

"This, the visiting newspapermen and women didn't like, they wanted reserved seats, but the court's orders stood. Photographers have also been barred from the courtroom. The court has the situation so well in hand, so far as controlling admittance to the courtroom is concerned, that any newswriter desiring to get into Courtroom Number Two had no difficulty."

The youthful Herb Cohen, who had hoped against hope to have his client tried last but who was outmaneuvered by the District Attorney, asked for and, since Mr. Herrmann offered no objections, was granted a severance. As if to emphasize the fact that the three prisoners would be tried separately, Judge Sherwood ordered their cuffs removed in open court. John Blymire was on his own and the selection of his peers began.

Ten minutes later, the first juror, William E. Sprenkle of 615 Market Street, York, who listed his occupation as "gentleman," was seated in the box. Before court adjourned for the noon recess Sprenkle was joined by four others, and at 3:45 P.M., after an examination of only forty-four potential talesmen, John S. Fishel, a York Haven insurance agent, became the twelfth man. Mr. Fishel seemed a bit too eager to serve but when His Honor overruled defense counsel's challenge for cause, Mr. Cohen raised no further objections and the juror was sworn. Questions asked by Mr. Cohen and Mr. Herrmann of potential panelists were strictly routine:

"Are you related by blood or marriage to the defendant?—Have you been spoken to or written to by the defendant or by any other person on the behalf of the defendant?—Do you have any conscientious scruples against capital punishment?—Could you, if the evidence warranted, render a verdict that would carry with it the death penalty?"

In addition to two other "gentlemen," Blymire's jury was comprised of a pair of farmers, a printer, a grocery store clerk, a wireworker, a weaver, a loom fixer and an insurance salesman, plus one banker, Harry P. Kissinger, who was selected as foreman. Kissinger, then only the chief bookkeeper of the York Bank and Trust Company, later became its vice president. He retired "officially" if not actually in 1967.

"I was only thirty-two years old at the time and I think I was the youngest man in the box," recalled the semiretired banker, still active at seventy-three. (He was not the youngest; juror number two, Earl E. Brown, the weaver, was only twenty-five.)

At least half the panelists bore surnames indicating Pennsylvania Dutch ancestry—Reisinger, Emig, Stauffer, Myers, Sprenkle and Kissinger—and it is more than likely that the rest, with the probable exception of Charles McWilliams, the wireworker, and Walter Cunningham, the printer, all had some German blood in their veins.

Visiting members of the fourth estate were singularly unimpressed by the physical appearance and habits of some of the jurymen and commented on them quite freely. Some panelists were "grossly fat," and one was "too thin and looked undernourished." The Cleveland

Plain Dealer declared that "the twelve who sat in the box, with few exceptions, seemed to experience considerable difficulty grasping the meanings of words containing more than two syllables."

Said the Associated Press, "Harry Warner has a hooked nose and a look about his jaw as though he had just swallowed a green persimmon." However, the A.P.'s man in York did not go so far as to suggest that the shape of Mr. Warner's nose or his possible enjoyment of unripe fruit should be enough to disqualify him from jury duty.

"Curtis Leathery, a Washington Township farmer . . . has a red face and the look of a Norse seaman," stated a United Press correspondent. Whether this was a favorable or unfavorable evaluation of Mr. Leathery's ability to render a proper verdict would depend, of course, on this reporter's personal attitude toward ruddy complexions and Scandinavian seamen.

Ken Mack of the Philadelphia *Record* was annoyed by at least two men in the box. "H. K. Stauffer holds his hand to his ear as though he had trouble hearing and chews tobacco constantly . . . . Philip Myers, of Washington Township, the sixth juror, chewed a little more furtively than Mr. Stauffer and his drooping mustaches are tobacco-stained."

Since all of the jurors were over twenty-one years of age and had spent part if not all of their lives in York County, it would not be unreasonable to assume that every man sitting in the box had been exposed to witchcraft in one form or other at some period in his life. Nor would it be too far-fetched to believe that at least one panelist, within the year preceding his call to pass judgment on John Blymire, had been tried for by his favorite powwower or had recommended a *braucher* to his wife, son or daughter.

But so dominant was the Establishment and its dependents' fear of bringing witchcraft into the open, thus exposing its powerful grip on the people of York County, that the one question of vital importance to the man in the dock was never raised. No prospective panelist was asked, "Do you believe in hexerei?"

As a result, until a witness blurted out the detested

word "witch," to the ill-concealed fury of Judge Sherwood, Prosecutor Herrmann had been able to lead the jury into believing that Blymire and his youthful associates killed Rehmeyer solely because they wanted the old man's hidden gold.

Unfortunately for Blymire and the two other defendants, the damage was done; black magic sneaked in through the back door instead of by the main entrance, where it could have been examined openly and its potent influence upon the prisoners in the dock measured with understanding and care.

To this day, Kissinger, a man of unquestioned integrity, firmly believes robbery was the sole motive for the crime. "After what Mr. Herrmann brought out and the Judge informed us in his charge, we did not seriously consider the hex angle for a single moment," the ex-foreman declared.

When the last juror was seated, His Honor ordered a brief recess. Fifteen minutes later District Attorney Herrmann announced his readiness to open the case of the *Commonwealth of Pennsylvania* v. *John H. Blymire, defendant.*

"Then," as the Philadelphia *Record* said, "jurisprudence rang up the curtain . . . on a carefully rehearsed American folk drama, nationally billed as 'York County's witchcraft murder trial,' and disclosed an all-star judicial and legal cast struggling desperately but vainly to keep the leading character in the wings. . . .

"But that chief character in the play whose presence the officialdom of York County is laboring so tremendously to conceal, is neither the sharp-featured, squinteyed Blymire nor the bearded eccentric who was beaten to death when he refused to surrender to his rival 'witch' a lock of his long and graying hair.

"The star of the weird piece of realistic tragedy being enacted here is the 'specter' of witchcraft which lurks in odd corners throughout five counties of this presumably civilized state."

Mr. Herrmann presented his case to the jury in low, unemotional tones. His delivery was in the singsong manner so characteristic of "up-staters" and his accent, although modified somewhat by exposure to other cultures at college and law school, was strictly Pennsylvania Dutch—the w's came out as v's and vice versa.

For the jury's enlightenment, District Attorney Herrmann stated the Commonwealth's carefully edited version of Blymire's confession. Every passage referring to witches, black magic, powwowism or necromancy was not merely cut, it was cut out.

And so the twelve good men and true, ordered by the Judge to disregard previous "knowledge" of the crime and render a verdict based solely upon what they heard in court, were misled deliberately by a representative of the People at the very start of the trial. This was a capital case with a man's life at stake and, as most trial lawyers know, what is first said to a jury remains longest in the panel's composite mind and is most difficult to eradicate or mitigate.

Not only did the prosecutor fail to present the prisoner's motivation for the murder, all carefully spelled out in the naïve Blymire's detailed confession, but he also forgot to mention the State's theory—that this was a murder for profit. However, Judge Sherwood, who had listened to Mr. Herrmann's long, dull opening, impatiently waiting for him to come to the point, sharply reminded that gentleman of his significant omission.

"Doesn't the Commonwealth intend to show any motive, Mr. Herrmann?" the Judge asked sarcastically. "If it has, I haven't heard it yet."

Sheepishly the People's representative returned to the box and faced the panel once more.

"There is one thing I did forget," he admitted, a slight deprecatory smile playing about his lips as though to imply everyone really was making much ado about nothing. "Speaking of things that took place at City Hall following the arrest of the three, there in the presence of Curry and Blymire, Wilbert Hess said, 'After Rehmeyer was dead, we searched the home and found money in a box. . . .' "

The Commonwealth called its first witness, the Widow Rehmeyer. Her testimony was strictly routine and, as the

Pittsburgh Press, apparently anticipating pyrotechnics, declared, "disappointingly tedious."

The first of a series of attempts by Mr. Cohen to bring the witchcraft angle out into the open was thwarted by His Honor. Upon cross examination, defense counsel asked Mr. Rehmeyer's relict why her late husband lived on one farm and she on another.

Her answer, of course, would have been the one she had given unhesitatingly to anyone who asked her why she and Nelson didn't live together. "He's too damned peculiar," was her usual response. "He's always down in that damned cellar of his puttin' a hex on somebody or takin' them off'n folks."

Mr. Herrmann stepped in quickly. "I think this question is improper, unless they bring it down to approximately the date when this man was killed."

"How do you contend it is material, Mr. Cohen?" asked His Honor.

"If the Court pleases, I wish to show the cause for her having left her husband."

Judge Sherwood upheld the prosecution.

"No, Mr. Cohen, I don't think that is material one way or the other. We will permit you to ask the witness whether there was any animosity or ill-feeling between her and her husband, but what the cause of their separating might be would have no bearing on this issue one way or the other."

Mr. Herrmann's second witness was a clerk, Frank Lehr, who had watched the sale of twenty-five feet of hemp Blymire and Hess bought at Swartz's grocery store. A perspicacious witness, Mr. Lehr, without being requested to do so by any one, brought with him into the courtroom a small piece of rope cut from the same spool.

Requested by the District Attorney to identify the rope's purchaser, the witness promptly arose from his chair, walked to the prisoner, tapped Blymire's shoulder and exclaimed, "This is the gentleman."

"The latter," wrote John M. McCullough, star reporter of the *Philadelphia Inquirer*, "slender, anemic, with a long pointed nose, seemingly undisturbed by the proceedings, if not actually oblivious of their real intent, was clad

110

in a new gray suit. He barely even looked at Lehr, glanced occasionally at the jurymen, but was by long odds the least concerned individual in the courtroom."

After a brief and meaningless cross examination by Mr. Cohen, the District Attorney called his third witness, Clayton G. Hess, Wilbert's older brother.

"When Clayton Hess strode with his powwow walk [whatever that might be] to the witness stand," said the Philadelphia *Record*, "there was no indication that his testimony would be less perfunctory than that of the others. Everyone who has been remotely connected with what York County officialdom calls 'the case' knows that the Hess family still believes firmly in the mystic power of witches.

"Almost everyone in York must know by this time that young Wilbert Hess was sent on his murderous mission to obtain a lock of Rehmeyer's hair in order that a 'hex' or evil spell might be lifted from the Hess family and the Hess possessions.

"Yet so cleverly had any mention of witchcraft been avoided by the officials who consider that their county has been held up to scorn by revelations of the prevalence of superstitious beliefs and who believe the way to stop the disclosures is to attempt concealment, that little of interest was expected even from this tall and gawky witness."

Deftly skirting every possible reference to witchcraft, a task that certainly required considerable ingenuity, Mr. Herrmann led Clayton through a labyrinth of questions and answers without once touching upon necromancy in any form.

From the Hess farm down the Susquehanna Trail and off to Rehmeyer's Hollow, the witness traced Blymire's and Curry's movements, as well as those of his young brother, Wilbert, and other members of the Hess family on the Monday evening preceding the murder and on Tuesday, November 27, the night of the actual slaying.

"Did you know John Blymire by another name?" Mr. Herrmann asked.

"By the alias of John Albright," replied Clayton.

111

"And when did you find out first that his name was John Blymire?"

"When I read in the paper what he done."

"About the killing of Nelson Rehmeyer?"

"Yes, sir."

It was when Clayton neared the end of his testimony and was almost ready for cross examination that Mr. Herrmann, who up to this point could have been proud of his ability to dodge and to conceal the true issue, slipped. The District Attorney had a plethora of witnesses—Coroner Zech, Drs. Langston and Ellis, David Vanover, Spangler Hildenbrand and other neighbors who had "turned over" the body and could testify that it was partially burned.

Since none of these real or potential witnesses was present at the murder or had previous knowledge of the crime and the criminals, none was likely to testify to the motive for the murder. Actually, the three defendants themselves readily confessed that they tried to burn Rehmeyer's body to conceal their crime.

But Mr. Herrmann was not satisfied; why, no one will ever know. He insisted upon using Clayton to impress the jury with the horrid fact that after committing a murder, the trio, including the witness' brother, tried to burn the body of their victim. For devout Lutherans (and a high percentage of the panel were of that denomination), cremation is a sin of considerable magnitude, whether with or without the victim's consent is a moot question.

"Did Blymire ask you to do anything for him on that Thursday evening of November 29?" queried the prosecutor.

"Yes, sir. He asked me if I would take him down to see if the house is burned down. . . . And I says, 'No, I don't care to take you down.' And he says, 'We want to go down. If it ain't burned down, why I'll burn it down," and I says, 'No, I won't go.' "

"All right," pursued Mr. Herrmann, "did Blymire or Albright, by whatever name you knew him best, say anything about Nelson D. Rehmeyer?"

At this point in the interrogation the learned Judge Sherwood must have regarded Mr. Herrmann with considerable amazement. He surely realized what fearful prosecution pitfalls might be opened by Clayton's answer.

The witness scratched his head in a troubled fashion and hesitated for several seconds before answering.

"Well, sir, Blymire says—when he comes out to the farm—he says, 'I got the man,' oney he has a certain name for it."

Mr. Herrmann continued. "What do you mean, Clayton, 'he has a certain name for it'?"

Still bewildered, unquestionably advised never to mention the "word," its synonyms or derivatives, Clayton glanced up at the Bench. Judge Sherwood was silent.

"Hess looked at the District Attorney in open amazement, not unmixed with doubt," reported John M. McCullough in the *Philadelphia Inquirer*. "Then he looked at the slender, immaculately dressed, black-haired Cohen, who was lolling back in his chair gazing into space with a tiny smile on his face.

"The witness colored to the roots of his hair, ground his hands together nervously, opened his mouth and shut it; opened it again, and finally managed, 'He says, "I got—," ' then turning to Herrmann in sudden embarrassed desperation, 'Should I say that word?'

"Cohen was on his feet. 'Say it, Clayton, absolutely.' "

Mr. Herrmann stood up, his face livid with anger, furious at his lack of foresight. "Go ahead, Clayton," he said. "Spit it out."

The witness still paused.

"No one in the courtroom," continued McCullough, "with the exception of a few privileged persons, had the slightest idea what 'the word' was, the majority imagining it to be some horrible epithet which might embarrass the dignity of the Court."

Clayton went ahead resignedly. "O.K., Mr. Herrmann. Blymire says, 'I got the witch!' "

"The words and Hess's evident embarrassment caused a tense situation in the courtroom and Blymire's attorney jumped to his feet and obtained a postponement of further examination until tomorrow morning," reported the *New York Times*.

Cohen's request for postponement was not heard by

members of the working press. They had gotten the break they were waiting for. Without even glancing at His Honor, who many times had warned everyone to remain in the room when court was in session, reporters hopped out of their seats and scurried through the aisles, out the door and down the broad marble staircase to phone new leads from booths on the first-floor corridor. Not that witchcraft had been ignored in previous stories even though it was not mentioned in the courtroom. But Clayton's use of the word made necromancy official and put it in the record where it belonged.

Clayton was back on the stand when court reconvened the following morning at 9:30, and Cohen put him through as searching a cross examination as His Honor would permit. The "word" was uttered once more, this time through the thin lips of Judge Sherwood. It was spoken shortly after the morning session began, when the District Attorney attempted to restrict Clayton's testimony following the latter's disclosure of events leading to the actual murder.

Mr. Cohen asked Hess why Blymire needed transportation to the Hollow and the witness replied, "Well, he was after the—" But before he could say the "word," Herrmann jumped up.

"If the Court please, I think this witness has gone pretty far. The defense has a right to subpoena him and use him in defense."

This was the Court's opportunity to admonish the District Attorney for his indiscretion the previous day.

"The difficulty with that proposition," replied His Honor, "is that you opened the door, Mr. Herrmann, by which the word 'witch' was used. If it were not for that, this would not be competent testimony."

Nevertheless Judge Sherwood sustained the prosecution's objection and barred Clayton's answer to defense counsel's question.

While His Honor did not hesitate to chastise Herrmann, it was obvious that he had no intention of allowing the defense counsel to take advantage of the District Attorney's tactical error.

"We will permit you, Mr. Cohen, to ask the witness

whether anything else was said by the defendant Blymire with reference to the trip down the Susquehanna Trail that night, but limit it entirely to that."

Bitterly disappointed, Cohen, who had fully expected to take advantage of his antagonist's slip, made one more attempt to show the jury the real motive for Rehmeyer's slaying. By adroit questions, the defense counsel was able to force Clayton to explain why Blymire needed physical assistance to complete the mission.

"Blymire says Rehmeyer is so strong he needs help to hold him down," declared Hess.

Defense counsel, to the consternation of the District Attorney, was moving toward his objective. Had Cohen been allowed to proceed in his own fashion, his next step would have been to show how easily such a God-fearing, law-abiding and typically York County family as the Hesses could be led into crime merely because of their long-held and generally respected belief in the devil's powers.

"Did he say you were hexed, too, Clayton?"

"No, sir."

Up jumped the prosecution, knowing quite well Cohen's next question would be, "Was any member of your family hexed?"

"I object," shouted Herrmann. "That is improper. I ask that that be stricken from the record."

Said the Court, agreeing, "Strike that out. Exception for the defendant. The jury will pay no attention to that question and answer."

Several times more, the defense counsel tried to inject witchcraft into the picture but at each attempt the Court upheld Herrmann's objection. Frustrated during direct examination of the witness, Cohen hoped to have some measure of success during cross examination if he could let the jury hear what Blymire had said to Clayton when the pair met at the Hess farm.

"Mr. Hess, when was the first time that you met John Blymire?" Cohen asked, and when the witness replied, "Sunday evening—that was before Thanksgiving," the defense counsel, after a few more feints, asked the important question.

"Did Blymire tell you anything that evening?"

But the District Attorney was on his feet. "We ask for an offer," he demanded, and Cohen gave it to him.

"In direct examination," said the defense counsel, "Clayton Hess testified as to certain conversations with John Blymire."

Here the Court intervened. "The first of which was on Monday, November 26," said His Honor. "Go ahead, Mr. Cohen."

"It is my purpose," continued Cohen, "to show that the arrangements which were made on Monday, as testified to by the witness, were in reality made on Sunday, and that the witness is incorrect in saying that they were made on Monday."

Cohen was now prepared to ask exactly what the arrangements were. The Court blocked this move.

"We will permit you to ask the question whether the statement he made as occurring on Monday, November 26, did not actually occur on Sunday, November 25. I might say, Mr. Cohen, that the Court will limit you in your cross examination to the occurrences as testified to by the witness in chief. Any other matters which you have cannot be brought out as under cross examination. They are entirely and simply matters of defense."

A few minutes later Cohen tried again, making use of the fact that Clayton seemed uncertain whether it was on Sunday, November 25, or the following day that he had spoken to Blymire.

"You testified, Clayton, didn't you, that John Blymire on Monday requested that you take him down the Susquehanna Trail?"

"Yes, sir," answered the witness.

Herrmann, aware of what was coming next, raised an objection. It was denied and defense counsel continued.

"Was that request made to you on Monday, or was it made to you on Sunday?" Cohen continued.

"Well, it wasn't exactly on Monday. . . ."

The witness hesitated for a moment and seemed ready to plunge ahead as he had done before to the consternation of the Court, but the District Attorney waved his forefinger in Clayton's face and shouted, "Just answer the question, Clayton. Answer *only* the question."

Cohen turned to the Bench. "He has answered that, Your Honor. He says it wasn't exactly on Monday, and we have to allow the witness to explain what he means by that." But the Court was not to be taken in by this one.

"I think we are getting aside of the issue," replied Judge Sherwood. "The Court remembers no testimony about the request. What the witness testified to was that on Monday, November 26, Blymire asked the witness to take him down the Susquehanna Trail, that he did take him and John Russell down the Trail. . . . The important and relevant part of the Commonwealth's testimony is what he did in connection with the occurrence on the twenty-sixth. . . . You can ask him on what date he actually did take him down the Trail."

Undaunted, Cohen continued.

"I realize, Your Honor, that he did take him down on Monday and Tuesday, but he has testified, too, as to the time the arrangements were made, and that is the material part we wish to bring forth, showing from what source he is testifying that the desire to have this trip accomplished came."

Judge Sherwood shook his head.

"I can't see the materiality of it, Mr. Cohen, whether he asked him on Monday or Sunday, or a week before. . . . We will permit you just as much leeway as you wish to take in connection with an examination as to what occurred in the actual taking down on the twenty-sixth, if that was the proper date. You must appreciate the fact that this is not defense that we are offering at this time. This is the Commonwealth's case. Your cross examination is absolutely limited to what the Commonwealth has established from the testimony of the witness."

Despite his unwillingness to permit witchcraft to play an appreciable part in the trials of Blymire and his colleagues, it would be unfair to say that a man of Judge Sherwood's personal integrity was a willing member of a cartel designed to preserve York's fair name regardless of what it cost the defendants.

That His Honor simply could not grasp the basic truth

in the Rehmeyer murder is far more likely than the alternative explanation—that his was a deliberate and highly successful attempt to obfuscate the issue and confuse the jurors. Judge Sherwood was raised in a Scotch-Irish, rigidly Presbyterian household, and was completely unable to comprehend the fact that a large portion of his neighbors, as well as his intimates, actually had faith in hexerei.

His exposure to powwowism was admittedly scant and while he certainly was aware it existed, in his childhood at least, he could not imagine that anyone in the year of Our Lord, 1928, might commit murder in its name. Therefore, he had to agree with the prosecutor's false premise and, consciously or unconsciously, to shape his rulings accordingly.

With the young, inexperienced and often inept Herbert Cohen, defending a murderer who in the Court's measured judgment deserved the severest of punishments, His Honor was surprisingly patient. He showed this quality by a tolerance of the defense counsel's frequent clumsy, albeit sincere, attempts to circumvent courtroom procedure that he never would have permitted in a more seasoned criminal lawyer without severe condemnation.

From his seat of autocratic power, the Judge could and did block Cohen's efforts to establish empathy between his client and the jury, many of whom unquestionably held the same belief in witchcraft as Blymire, if not with the same intensity of worship. Yet His Honor rarely lost patience with Cohen and his rebukes were almost in the nature of a professor expressing impatience with a well-meaning student unsure of that day's assignment.

"Stay away from fishing expeditions, Mr. Cohen," Judge Sherwood would warn with a half-smile on his lips when the defense counsel strayed from rigid rules of evidence to try to make a point in behalf of his client.

But His Honor never forgave Mr. Herrmann for his error in permitting entry of the "word" into the court records, and he showed his spleen throughout much of the time Clayton was on the stand. Even though Clayton was a witness for the prosecution, had he been permitted to relate the whole story in his own words, there is little doubt that he would have scored heavily for the defense, setting a pattern not only for the Blymire trial but for the two other trials as well. Cohen was aware of this, as were Herrmann and Judge Sherwood.

Clayton Hess was on the stand for several hours, far longer than any witness who preceded or followed him. Shortly before he was permitted to step down from the box, Cohen made his last sortie.

"Did Blymire offer any explanation for his action in regard to Rehmeyer?" he asked. Clayton had just testified that the defendant wanted to burn down the house in the Hollow.

Of course Herrmann objected and was sustained.

By this time Cohen, whom the Court had committed to a defense not based on the facts as he saw them, knew that his case was almost hopeless. The most he could wish for was Blymire's escape from the electric chair.

Herrmann, however, was free to pound away relentlessly at the "murder for profit" angle. Thus, he was able to appease the conscience of each juror aware he was being called upon to decide the awful fate of a man who, but for the grace of God, might well have been himself.

15

DAVID VANOVER, REHMEYER'S NEIGHBOR, WHO had heard the braying of that unfed mule, followed Clayton to the stand. His testimony and the testimony of Coroner Zech and the latter's physician offered little to whet the appetites of the working press. Undertaker John Wagner (no mortician, just a plain undertaker, in that simple bygone era) appeared briefly to verify several of his medical collaborators' gruesome finds.

York City Detective Ralph Keech, the arresting officer, was the next witness of any importance. Interrogated by the prosecutor, he repeated his highly improbable version of Blymire's, Curry's and Hess's confessions following their arrest, swearing that at no time was pow-wowism in any form mentioned.

Blymire and Curry admitted everything, Keech said, shortly before midnight on November 30, in the presence of District Attorney Herrmann and Police Sergeant W. C. Craver after the usual warning that what the prisoners said could be used against them.

According to Keech, whose testimony was corroborated by Sergeant Craver, Blymire and Curry (and later Hess) told the arresting officers that robbery was the sole motive for their crime. This preposterous claim is in such complete contradiction to the facts that it is almost impossible to account for its admission into the evidence.

Blymire and Curry were interrogated by the District Attorney and members of the York Police Department in a session that according to them lasted from midnight until dawn. Yet Blymire's confession was reduced to three brief paragraphs; Curry's occupied less than a full page of type.

Blymire's confession, read aloud to the jury after Judge Sherwood overruled the defense counsel's vociferous objection, follows:

"City Hall, York, Pennsylvania, November 30, 1928: This statement is made without any threats, force or any promise and made after being explained to me that whatever may be said by me may be used against me.

"John Curry and I bought twenty-five feet of rope at Swartz's store and paid for the rope.

"We went to Nelson Rehmeyer's home on Tuesday evening and we threw Rehmeyer down. I helped to tie Rehmeyer. I poured water. I don't know whether I set fire to the body. On Wednesday evening, I burned my pants because they were bloody from the killing of Rehmeyer and I burned them in the furnace at Spangler's at the corner of Chestnut and Pine Streets. I hit Rehmeyer with a chair."

Not a word of necromancy, not a hint of the troubled murderer's long search for the witch who hexed him, not a line about powwowism, sorcery, "curing for," or anything else pertaining to the powers of evil he believed in, is to be found in the now yellowed stationery of the District Attorney's office at the bottom of which skinny John Blymire scrawled his signature on a cold November morning some forty years ago.

What did judge and jury think Blymire and his interrogators discussed for more than seven hours? Cohen and everyone else, with the possible exception of the twelve men in the box, knew that what the District Attorney produced had to be a highly blue-penciled version of the text. However, defense counsel, boxed at every turn by the prosecutor whose objections Judge Sherwood almost invariably upheld, was able to extract from Keech or Craver little more than the official version of the homicide, the murder for profit angle. That, of course, was dangerous ground for Cohen to tread and he knew it.

Despite the District Attorney's frequent and usually sustained objections, Herbert Cohen, through Clayton Hess, was able to prove beyond the slightest doubt the power witchcraft had upon the families of Blymire and Hess.

Keech and Craver were "cops" and perhaps in those unenlightened days they saw and heard only what they wanted to see and to hear. At this early stage in the game, prior to the arrival of Mr. Dudley Nichols and his cohorts and before civic pride clouded the proceedings, it could not have made an iota of difference to either of these police officers why Rehmeyer was murdered.

Two of the three culprits were already under arrest; the third was known and his apprehension anticipated within hours. None of the prisoners needed prodding to confess. Each spoke freely about his own role in the murder, and except for trivial discrepancies, the trio of killers was in almost complete accord as to methods and motive.

One also must assume that being old-time York policemen, the detective and the sergeant had been exposed professionally as well as personally to nearly every conceivable brand of hexerei. Furthermore, they must have known exactly who Blymire was; he had a record. He had been arrested as a potential threat to his wife when

121

he thought she had cast the spell on him, and later was listed as an escapee from a lunatic asylum.

But while Blymire was a self-proclaimed witch (a profession not without respect throughout the region) and a loner, who for years had wandered about the city streets bent on his peculiar mission, he was no felon; prior to Rehmeyer's murder, he had never been questioned for possible participation in a crime of violence, except in the matter of his ex-wife.

Curry was "clean" as far as the cops were concerned. So was Wilbert Hess, whom authorities considered a hard-working youth with a fine reputation. Clayton, his brother, was a mill foreman; Milton J., his father, a stupid but honest farmer temporarily down on his luck because of a "hex"; and Alice Ouida Hess, his mother, the highly respectable operator of a stand in the Farmer's Market.

This is not to preclude the possibility, remote though it may be, that such a trio could have robbed and murdered Rehmeyer for his gold. Today's newspapers, and to a lesser degree those of the twenties, are filled with violent crimes committed by scions of our best families.

But in view of the facts developed before and after the trials of Blymire, Curry and Hess, it would be a real challenge for the police to produce a trio of felons more unlikely to rob and murder old man Rehmeyer for his gold.

Judge Sherwood's point of view is understandable, if indefensible. To use the vernacular of that and this day, as far as witchcraft was concerned, the learned jurist didn't know his ass from a hole in the ground.

Amos W. Herrmann's position is far more difficult to interpret. That he was gnawed by ambitions beyond his job is a dead certainty. The lawyer willing to limit his political aims to a single term as county prosecutor is indeed a *rara avis*. Almost without exception they want something more—the governorship, a seat in the United States Senate or a spot on the Bench, and a sadly large number of these gentlemen have gone extremely far to get there.

Even granting all this, Herrmann's deliberate (what

else could it be?) suppression of such vital evidence as he withheld from the jury is inexplicable. Herrmann was hardly a brilliant addition to the American Bar but he was not a fool. He *had* to know why Rehmeyer was murdered. He was present when the three suspects confessed, he knew their milieu (not dissimilar from his own) and he had heard them discuss the hex the Witch of Rehmeyer's Hollow had put on the Hess and Blymire families. Yet he assiduously ignored these facts.

The introduction of Blymire's confession and Craver's testimony was followed by the appearance of York Chief of Police Michael J. Schwint as a Commonwealth witness. Apparently no one had troubled to wake the Chief the night of November 30, and when he reached his office at 8:05 the next morning, the arrest and subsequent confessions of the two culprits were a *fait accompli*. It is to be hoped someone briefed him, if only slightly.

Schwint was asked where Blymire was when he reached City Hall.

"He was in Cell Number Two and I went back to see if I knowed him. I knowed him by sight; I never knowed him by name. He didn't say nothin'."

Schwint took a quick look at Curry, who was lodged in an upper tier, left the cell block and returned to his office. The next time he saw either of these prisoners was a little more than an hour later. Meanwhile, the Chief discovered that Blymire and Curry were not the only ones involved in Rehmeyer's murder; there was a third party still at large. He learned this interesting fact in a casual fashion, although it was not until Curry's trial that the Chief's belated involvement in the arrest was revealed.

After he left the prisoners and returned to his office, a visitor was announced; Mrs. MacLean had come to pay a call on her son John.

"His [Curry's] mother come in about twenty or twenty-five minutes of nine and asked whether she couldn't see the boy. I went upstairs and got the boy and I fetched him down and he talked to his mother."

The Chief was forced to eavesdrop and heard, for the

first time, it would seem, that someone else had participated in Rehmeyer's murder. Even such a fat, easygoing gentleman as Chief Schwint must have been startled by this news.

"While Curry and his mother was settin' there," Schwint testified, "I says to him, 'Third party? *Who* was the third party?' and he tole me."

The Chief reached for his jacket and donned his uniform cap. Then he summoned a patrolman to take charge while Mrs. MacLean and her son were in the office, excused himself and left to perform his duty.

"Me and Officer Myers went out after Hess," Schwint testified, "and the next time I seen him was when he was fetched into my office."

Nearly all the conversation that took place then, at least according to Chief Schwint, was devoted to the division of the spoils, the few dollars or less in change, taken from Rehmeyer's house.

"It was about ten o'clock in the morning," the Chief testified. "We had Hess there. Blymire was fetched in. All three of them was together. The District Attorney says to Hess, 'Do you know these two men?' Hess says, 'Yes, I do.' 'Were they with you down to Rehmeyer's?' and he says, 'Yes, sir.' . . .

"Then you [District Attorney Herrmann, who was asking the questions] says to Hess, 'Were these two along upstairs with you when you got the money?' and he says, 'Yes, sir, and they gave me one dollar and I think they "gypped" me out of the rest. I think they "gypped" me.' This is the way it was.

"Then, Mr. Herrmann, you said to Blymire, you asked Blymire if he has got anything to say and he says, 'No,' and you said, 'You talked too much already.' "

"Did I say that?" asked Mr. Herrmann.

"No, sir, you said, 'You talked enough already,' " replied the Chief.

This closed the conference. "That's all that was said there," testified Schwint.

According to Schwint, the meeting he held in his office that morning, with the three defendants and the District Attorney present, lasted about fifteen minutes. According to Curry, they, and possibly another policeman, were together for more than an hour. In either event, the total amount of time consumed in talk could not have been more than one or two minutes if the Chief and the District Attorney are to be believed.

The point is important because it reveals the lengths to which this District Attorney, an elected representative of the People, sworn to present all the evidence regardless of its value to himself, was willing to go. In cross examination, Cohen brought out the absurdity of Schwint's testimony.

"How long did the conference last?" Cohen asked, and the Chief replied, "I would say a quarter-hour. It didn't take no longer than that."

Continued defense counsel: "Now, Chief, what was said during those fifteen minutes?"

"Well," answered Schwint, "just what I got done telling. When Blymire and Curry come in, the District Attorney asks Hess whether he knowed Blymire and Curry. He said, 'Yes.' Then he asked Blymire the same quesion. He answered, 'Yes.' Then the District Attorney says to Hess, 'Was these the fellows that was down to Rehmeyer's?' and they said, 'Yes.' They were all three together, all three said, 'Yes, sir,' about the same time. They all knowed Mr. Hess, anyhow."

Cohen then injected the State's motive for the slaying to show that even the theme most important to the prosecutor had been dismissed in a few words.

"Then Hess spoke a little bit about the money, didn't he?" asked Cohen.

"Yes," answered Chief Schwint. "The District Attorney asked Hess whether they was the people that got the money and he said, 'Yes, sir.' Then Hess talked. He said he got about a dollar, but he thinks they 'gypped' him."

It was the word "gypped" used so frequently by the District Attorney and his police witness that had such a telling effect upon the jury. If Hess believed that he was "gypped" (and those twelve in the box knew what that meant), here was an admission that the murder was for profit and that the thieves had fallen out over a division of the spoils.

125

While the three prisoners were self-admitted murderers, they were honest, and, until much later, Blymire and Hess at any rate were convinced they had done only what was necessary to protect themselves and their families from the machinations of an evil witch. As far as Curry was concerned, all he had done was "come along for the ride," and become trapped into participating.

The trio presented a solid front. When arrested and subsequently questioned by the District Attorney, Detective Keech and Sergeant Craver, they answered in full every question put to them and used neither subterfuge nor deceit. It is true that they attempted to burn the body to conceal their crime but that was before they were caught and they now wanted to make a clean breast of everything.

Their motive for the murder was clear. Properly interpreted it could strike an empathetic juristic chord, disastrous to the District Attorney, who had charted his course to reach first-degree murder convictions, with the electric chair a distinct possibility.

Herrmann was anxious to create dissension among the three and so eclipse their motive. He chose Hess as his tool, probably because the latter's prior association with the others was limited to a single night. That he succeeded in creating an illusion of dissension was due to many factors. Judge Sherwood's self-constructed isolation booth into which no words of powwowism could enter except through cracks in the woodwork was one; Counselor Cohen's lack of trial experience a second; Wilbert Hess's gullibility was a third; and perhaps most important of all was the highly unethical conduct of Amos W. Herrmann.

It was not until Hess, himself, was placed on trial that the truth about the prosecution's dishonest use of the offending verb "gypped" was revealed. Gross, no Darrow but head and shoulders above the other defense counsel, knew he had to break down the impression of group thievery, the motive created by Herrmann, abetted by Schwint and supported by His Honor.

The Bulldog also was aware of the importance of establishing his client's honesty; he began the buildup for this the moment the first member of the Hess family took the stand. Finally, when he placed the defendant in the box, he asked, "Wilbert, did you know prior to that time up there in City Hall [the morning of his arrest] what 'gypped' meant?"

"No, sir. I don't know what it means yet."

Then Gross, with a sardonic smile, turned to the jury and shook his head sadly at the shared revelation of how *that* word had been painted into the picture.

But young Herb Cohen failed to pursue the point. Nevertheless, he did establish that if Schwint were a credible witness, the conference held that morning had bordered on the ridiculous with all participants sitting around, staring at each other and saying nothing.

Cohen had just proved, through Schwint, that the total time consumed in the question and answer period could not have been more than one or two minutes at the most.

"What was said during those other thirteen or fourteen minutes, Chief Schwint?" the defense counsel asked.

"They chust stood there."

"Do you mean to tell me that there was nothing said about hexing?"

"Not a word, Mr. Cohen, not a word. Not there, not before all three of them."

"Chief, you testified to a conversation that has taken exactly one minute. What was said in the other fourteen minutes?"

"Nothing was said. I told you onct chust what was said there."

"Was anything mentioned by Hess about their going down there to get a lock of hair?"

"No, sir. Not a word. . . ."

"Was anything mentioned about going down to get a book called *The Long Lost Friend?*"

"No. . . . Nobody asked them questions outside of District Attorney Herrmann. . . . I tell you there was nothin' mentioned at all about any hexing or any hair or anything else. . . ."

Cohen made a last try.

"Were you present at any other meeting in which Blymire and Curry were present?"

"No, sir."

"You never interviewed Blymire, Hess or Curry?"

"No, Mr. Cohen, the only time I talked to any of them was there."

"Well, when *did* you speak to them?"

At this Herrmann was on his feet. "I object," he shouted. The court, aware of what defense counsel was attempting, sustained Herrmann and sharply reprimanded Blymire's attorney.

"Mr. Cohen," he said, and this time there was no hint of tolerance in his voice. "I have told you often enough not to get your defense before the jury under the guise of cross examination. Confine yourself to what he has testified. . . ."

Cohen shrugged his shoulders hopelessly. "No further questions, Mr. Schwint," he said, and the Chief stepped down from the box.

Over defense counsel's objections, the clean rope furnished by Frank Lehr, that thoughtful clerk who worked at Swartz's grocery store; the burned hemp found beside Rehmeyer's body; some bloody cloth from the murdered man's jacket; his flashlight; and rungs from the chair used to beat him to death were admitted as evidence and paraded before the jury.

The prosecution rested.

16

AT 2:52 P.M. ON THE SECOND DAY OF THE trial, Cohen opened for the defense.

"Herbert B. Cohen, Blymire's counsel, a slender, dark-eyed young attorney, arose in his place," said John M. McCullough in the *Philadelphia Inquirer*.

"A deathly stillness fell upon the court as he placed a sheet of scribbled notes on the rail before the jury box. The stolid Pennsylvania Dutch faces sprinkled through the courtroom remained expressionless but a kind of electric tenseness suffused the throng as the pale saffron light from the buff window blinds cast a jaundiced shade upon them.

" 'My defense—the defense of John Blymire—is going to be the same thing that I've been pounding at, pounding at, pounding at, and trying to get from every witness on the stand,' Cohen began, his voice breaking into a scream with the intensity of his emotion."

Theodore MacFarland, who covered the Blymire trial for the now defunct Philadelphia *Evening Ledger,* was disturbed by defense counsel's lack of emotional control.

"Hindsight's a pretty easy way to determine what ought to have been done," MacFarland said, "but I don't believe this was any way to reach into the minds of those thickheaded Dutch jurymen. You could see them shudder at Cohen's dramatics. They weren't used to it; they squirmed under it; they were uncomfortable; they preferred the District Attorney's slow and easy approach, and his accent, too, and you could see they couldn't wait until Herb stopped talking."

MacFarland's opinion was shared, he recalled, by most of his colleagues. *The Inquirer*'s story continued.

" 'My defense,' said Cohen, 'is what was in John Blymire's mind when he went down to Nelson D. Rehmeyer's house, what was in his mind when he got Clayton G. Hess to drive him down the Susquehanna Trail. I will show you what was in his mind, and why nothing else in the whole wide world could have been in his mind.

" 'I will show him as a little boy, how he grew up in body and in years surrounded by thoughts of pow-wows.' "

This may well have been Cohen's best approach since it was the truth. But it was the kind of talk those men in the box did not want to hear. It embarrassed them because it was uncomfortably close to their childhood. It angered them to see Cohen, a Jew, spreading the word about a secret they all shared; making public property of their private beliefs in the presence of a horde of "furrin" newspapermen who they knew would be delighted to tell the world just how dumb the Dutch really are. Their own

Amos W. Herrmann's explanation of the crime was far more palatable.

"At this point," McCullough wrote, "Cohen halted for a barely perceptible moment. There was not a sound except for the rhythmic munching as an ancient juror ground his few remaining molars upon a peppermint drop and the hoarse breathing of a grizzled and dirt-stained farmer leaning forward in his chair.

" 'Blymire was surrounded by witches,' Cohen continued, 'by ideas of witchcraft, by hallucinations and delusions and by voodooism. I am going to show you that as all these years transpired, and he was exposed to all these outside influences, his mind did not grow. It was the same mind that he had when he was an eight-year-old.

" 'He is now thirty-two, and from the time he was eight up to the present—twenty-four years—he has been listening to these powwows and this witchcraft and he has only been able to decide what to do with the mind of an eight-year-old boy.' "

This really was hitting the jurors below their belts. To some degree most of them had been exposed to the same influences that had made Blymire murder the old man in a childish rage. If he could do that, so might they given a similar set of circumstances. Herrmann's explanation suited the panel better.

Cohen then revealed another, and anticipated, angle of defense strategy.

" 'In addition to the fact that for twenty-four years John Blymire, an eight-year-old boy, has been exposed to powwowism, witchcraft and mysticism, I am going to show you that these same facts were realized by the people with whom he came in contact, and for that reason five years ago he was brought into the York County Almshouse and examined by the steward and two York County physicians, who committed him to the insane asylum. . . .

" 'Gentlemen of the jury, this isn't a defense brought here to help a man escape from the consequences of his acts. It is not the same kind of insanity plea as one that might be injected into a social murder, but one that has existed over a period of time.

" 'It is an insanity that has existed in John Blymire's life all his life. Just as coolly unconscious as he is now he was, and he always *will* be. He has no conception of what he did. . . .' "

How did John Blymire react to this disparagement of his mental powers?

"Not an expression or the shadow of an expression passed over the defendant's pallid face on which the stiff dark beard bristled unhealthily," observed McCullough.

"He was neither defiant, sullen nor brazen. He was simply detached. Not a word of the fearful arraignment which had swept about his slender shoulders by his own counsel had penetrated the impenetrable shell of his isolation in a world of demons and wraiths."

When Cohen concluded, he stood in silence before the jurors for several seconds, staring into their faces. During the past hour his passionate appeal to reason had held their attention at least part of the time despite some squirming, occasional coughing and surreptitious efforts to rid a few mouths of what they called "tobacco juice." But these stolid faces Cohen now looked at revealed nothing.

With a deep sigh—he no longer remembers whether of exhaustion or frustration—defense counsel turned around abruptly and joined his client. A few feet behind them sat Alice Ouida Hess, who only that day had told a representative of the *Boston Herald*, "We're all all right now; the hex is gone. Our cattle don't die and nobody's sick no more in our house except maybe for a cold."

Cohen had made a bold start but it was stopped with a dull thud a few minutes after Emanuel Blymire, the first witness for the defense, took the stand. The defendant's aging father, a character right out of Dogpatch Hollow or Tobacco Road, was not likely to inspire confidence in anyone.

"This gaunt, shambling, wretched figure of a man with the colorless, uncombed hair, stumbled up the aisle to the marble-encircled witness box," said the *Inquirer*.

"His trousers, not reaching to his shoe tops, were out at the knees and clumsily patched. His coat, too small by several sizes, was out at the elbows, and its sleeves revealed the huge knobby bones of his wrists and his long, heavy-knuckled, dirty hands. It could not conceal the soft-colored shirt, unadorned by any tie and indescribably filthy.

"His face, like that of his son, was utterly without expression under curiously light brows. It was as if John Blymire's own face had been worked into wrinkles and smudged carelessly with a muddy hand."

Ken Mack of the Philadelphia *Record* noted another one of Blymire's *père*'s hitherto unmentioned handicaps.

"Emanuel has a speech defect which makes his answers all but unintelligible. A stick he was whittling went through his throat when he fell down, he told this correspondent, and 'powwowing didn't do it no good.' "

Cohen's point in placing this sad figure of a man on the stand was, of course, to emphasize John Blymire's heritage, his early training and the entire family's obeisance to hexerei with all its ramifications as their normal way of life. The first dozen questions defense counsel asked went unchallenged and were answered to the best of the witness' strictly limited ability.

Emanuel was cognizant of the fact that John was his son but he wasn't quite sure how old the boy was. "Along 'round thirty or so," he surmised. Emanuel wasn't too certain of his own age either. "I don't know exactly how old I am, Mr. Cohen," he said. "Must be somewhere near fifty-eight or there-abouts." (Baptismal records show that he was then close to sixty-three.)

When Cohen asked the witness how many children he had he replied, promptly enough, "Seven." But he'd completely forgotten his first-born, a daughter who'd married and left home many years before.

He was aware he was living presently in East Prospect Township and that immediately prior to this he'd had a home in North Hopewell, but he could not recollect the names of the various York County towns and villages where he had lived for periods ranging from three months to one or two years.

His vocation came through loud and clear. "Me and the missus is basket makers," declared Emanuel rather proudly.

A probe into Emanuel's avocation was coming soon but defense counsel never got that far.

"Did you know Nelson Rehmeyer?" was his next question, and the witness nodded and said, "Yes, I did."

"How did you happen to know him?"

"Well, I worked for him already."

Herrmann had had enough of this; he was aware of his opponent's objectives.

"I ask for an offer, Mr. Cohen," he said. Cohen replied, "I want to show by this witness the environment under which John Blymire was reared, his possibilities for education. I want to show by this witness the fact that he knew Nelson Rehmeyer, and knew of Nelson Rehmeyer's reputation as a dispenser of powwow treatments.

"I want to show that they were all acquainted with it when they lived down in the Rehmeyer Valley, and that John Blymire was reared in the atmosphere of powwow and hex, in order to show a basis for the motive of John Blymire's going down to the Rehmeyer house."

Herrmann shook his head violently.

"The Commonwealth objects to the admission of the greater part of this offer, it being impossible to distinguish which is admissible and which is not. . . ."

One way or the other this must be the turning point in Cohen's case and he knew it. If His Honor ruled against the prosecution, Cohen's path was open and, through Emanuel Blymire, he could parade all his facts before the jury, including his client's mental aberrations and strictly limited mentality.

This is not to conclude the jury then would have found the prisoner innocent and turned him loose. But they would have been denied the opportunity to salve their consciences with the juridical ointment applied so far in such profusion to ease the pain of an honorable, albeit unpopular, verdict.

His Honor had no intention of permitting the panel to hear defense counsel's pleas and ordered the jury removed to another room while he and the pair of antagonists held a conference.

"I would like to hear from both sides on that proposition, gentlemen," he began, reasonably enough. But before either could answer, Judge Sherwood threw cold water on Cohen's hopes without even hearing his arguments.

"I might say, Mr. Cohen," the Judge continued, "that the Court has grave doubts about your proposition's materiality at this time."

Defense counsel, gulping hard, went ahead nevertheless.

"I have in mind, Your Honor, calling the witness to show the conditions under which John Blymire lived and the truth of the statements which will come from John Blymire that he believed Rehmeyer had him hexed."

Judge Sherwood, aware that the basis of Cohen's argument was a plea of "innocent by reason of insanity," anticipated him and shook his head.

"Suppose he did believe all that, Mr. Cohen? Unfortunately the early English McNaughton case holds that that is not a defense, unless, in reality, the delusion is true. He would have been justified in taking human life under those conditions. . . . Now I would like to know in the first instance from counsel what your defense really is.

"Is it general insanity, is it partial insanity in the shape of delusions or hallucinations, or is it homicidal mania? Because the question of admission of testimony depends entirely upon what your real intention is in reference to these three branches of insanity."

Cohen's purpose, he said, was "to show the condition under which John Blymire lived, and the truth of the statements which will come from John Blymire that he believed that Rehmeyer had him hexed."

His Honor was unconvinced.

As a correspondent for the *New York Times* phrased it on January 8, "A defense of insanity, caused by lifelong association with ideas of witchcraft, powwowing and voodooism was offered today for John Blymire, the 'Powwow Doctor,' in his trial . . . but it received a setback in a ruling by Judge Ray P. Sherwood who held that belief in witchcraft or similar 'delusions' did not constitute legal insanity.

"The ruling, which interrupted the examination of the first defense witness after Herbert B. Cohen, Blymire's

134

lawyer, had eloquently opened his case solely upon the rejected basis, so upset the defense plans that Mr. Cohen asked for and received an adjournment until tomorrow morning."

Cohen was angry and he showed it when Court re-opened at 9:30 the following morning.

"If Your Honor please," he said, his voice pitched high with emotion, "I wish to offer an objection to the fact that the Commonwealth, in the production of its case, has not produced all the evidence and all the facts which were in the knowledge of the Commonwealth's officer concerning this crime; that there was absolute knowledge on the part of the Commonwealth's officer Mr. Herrmann, as expressed by John Blymire and his associates, that the purpose for which John Blymire went to the house of Nelson Rehmeyer was to get a lock of hair and the book called *The Long Lost Friend*."

White-faced, he paused and turned to look sharply at Herrmann seated on a chair behind the prosecution's table. Then he continued.

"I object to the fact that the Commonwealth has not produced *all* its evidence and has abused its discretion in selecting only that part of the evidence which would tend to substantiate its case and prove a motive other than to get the lock of hair and the book called *The Long Lost Friend;* that this abuse of discretion is in violation of the rights of the defendant, which rights require that the Commonwealth produce *all* the evidence that it has pertaining to the crime."

This was a serious charge to level against Amos W. Herrmann. The latter did not deny Cohen's accusations; he simply laughed at them, called opposing counsel's claims ridiculous and declared further, "If there is any knowledge available for the defense which should have been brought out in chief by the Commonwealth, they have the right to subpoena such witnesses and offer their testimony in defense."

But once begun, Cohen was not to be stopped until he'd had his full say.

"Furthermore," he continued to remonstrate, "I wish to include the fact that the Commonwealth had subpoenaed

135

twenty-three witnesses, as their names appear on the back of the bill of indictment. The Commonwealth has allowed only approximately thirteen of these witnesses to testify and withheld from the consideration of the court and jury the testimony of the other ten witnesses."

Defense counsel was overruled; resignedly he called his next witness, one of Blymire's former landladies, who was followed in a few minutes by the prisoner's ex-father-in-law. But their testimonies were so circumscribed by Judge Sherwood that they might just as well have stayed at home.

Then Cohen put his medical guns into action. The first shot was fired by Dr. Joseph Comroe, second in his class of one hundred seventy-five at the University of Pennsylvania and a practicing psychiatrist in the City of York for almost a quarter of a century. His appearance on the stand and that of a colleague, Dr. Richard Ridgeway, a Johns Hopkins man (class standing unknown) were brief.

Assuming correctly that the jury wouldn't know what they were talking about anyway, this pair of psychiatrists was permitted to answer most of defense counsel's questions with few objections from the District Attorney.

As McCullough of the *Philadelphia Inquirer* saw it, "While the panel puzzled over the words, Blymire was pronounced a psychoneurotic, a paranoic, a schizophrenic, a borderline lunatic and a hypochondriacal melancholic who, beset by hallucinations, delusions of persecution and a firm belief in black magic, had no more known the moral implications of his act of violence than an untutored child."

Did the jury believe Blymire was crazy? "No, sir!" recalled foreman Harry P. Kissinger. "Not for a minute. Those head shrinkers seemed far worse off than he was."

Emanuel Blymire was recalled to the stand. Through him Cohen finally succeeded in placing into the record a few pertinent facts about his client's childhood and the baleful influences surrounding it. Emanuel, asked if he had ever taken his son to be powwowed, replied, "Yes, sir. Maybe a dozen times." But when counsel followed this with "What was wrong with John?" the Court intervened and refused to permit the witness to answer the question.

Cohen knew that he was getting into deep waters and that Judge Sherwood was becoming angry, yet he persisted.

"Did John complain about the witches?" he asked, and Emanuel replied, "Yes, he did . . . a couple times."

"Did he complain to you about the witches while he was at your home sick?"

"Yes, Mr. Cohen."

"Emanuel, did he say why he was sick?"

His Honor had had enough. "You can hardly lead the witness, Mr. Cohen," Judge Sherwood warned. "We have allowed you to go as far as we will in this examination."

Cohen protested. "I have never examined this witness before. I have had no opportunity to prepare. . . . I personally felt that any preparation would be useless. What I am getting out of this witness is just as new to me as it is to the Court and the jury, and I think everybody should be entitled to hear it."

But His Honor denied the relevancy of Emanuel's testimony. Cohen abandoned his efforts and called his next pair of witnesses, Milton J. Hess and wife Alice Ouida Hess. Before the Court intervened, he got about as far with them as he had with Emanuel Blymire.

The next and almost the last defense witness was a reporter, John C. Hoffman. He was one of the ten witnesses who Cohen claimed had been subpoenaed by the Commonwealth and then, because Herrmann felt their testimony would be damaging to the prosecution's case, were not permitted to testify. So Blymire's counsel subpoenaed him for the defense.

Hoffman covered the courthouse and City Hall beats for his paper, the *York Dispatch*, and had been in Chief Schwint's office when Hess confessed. Cohen's purpose in placing Hoffman on the stand was to attack the credibility of Detective Keech and Sergeant Craver directly and Amos W. Herrmann indirectly.

Hoffman, personally disinterested in any of the three defendants or their families and as objective as most members of his craft, was a serious danger to the Commonwealth's theory of murder for profit. He had heard the lengthy conversations between the arresting officers, the District Attorney and Wilbert Hess on the morning of Hess's apprehension. He knew the talk was not limited to a one- or two-minute discussion of the few cents in change stolen from Rehmeyer as sworn to by the Commonwealth's witnesses. He knew that powwowing, witchcraft and the other forms of black magic shaping Hess's life were talked about; he was ready to swear to this in open court.

Hoffman had given only his name, occupation and the fact that he had been there when Hess related the part he played in the crime, when His Honor brought the questioning to an abrupt halt, rebuked the defense counsel and gave the jury the out it sought.

"Mr. Cohen," said Judge Sherwood angrily, "you have gone far enough. You have been talking about this powwow business. The Court says to you that powwow business has *nothing* to do with this case. . . ."

17

LATE IN THE AFTERNOON OF JANUARY 9, 1929, John Blymire took the stand in his own defense. Courtroom Number Two was still crowded, although as dusk fell there were a few empty seats vacated by wives scurrying home to get the Mister's supper ready. A light snow had begun to fall, and could be seen in the yellow glow of lights shining through the tall windows.

For a short while the remainder of the audience was beset with a problem. Sounds of a crowd gathering outside reached into the courtroom and a number of spectators were afraid they might be missing something of importance. However, a tipstaff relieved their fears. He passed the word that the noise was due to a minor accident caused when a farmer's cart skidded into a police motorcycle parked at the bottom of the courthouse steps. Only one man, a police officer, had been injured. Thus, spectators could settle back in their seats to enjoy in full the drama they knew was drawing to a close.

"John Blymire, take the stand!" called his counsel.

"Cohen's enunciation and manner were like those of a stage magician informing his audience that the rabbit was about to be produced from the hat," reported the Philadelphia *Record*.

"In response to his name there stepped quickly to the witness stand as strange a figure as ever has occupied a similar seat in a modern American court of justice. Graceful as a dancer, his slim hands folded before him, Blymire sat waiting with an air of complete placidity for the questioning to begin.

" 'John,' said Cohen in a tone with which one might address a child such as the defense contends Blymire actually is in mentality, 'How old are you?' "

With Blymire's answer, "Thirty-three," the murder story as seen through the eyes of its chief protagonist began to unfold.

Prodding gently and never displaying the impatience he must have felt, Herbert Cohen, for more than two hours, took his client along the powwow trail from early childhood to that moment when he cried out in exquisite relief, "The witch is dead!"

"This was the big point of the defense case," the *Record* continued, "but there was nothing else in Blymire's tone that was anything but conversational. He might have been reporting that he had suffered a cold in the head.

"Neither Blymire nor the young attorney who was risking his entire case on the bold stroke of placing his client on the stand and thus subjecting him to cross examination, appeared to tire of the long siege of questions and answers. . . . Spectators and witnesses listened breathlessly. Near the front of the courtroom sat one aged farmer who uttered a little gasp every time the words 'hex' or 'the book' or 'witch' were uttered."

No doubt that unidentified tiller of the soil reflected the

attitude of at least some of Blymire's peers, sitting stolidly in the box sucking peppermints or chewing cut plug and furtively depositing its salivary byproduct in places known only to courthouse janitors.

When Cohen signified that he was finished with his witness the prosecution took over. Herrmann handled the accused far more gently, and his interrogation was much less grueling than the press had anticipated. In it there was little mention of necromancy in any form. Herrmann obviously preferred to limit his questions to the actual murder, those naïve attempts to burn the body or wash out fingerprints, and, of course, the cash the trio stole and "divvied up."

Blymire answered every question freely except those he failed to comprehend. When this happened the District Attorney, with an assist or two from the Court, reduced the words he had used to substitutes containing fewer syllables.

To reporters who had sat in court from the selection of juror number one to the prosecutor's last question, both Cohen's final brief appeal for an acquittal and the District Attorney's short plea for the extreme penalty seemed anticlimactic. By no stretch of the imagination could either Cohen or Herrmann be classified as gifted spellbinders.

"In his closing plea Cohen fought hard for an acquittal on the ground of insanity," reported the *New York Times*. "'These are three feebleminded babes in the wood,' Mr. Cohen told the jury, referring also to Wilbert G. Hess, aged eighteen, and John Curry, fourteen, companions of Blymire on the night of the murder. Curry is to go on trial tomorrow. He went on:

"'You know them. Blymire had no conception of what he was doing. You heard him say he would murder the presiding judge if he thought that he had bewitched him. You heard him say that he would murder the District Attorney for the same reason.'"

There were few moments of drama in Herrmann's summation. "When he warmed up, unless you were a native, it was tough to understand what the hell Herrmann was trying to say. That goddamned Pennsylvania Dutch accent of his got thicker and thicker," recalled Theodore MacFarland of the *Evening Public Ledger.*

The *New York Times* boiled down the prosecution's half-hour plea to a few paragraphs.

"District Attorney Herrmann stressed the contention that Blymire murdered, not to save his life or his soul from the effects of an evil incantation, but for money.

" 'They went to get a lock of hair but then why didn't they get it?' he asked. 'If you think this man guilty of murder in the first degree, rise up in your might like men and say so. If you think him deserving of the death sentence, say so like men of courage.' "

Then Judge Sherwood charged the jury. In his hourlong talk he touched only lightly upon witchcraft and its allied disciplines and dismissed the subject with a few selected phrases. The "word" itself never slipped through his lips. His Honor had shown the panelists his personal attitude toward powwowing, hexerei and black or white magic early in the trial. They needed no further elaboration.

To refresh the jury's memory he reviewed with care all the testimony—too carefully, in the opinion of legal experts who later studied Judge Sherwood's charge. He pointed out the Commonwealth's theory of motive and that of the defense as well, or perhaps not quite as well.

He explained the meaning of legal insanity and acknowledged that the Commonwealth had produced no medical testimony, but added that the two psychiatrists placed on the stand in behalf of the defense differed greatly in their opinions of Blymire's ability to make proper judgments at the time of the murder.

"A mere weakmindedness, a mere feeblemindedness, is no excuse for crime," he added. "The controlling element, in the first instance, is, did the party committing the crime have sufficient intelligence to distinguish right and wrong, to know that his act was wrong and that he could be punished for it, if caught. That is the distinguishing criterion under the law of the State of Pennsylvania. . . .

"Therefore, if the prisoner, although he labors under partial insanity, hallucinations or delusions, might understand the nature and character of his acts, had a knowledge that it was wrong and criminal and mental power sufficient to apply that knowledge to his own case, and knew if he did the act he would do wrong and receive punishment;

"If, further, he had sufficient power or memory to recollect the relation in which he stood to others and in which others stood to him, that the act in question was contrary to the plain dictates of justice and right inherent to others and a violation of the dictates of duty, he would be responsible."

Down went Herbert Cohen's hopes for an acquittal based on insanity. Actually, as foreman Kissinger recalled, this idea never was considered seriously by himself or his eleven colleagues.

At 5:40 P.M., Judge Sherwood concluded his charge; Mr. Cohen asked for and was granted the usual general exception for the defendant, and the jury retired.

"At 7:30," reveals the trial record, "the jury indicated that they were ready to report, and the Court, District Attorney, the defendant and his counsel having appeared in court, at 7:40 o'clock P.M., the jury entered the jury box and the following verdict was rendered:

"DEPUTY CLERK OF THE COURTS SAUBEL. Prisoner, please rise. [The prisoner rose, facing the jurors, also standing.] Prisoner, look upon the jurors. Jurors, look upon the prisoner.

"Gentlemen of the jury, have you agreed upon your verdict?

"THE JURORS. We have.

"DEPUTY CLERK OF THE COURTS. Who shall answer for you?

"FOREMAN OF THE JURY. I will.

"DEPUTY CLERK OF THE COURTS. How say you in this issue joined between the Commonwealth of Pennsylvania and John Blymire, prisoner at the Bar, defendant? Do you find the defendant guilty in manner and form as he stands indicted, or not guilty?

"FOREMAN OF THE JURY. Guilty of first-degree murder, with life imprisonment.

"DEPUTY CLERK OF THE COURTS. . . . And so say you all?

"THE JURORS. We do"

An impassive Blymire listened to the judgment that in theory at least would place him behind bars forever. For a moment or two he stared at Kissinger. Then he turned to his counsel. "I think maybe they went a little strong, don't you, Mr. Cohen?" But Herb Cohen said nothing; he simply shook his head sadly. He had lost his case.

"The deputy constable who has guarded Blymire gazed at him with jaw agape, his eyes fairly bulging from his lined face," reported the *Philadelphia Inquirer*. "Then, tugging at his prisoner's sleeve, he slipped a steel manacle over his slender wrist. The handcuff clicked viciously in the stillness of the courtroom.

"A few minutes later, down in the Sheriff's office, Blymire turned to his youthful attorney and said: 'I am happy now. I am not bewitched anymore. I can sleep and I am not pining away.' "

In Harry P. Kissinger's mind, there never was the slightest doubt of Blymire's guilt or the motive for Rehmeyer's murder.

"What we really had to decide," recalled the foreman recently, "was how we should punish the defendant—put him away for life or give him the chair."

Nearly four decades have passed since Kissinger was summoned to serve in Judge Sherwood's Courtroom Number Two, but he remembers most of the details of that important event in his career. While he has retired from the York Bank and Trust Company, Kissinger, a pleasant, healthy-looking septuagenarian, is still active and maintains a desk in the institution's main office on East Market Street directly opposite the courthouse.

Unquestionably mellowed by the passing years, and probably superior mentally, socially and economically to most of the eleven other jurors, Kissinger is willing, even if he is not happy, to discuss the Blymire trial, the part he played in it and his own interpretation of the case.

"We paid no attention to the hex angle Herb Cohen was trying to produce; we were convinced it had nothing to do with the case. And we disagreed completely with

143

those psychiatrists. As far as Blymire and the other two were concerned, they killed the old man for his money; the powwow business was nonsense."

He paused for a moment or two, then went on.

"I really don't think Herb Cohen made much of a fight for it. He sounded to me like he almost felt convinced his client was guilty. On the other hand Amos Herrmann did a fine job. I'll tell you something else, though. When Judge Sherwood finished his presentation and we got into the jury room a couple of fellows started to insist on the electric chair. But the rest of us felt we ought to find him guilty and give him life imprisonment.

"I was foreman and I told those fellows who were holding out for the death penalty that if necessary I'd make them stay for a month. After two ballots they gave in and we were all in agreement. I haven't a single regret about the verdict. It was a just one."

"Not so," said Mr. Dudley Nichols of the *New York World*, whose story "Witches Win in York" appeared in the January 23 edition of *The Nation*.

"The prevalent belief in the powers of darkness is merely a matter of disclosure, not invective," he wrote. "But there is something more contemptible than medieval darkness and that is the flagrant injustice which in the opinion of the writer attended the witchcraft trial in consequence of the Commonwealth's smug determination not to recognize any such stigma upon York County as widespread witchcraft and powwowing.

"The Commonwealth in the person of District Attorney Amos Herrmann buried its head in the sand of self-righteousness against the powers of darkness, and refused to allow to the jury that there was any motive behind the inadvertent crime except plunder, as represented in the dollar apiece the three spell-breakers carried off after ransacking Rehmeyer's house for 'the book'. . . .

"That position of the Commonwealth amounted to suppression of the real facts. And Blymire, victim of York County's medievalism and the sad circumstances of life, who belongs in the asylum from which he escaped . . . became in turn the victim of a pharisaical society. The slain man, Rehmeyer, was a sacrifice to the powers of

144

darkness, while the three boys (Blymire has a mental age of eight) were sacrificed to the Commonwealth's smug self-righteousness and respectability, and there is not a straw to choose between the two bloody idols. It is an ancient story; scapegoats, like witches, are written into the Bible."

18

ON A COLD JANUARY DAY, WITH SNOW THREAT-ening the bleak countryside, fourteen-year-old John Curry went on trial for his life. York was filled with an increasingly tense atmosphere, an almost fanatical desire to get the whole "witchcraft business" over with as soon as possible and hatred for the "furrin" press.

"Mayor Weaver," reported Mr. Nichols, "summoned news photographers, called them rascals and hoodlums and told them the next man who walked down the street with a camera would be thrown in the 'cooler.'"

Ted MacFarland of the Philadelphia *Evening Public Ledger* witnessed one episode involving York's chief executive and his attitude toward the press. The reporter told this one with a laugh.

"The morning of the Curry boy's trial," he recalled, "it must have been around eight o'clock when a bunch of us, reporters and photographers, were having breakfast in the Yorktown Hotel, right next to the courthouse. The place was jammed, a couple dozen members of the working press from all over the country, traveling salesmen, etc., and, of course, lots of local citizens as well.

"In strutted the Mayor, a pompous nonentity. We knew who he was; we'd seen him around but he wasn't any part of our story. At best someone might have interviewed him once but generally we ignored His Honor. Well, the son of a bitch had a couple of his henchmen with him and he walked up to our table and stood staring at us.

"Then he sang out real loud in his thick Pennsylvania Dutch. Everybody stopped eating to hear what he had to say.

" 'Listen, you bums! You'd better watch your behavior in York. I've heard some pretty bad stories about your conduct. This is a law-abiding community and we won't stand for any nonsense. And don't let me catch any of you taking pictures of any citizens who don't want to.'

"With that, His Honor strutted out the door."

MacFarland smiled at the recollection and went on.

"Well, there was a skinny young photographer, from the *Inquirer*, I think. If I remember correctly his name was Wagner. At any rate, when the Mayor stepped out. Wagner, or whoever the hell he was, stepped right behind him. We could see all the action that followed through the windows by our table.

"Wagner circled the Mayor, went ahead and stopped a couple feet in front. 'Just a minute, Your Honor,' Wagner said, 'I'd like to get a shot of you for our paper.'

"With that, Mayor Weaver stood still, adjusted his tie, brushed aside his henchmen and put on a big smile. Then Wagner, about to snap the shutter, looked at his camera. He shook his head apologetically. 'Oh, Your Honor,' he said, 'I'm terribly sorry. I used my last film an hour ago and I forgot to reload. Please wait. I'll be right back.'

"Wagner returned to his table in the coffee shop, sat down and started working on his breakfast. Outside, the Mayor didn't budge and held the pose. After about ten minutes or so he glanced inside the coffee shop and could see we were all, including Wagner, watching. His Honor got red as a beet, shook his fat fist at us and walked away."

The first juror, Howard Harbold, a middle-aged Washington Township farmer, was selected a few minutes after court convened at 9:30 A.M. By a strange coincidence, juror number two, chosen foreman, was a York grocery store owner named Alexander McClean, a name so close to that of Curry's stepfather that it caused the defendant's counsel some misgivings. But he was allowed to pass

146

unchallenged. Slightly more than an hour elapsed before the panel was completed; only twenty-seven prospective talesmen had been processed.

The trial of John Curry was one of the speediest on record in Pennsylvania for an offense as serious as was the defendant's.

"When the final juror was in the box," said the *York Gazette and Daily*, "District Attorney Herrmann outlined his case for the jury and then the witnesses for the Commonwealth were heard. Taking of this testimony was concluded by 2:30 o'clock P.M., after which Mr. Van-Baman opened before the jury for the defense.

"Then Curry and his mother testified, after which Van-Baman made his final plea to the jury. The attorney had several witnesses ready to testify to Curry's good reputation but the District Attorney was willing to admit Curry's character was good and they were not called."

The trial of John Curry produced little that had not already been heard in Courtroom Number Two in the previous witchcraft trial. With few exceptions witnesses for the prosecution and for the defense were the same ones as those put on the stand in the case of the *Commonwealth of Pennsylvania* v. *John Blymire*. No medical testimony was offered, however, since VanBaman did not intend to claim insanity in any form.

For Counselor Walter W. VanBaman, even though he did the best he could under the circumstances, the task of defending young John Curry must have been extremely difficult. He then believed his client guilty as charged and has never changed this opinion.

In his office at 30 North Queen Street, a three-minute walk to the courthouse where he has been trying cases since 1901, Mr. VanBaman recalled his involvement with John Curry and the rest of the family.

"The Currys had no money at all and outside of the boy's mother, nobody cared really what happened," said VanBaman. "When the Judge asked me to represent the boy, there was nothing I could do but accept.

"That kind of law isn't my great love but I'd only recently finished a term as District Attorney; I'd had other criminal cases so I knew what I was up against.

147

Besides, I didn't believe the story Blymire'd been telling; I'm sure what those three wanted was the old man's money and that's what they went out there to get. That hex business was a lot of tomfoolery.

"What happened was the press blew the trials all out of proportion. There was no reason for it; these were just ordinary cases and should have been so regarded, but they weren't."

This white-haired handsome gentleman shook his head.

"I've never changed my mind about Curry and the others. Tell you what convinced me robbery was the real motive, that eight hundred dollars they wanted to steal from the old man." No mention of that sum is to be found anywhere in the press before, during or after any of the trials. "When I asked Curry—he was still in the county jail—if he wore gloves when they killed Rehmeyer, he said 'no.' But when the D.A. asked him the same question, he said 'yes.' That really shook me.

"Even though I thought the verdict was just, and I still do, I appealed the case. It was against my better judgment but some New York group—I don't remember what they were called—pressed me into it. So I got all the jurors to sign a petition saying the verdict they rendered was too severe. Then I presented it to the Pennsylvania Supreme Court and did I get taken to task! Chief Justice von Moschzisker said I had no case for an appeal."

Despite VanBaman's mental reservations about the righteousness of his cause, he put on a good show.

"Tears coursed down the faces of jurors and spectators alike in the courtroom . . . as Walter H. VanBaman made a moving plea to save the boyish defendant either from death in the electric chair or from imprisonment for all or a greater part of his life," reported Ken Mack in the Philadelphia *Record*.

"I am not here to tell you that this boy committed no crime," VanBaman declared. "But the crime is neither first-degree murder nor involving premeditation of commission during the performance of a felony such as robbery, nor even second-degree murder. In point of judgment these three defendants are imbeciles whose existence in this twentieth century of Christianity is an indictment of our civilization.

"There is no doubt that this crime was the product of that monumental mass of ignorance and superstition involved in the visit of these three to Rehmeyer's home in quest of a lock of hair to bury eight feet underground."

The defense counsel appealed to the jury to "consider the age of John Curry and look with sympathy upon the unhappy home life this boy led . . . this fourteen-year-old who rarely experienced a day's happiness or knew the joys of childhood to which all of us are entitled at least in some slight measure."

But, in his charge, Judge Sherwood destroyed any hope of leniency the jury might have shown Curry because of the defendant's age.

"The Court says to you," declared His Honor, "as a legal proposition, that where one has arrived at the age of fourteen years, the law presumes that he has the ability to distinguish between right and wrong, and he is responsible for his criminal acts.

"The law even recognizes the fact that earlier than fourteen years one may have the power to distinguish between right and wrong, but that until such time as a child arrives at the age of seven years, it has no power to distinguish between right and wrong. . . .

"It therefore follows that the law presumes that he [Curry] knew the difference between right and wrong. . . ."

Fortunately for York County's already tarnished reputation, the question of what this jury would have done had Curry been half his age is purely academic. But in view of His Honor's openly expressed view of a juvenile's responsibility, it is not improbable the panel would have judged Curry as harshly at seven as it did at fourteen.

Perhaps the worst blow the defense suffered was struck when the Court refused to rule out Curry's confession, obtained quite readily from the eager prisoner in response to an implied offer of leniency.

"You help me, John, and I'll help you," the District Attorney had promised.

"That's what you told me, Mr. Herrmann," Curry testified under cross examination, "and I thought by that you meant you'd get me out of trouble."

Herrmann, however, claimed what he told Curry was not "I will help you" but "I might be able to help you." The question of semantics is moot; both Herrmann and Curry understood exactly what the offer meant.

The District Attorney was not dealing with a mature criminal accustomed to methods, legal or otherwise, often used by police and prosecutors to obtain confessions. Herrmann was talking to an adolescent who never before had been in trouble and who was entitled to the full protection of the law the same as anyone else.

It is true Curry had just participated in a gruesome murder, but when he was taken into custody he was no more than a frightened child, remorseful over what he'd done and anxious to place his trust in someone who would respond. Amos Herrmann, the kindly gentleman who occupied such a high position in society, offered his aid, and the fourteen-year-old boy accepted it at face value.

When VanBaman showed how Curry's confession was obtained and objected to its admission as evidence, he was overruled by the Court. Replied Judge Sherwood: ". . . a confession . . . is not objectionable even where it is obtained by a trick, unless there is something in it that shows that it was made through fear or hope in connection with promises that were actually held out to him."

What did His Honor suppose District Attorney Herrmann meant when he said, "John, you help me and I'll help you"?

As Curry's trial drew to a close, VanBaman made one last try to exclude his client's confession, Exhibit Number Eight, from the evidence. This attempt succeeded.

While Judge Sherwood had a closed mind on the subject of powwowing, he knew the law and few of his past decisions ever had been reversed by upper courts. By the time VanBaman made his final plea to exclude Exhibit Eight from the evidence, the Judge had had the opportunity to reconsider the point. His reply to defense counsel's objection showed the Court's fear of a reversal by the State Supreme Court with the possibility that Curry would be granted a new trial and the whole horrid case rehashed publicly.

"Does the District Attorney *insist* upon the admission of this confession under these circumstances? The matter is pretty close to the borderline," said Judge Sherwood.

Herrmann, aware of this potential danger to his case, replied, "We will not insist upon it."

The Court continued. "I have some doubt as to its real admissibility," and Herrmann, getting the message, declared, "I will say this, whether it is in the record or off the record, that I want this boy to have a fair trial. I will withdraw that."

His Honor, who must have breathed a sigh of relief, answered, "That will simplify the whole situation."

Even though Judge Sherwood, District Attorney Herrmann and defense counsel VanBaman saved face by this buck passing, the victory was shallow indeed for John Curry; the jury had already heard his confession.

"Only two witnesses were called for the defense and of these one testified briefly," said the Philadelphia *Record* of January 11. "She was Mrs. Anna MacLean, mother of the youthful defendant and of twelve-year-old Elizabeth Curry who sat uncomprehending with the spectators and slept contentedly through much of the day.

"The other witness was the defendant, the dark-haired, good-looking boy, with down on his rosy cheeks, who smiled his way into Court this morning, who viewed the . . . proceedings as though he were a spectator at a movie show and who squirmed on the stand like a child being chided for playing hooky from school. . . ."

Not called but available and rather bored by the entire show, the previous day's star sat a few yards away from Curry.

"Brought into Court as a possible witness against his former disciple, Blymire yawned his way through another day, twisted his long hands in his eternal task of cleaning one fingernail with another, grinned now and then and shook his six-and-a-quarter-sized head when Curry said

151

something with which he did not agree," continued Ken Mack in the Philadelphia *Record*.

On hand in Courtroom Number Two were three responsible York County citizens prepared to testify as character witnesses for John Curry. They never got the chance. Instead of insisting that the panel hear their actual words, VanBaman unaccountably acquiesced to a suggestion made by Herrmann that to save time the District Attorney would admit to the defendant's previous reputation for "peace, quiet and good behavior" if these character witnesses were not put on the stand.

In the opinion of experts on criminal law, this was a serious mistake on VanBaman's part.

At 4 P.M. on the first day of the trial, the defense rested and VanBaman addressed the jury on behalf of his client. "His stirring appeal to consider this boy's tender age moved spectators to tears," declared the *Pittsburgh Gazette*. But, as subsequent events proved, it did not move the jury one whit. At 4:33 VanBaman concluded and court adjourned until the following morning at 9:30, when Amos Herrmann spoke his piece, adding little that he had not said to the Blymire panel.

"It is expected," prophesied the *Newark* (New Jersey) *Evening News*, "that the jury's verdict will be that for which VanBaman asked, one finding young Curry guilty of manslaughter, and that the sentence will be light."

But in the collective mind of the jury, if not in that of the *Evening News* correspondent, Judge Sherwood had already demolished the possibility of a manslaughter verdict.

"The Court," declared His Honor, "has no right to substitute its judgment for yours, and in what we are going to say we have no intention of trying to impress on your minds what your verdict shall be . . . but the Court, from the evidence adduced in this case, cannot see how your verdict should be one of manslaughter. That is intentional killing in hot blood, or in the heat of passion, resulting from some reasonable provocation. . . ."

At 10:50 on the morning of January 11, 1929, the jury returned and less than two hours later announced it had reached a verdict. As Curry rose to face the panel he faltered momentarily; his shoulders sagged and he leaned against his attorney for support. Then he regained his composure, stood up straight and looked directly into the eyes of Foreman Alexander McClean.

"Your Honor," reported McClean in a crisp, no-nonsense voice, "we find the defendant, John Curry, guilty of murder in the first degree, with life sentence."

Young Curry listened in disbelief; his face turned white as he grasped the meaning of McClean's words. His loud, quick breaths broke the silence of the courtroom, and he rubbed his hands across his forehead.

"Then," reported the *Philadelphia Inquirer*, "Curry smiled a faint, twisted smile—the last grand gesture of a beardless, dark-haired boy to a youth that is ended. . . .

"Behind him, amid the gaping dull-faced spectators of the courtroom, his mother bent forward and sobbed distractedly, her red, tear-stained face hidden in the folds of a handkerchief not yet dry from yesterday's weeping."

Deputy Sheriff Altschuler led the manacled Curry down the broad, marble courthouse corridor. "Don't worry, son," comforted Altschuler, "maybe they'll let you out when you're twenty-one."

Quite understandably the verdict met with District Attorney Herrmann's full approval. "It was just," he said. "Curry got what he deserved; the jury should be complimented for its courage."

But VanBaman's reaction to the verdict was, in the opinion of the Philadelphia *Record*, "a little unusual for a defense attorney. 'There is no reason for appeal,' he announces, 'the whole thing is that an atrocious murder has been done and they are going to knock the whole thing on the head. That's all there is to it.' "

Shocked and deeply troubled by the harshness of the Blymire verdict, the public beyond York County's borders was aghast at the harsh punishment meted out to the youthful John Curry.

"I see by tonight's papers," wrote philosopher-columnist Will Rogers on January 11, "that a Pennsylvania jury sentenced that fourteen-year-old boy to life imprisonment because he believed in witchcraft. That's all he'd ever been raised up to. It's like sentencing one of

153

our children for acting according to their religious beliefs. No doubt about there being witches in that county—the jury's verdict shows that plainer than the boy's deed.

"What's become of an old-fashioned law they called, 'Change of venue'? I think it's still in vogue among the rich, at any rate.

"The Lord certainly had that dozen in mind when he said, 'Father, forgive them, for they know not what they do.' "

Said the Cleveland *Plain Dealer*, "The box score in the York County witchcraft trials is now two down and one to go."

Speed was the order of the day; "get 'em over with fast," the attitude of People, Judge and jury.

Declared the *York Gazette and Daily* with pardonable pride, "The Court established another record . . . in handling a murder trial. It was the fastest time ever made in a trial of this sort here."

The People would permit little time to be lost before they gave the third defendant his day (almost literally) in court.

"Hess, the last of the trio, will probably know his fate by tomorrow night," said the *New York Times,* "for even before the Curry jury reported, more than half the talesmen for Hess's trial had been chosen and when court adjourned at 5:15 o'clock, the Commonwealth had rested its case against Hess."

19

A WARNING TO THE FAITHFUL THAT THE POWers of darkness were keeping their eyes on events up in York County, Pennsylvania, came with a visual demonstration of black magic the very morning Hess was brought to trial. The nearly fatal victim of hexerei was that necromantic belittler, Herbert B. Cohen, on his way from office to courthouse.

"Cohen," reported the *York Gazette and Daily*, ". . . had a narrow escape in the hallway of the Central National Bank Building, when a bolt from a riveting machine crashed through the glass in a hall window and through his office door. As a result of this experience, he was plainly nervous when he appeared before the court a short time later to present a motion for a new trial for Blymire.

"Mr. Cohen left the elevator on the second floor of the building. . . . Suddenly there was a terrific crash of glass in front and on his left side. In the twinkling of an eye there was another crash and the glass in his office door was splintered and showered over the stenographer.

"For a moment Cohen was unnerved. The two sudden crashes appeared to be the result of a shot."

The newspaper then purported to explain the reason for the mishap which nearly took the life of Blymire's counsel. Almost everybody in York County who had heard what Mr. Cohen said about witches or had read his ill-advised remarks in the newspapers knew what *really* happened; nonetheless, for the benefit of its few skeptical subscribers, the *Gazette and Daily* felt obliged to offer a more earthly excuse for the near tragedy that had befallen Mr. Cohen.

"The crashes," this newspaper continued, "were caused by a bolt that had been shot out of a riveting machine being used in the construction of the Hotel Yorktown addition. The bolt was found on the floor of Mr. Cohen's office a few minutes later."

Lawyer Cohen's close brush with death was not the only example of necromantic ire displayed in or around the York County courthouse the day the third defendant was brought to trial. Obviously under the influence of some evil spirit, "Mayor Jacob Weaver, red-faced and bristling with anger," as the *Chicago Tribune* reported, "shook his fist at a group of newspaper photographers snapping pictures of participants in the witchcraft trial of Wilbert G. Hess. . . .

" 'I warned youse fellers wunst,' shouted His Honor,

'and I won't warn you no more. The next time any of you chentlemen annoys my beeple, I'll toss him in the chug myself.' "

Except for a constant display of Bulldog Gross's superior ability as a criminal lawyer, there was not much to differentiate the trial of Wilbert B. Hess from the trials of John Blymire and John Curry.

Ethnically and culturally, the third defendant's peers were mostly of the same stock as that of the twenty-four gentlemen who had decided Blymire's and Curry's fate. An argument might be advanced that the presence of two bankers (Earl Shatto, Dallastown, and Stewart Hoffeins, Hanover) raised the economic and intellectual level of panel number three. Since this was about eight months before the Great Depression's start, there are many who would have gone along with that premise. Those who wish to refute the theory that this jury was on a higher social level than the others could point out the unassailable fact that not a single member of Hess's jury claimed to be a "gentleman."

No previously unheard witnesses were placed on the stand; no new testimony was offered and, with one exception, no fresh evidence presented at the Hess trial. The single bit of additional evidence Gross was able to bring out concerned the length of time it took to kill that tough old witch, Rehmeyer. According to Blymire's and Curry's own testimony, the struggle between Rehmeyer and his three attackers lasted nearly an hour.

If this were true (and neither the Blymire nor Curry juries were given any reason to question the defendants' own statements), it would clearly demonstrate the utter heartlessness of the murderers who kept beating their victim until they drove life from his body. On the other hand, should Gross be able to show that the struggle ended so quickly that neither the killers nor their victim were aware of what was happening, then the defendants were far less cruel than they had been purported to be.

"To gain this point," reported Ken Mack in the Philadelphia *Record*, "Gross resorted to a dramatic device.

" 'Wilbert,' he said, 'I am going to take out my watch and when I say "go," I want you to think that the fight has begun. Then, when you think the time that the fight took has elapsed, I want you to stand up.'

"Some of the jurors took out their watches, and Gross, standing near the jury, removed his from the pocket of his waistcoat.

" 'Ready,' he said. And then, 'Go!'

"There was complete silence in the courtroom. Murmurs of conversation had ceased and even the coughs were stilled. Every pair of eyes was upon Hess. In his mind, the crowd knew, was the struggle in that remote cabin where the murder was done in the light of a kerosene lamp and the darkness of superstition. After what seemed at least five minutes, Hess rose quickly, swung his hand behind him, stood with his legs far apart. The fight was over.

" 'My watch made that fifty-five seconds,' Gross announced, and the other timekeepers agreed."

The Bulldog recalled the trial incident with a chuckle. "Actually," he said, "my watch showed fifty-three seconds, but the jury thought I was leaning backwards to be fair when I announced it was fifty-five."

Unlike Cohen and VanBaman, Gross allowed the introduction of Hess's confession as evidence without argument. His reasoning was sound. In the minds of the panel, since the other lawyers had raised such a fuss over permitting the juries to hear the confessions, there must have been a great deal in them that Cohen and VanBaman didn't want the talesmen to hear.

The Bulldog played this important card with far more sagacity and parleyed what began as a liability into an asset. He let the jury listen to his client's confession, then destroyed the document's value. Shortly after Herrmann was granted permission to introduce this seemingly damaging exhibit, Gross, with an expression of tolerance and understanding on his face, quietly picked up a chair from behind defense counsel's table, carried it over to the witness stand and seated himself next to his client.

"Then," said the Philadelphia *Record*, "with all the bedside manner of a family physician inquiring into a patient's symptoms, he began the laborious task of going through the document, phrase by phrase. His purpose was apparent. He was laying the groundwork for his contention that the boy's mind had not been clear when he made the statement; that he had made certain 'mistakes' which the witness could not explain away. . . .

"Sentence by sentence the confession was read by Gross. 'Is that true?' or 'Is that right?' or 'Did you say that?' the attorney inquired as he came to each period and each time Hess replied either 'Yes, sir,' or 'No, sir, that wasn't the way.' "

As juror number nine, O. C. Livingston, a Paradise Township farmer, later told *Philadelphia Inquirer* reporter Herman A. Lowe, "Ole Harve convinced me the police pushed the boy so hard by shooting questions at him so fast that he didn't give Wilbert time to know what he was saying, and that wasn't fair."

Nor would the Bulldog accept Judge Sherwood's and District Attorney Herrmann's proffered "time-saving" device—the one to which VanBaman had readily acquiesced—of dictating character witnesses' statements to a court stenographer instead of letting the jury know exactly what responsible citizens felt about Wilbert G. Hess.

Two of Gross's character witnesses were well-known and highly respected schoolteachers who testified that Wilbert's reputation was not merely good, it was "extra" good. These were followed first by a farmer, then a contractor, whose opinions of the defendant coincided with those of the schoolteachers.

Gross did nothing to hurry them along. They listened to his questions carefully, then gave their answers in measured tones as though to assure the jury that they were not prone to render snap judgments about anyone, least of all the defendant. The District Attorney obviously had no desire to tangle with these self-assured, respectable gentlemen who had known Wilbert G. Hess since the defendant was a small boy, and who clearly felt that it was their duty to give as much time as Mr. Gross needed to tell the jury what they thought of young Hess, in trouble for the first time in his life.

Mr. Herrmann, who listened impatiently while his antagonist methodically built up the defendant's past record, finally had enough.

"The Commonwealth will admit to the good reputation of the defendant," he said.

But the Bulldog was too wily to be taken in by this gesture.

"Your Honor," he protested, "I should have the right to let this Court know that, in addition to the witnesses whom I have called, I have a large number of people . . . in this court to testify to the good reputation of this defendant."

"Just how many are there, Mr. Gross?" asked His Honor with some concern.

The Bulldog slowly turned around and looked toward the rear of the courtroom. Then he faced Judge Sherwood.

"In all," he replied, "I have about seventy-seven more from Wilbert's neighborhood."

Herrmann, dismayed by this disclosure, raised his eyebrows and regarded the defense counsel with amazement.

"Are they here now, Mr. Gross?" he asked.

The Bulldog turned around once more. There was a loud shuffling and buzzing in the rear of Courtroom Number Two and a considerable number of ladies and gentlemen either stood up or raised their hands. Gross nodded his head in approval.

"Well, they're *supposed* to be here," he answered, knowing full well that the jury had seen they *were* in court and that no one, least of all Herrmann, was going to demand a head count.

The District Attorney was in a box and, in a sense, so was Judge Sherwood. The latter could not deny a lawyer of Gross's stature the right to summon as many character witnesses as he felt necessary. On the other hand, if the Court permitted him to place seventy-seven more unhurried citizens on the stand, the session could drag on for days.

His Honor frowned unhappily.

"Well, we will permit you to call some more if you want to, Mr. Gross," he said, then faced the box. "We will say to the jury that there is no question about the prior reputation of this defendant and that reputation has already been proven by the witnesses called and by a large number of additional witnesses whom Mr. Gross would call."

The Bulldog was satisfied; he had made his point. He never had had the slightest intention of antagonizing a weary jury by placing all those character witnesses on the stand. However, he had shown the panel they *were* available to testify in his client's behalf and, furthermore, that it was within his legal right to place each and every one upon the stand. "When the time came for the talesmen to make their decision regarding the fate of Wilbert G. Hess, they'd keep these facts in mind," recalled Gross.

That the panel did keep these facts in mind was admitted to Lowe by Juryman Livingston.

"If ole Harve lined up all those people to say a good word for young Hess, well, then I guess the boy wasn't too bad before he got mixed up in bad company. And Harve was smart to know he didn't have to waste all that time provin' it. We could see the Judge awreddy give up and so did that foxy Herrmann."

Gross had nothing further to add in defense of Wilbert G. Hess. At twelve o'clock noon on the second day of the trial he rested his case. While the jury retired from Courtroom Number Two, the defense counsel presented seventeen points for the Court's charge.

"Gross, his short and stocky figure dominating the courtroom, wrestled with Judge Ray P. Sherwood for a charge to the jurors that would instruct them to find his client guilty of no greater crime than murder in the second degree," reported the Philadelphia *Record*.

While the Court refused to agree on the question of degree, His Honor did affirm all seventeen of the points defense counsel had raised. As a result, the Judge's charge to the Hess jury was far more tempered than it had been for either the Blymire or Curry panels.

At 12:30 P.M., Judge Sherwood declared a brief recess, and at 2:05 P.M., the Bulldog began his plea to the men in the box.

For the next hour and twenty minutes Gross spoke to the jury. These twelve were his own people and not for one moment did he let them forget it. His accent was thicker than usual and from time to time he resorted to a

Pennsylvania Dutch phrase or expression to strengthen the bond between the panel and himself. He was aware that the dramatic approach Cohen had used was distasteful to the jury and only once or twice did he resort to mild histrionics. When he did, it was obvious, from the way the twelve nodded their heads, he had their approval for this bit of stage play.

"The eyes of the world are on you, and on me and on York because of the atrocious and peculiar nature of this crime," he said. "York must be vindicated, but that vindication must not come at the expense of justice. We must acquit York County, I would say, of what we might call 'York County dementia.' We must not, on the other hand, sacrifice justice. . . .

"Yet, in truth, York really does not have to be vindicated. It does not have to draw the last drop of blood from the heart of a boy to save a good name that has stood for generations. Superstition has been in the world down through the ages. Paul prayed at Philippi and the sorcerer followed him to cast out the evil spirit and to be thrown into prison as his reward."

For only a few seconds during his eighty-minute address did the jury's attention leave the speaker, and that brief, inadvertent interruption helped rather than hindered the Bulldog's efforts. It occurred when Gross emphasized the use of powwowing to rid the Hess's cattle and chickens of a hex.

"A heavy-faced countryman in the courtroom snickered," reported the Associated Press, "and his guffaw was as out of place as a curse before the altar. His face flushed with shame as spectators turned at him with scowling faces."

Gross was not averse to staging a few side effects he felt the jury would appreciate.

"Naturally, Hess's mother was in court the whole time, sitting up front near her boy," Gross recalled. "She was a big, domineering woman, rather handsome, and she wanted to dress in her Sunday best. But I wouldn't let her. I made her wear a clean house dress and insisted that she keep her apron on. I also told her she could cry as *much* as she wanted *whenever* she wanted.

"Another point I had to make clear to the jury was that I was defending them and myself from the persecution of those city reporters who kept calling us 'hicks' and 'backwoodsmen.' "

These same city reporters hastened to give the Bulldog full credit for his abilities.

"Gross's summation to the jury," declared John M. McCullough of the *Philadelphia Inquirer*, "was one of the mightiest appeals ever heard in the law courts of this county. He ripped aside the thin veil . . . the prosecution attempted to spread before the ghoulish figure of a mysticism which for generation after generation has persisted in the villages and the farmhouses of York County."

Another admiring journalist was the *Pittsburg Gazette*'s correspondent.

"In quiet, measured tones," said this reporter, "Counselor Gross made a mighty plea for mercy and justice to twelve of his compatriots who listened in rapt attention as words poured from the lips of this squat little man. There was hardly a dry eye in the packed courtroom. It was one of the most brilliant addresses ever made in the courts of the Keystone State."

The Commonwealth's plea came next but almost from the moment Herrmann stood in front of the panel to demand "the full penalty of the law for this evil youth who helped kill a harmless old man for his money," the District Attorney discovered that Bulldog Gross was a tough speaker for anyone to follow. Herrmann's problems were pointed out by the *New York Times*.

"The prosecutor," said this newspaper, "faced a wet-eyed courtroom and a none too complacent panel of talesmen when he made his demand that Hess be found guilty of malice and premeditation."

At 4:05 P.M. the Court charged the jury; at 4:52 the panel retired, and at 7:18 the jury announced that it had reached a verdict—"Guilty of murder in the second degree."

In the face of great odds, with two of his client's partners in crime already convicted of murder in the first degree, the defense counsel had won a remarkable victory and he knew it.

"Little Harvey A. Gross, pint-sized Clarence Darrow of York County's Bar, beamed happily and shook hands with each juror as soon as Court had taken its adjournment," reported the Philadelphia *Record.*

" 'Fine, fine,' was his message to the world.

" 'Absolutely fine, and I win.' "

At first Wilbert appeared dazed. He turned to a sheriff's deputy and said, "Won't they let me go home at all now or will I have to go right to jail?" The deputy said nothing as he led his prisoner away.

Mrs. Hess, who had had good reason to expect the worst for her son, was not too unhappy with the jury's decision. "We'll have to be satisfied," she said. Then she walked over to Mrs. MacLean, who sat sobbing near the counsel's table. The two mothers embraced quietly, then arm in arm slowly walked out of Courtroom Number Two.

If anyone representing John Blymire was on hand, his presence was unnoted by members of the working press.

20

ON TUESDAY, JANUARY 14, 1929, JUDGE SHERwood passed sentence on the prisoners: Blymire and Curry were to serve life terms; Hess, a term of from ten to twenty years. Justice had been dispensed swiftly in York County. Only nine days elapsed between the opening call of the Crier's "Hear Ye! Hear Ye!" and the metallic clank of Eastern State Penitentiary's iron gates swinging shut upon the trio of convicted murderers in Philadelphia, ninety miles away.

Local reporters went back to routine jobs; the "furrin" press went home; Judge Sherwood returned to his Bench in an uncluttered courtroom; Messrs. Cohen, VanBaman and Gross resumed their normal law practices; Amos W.

Herrmann began his short descent into oblivion and the York Chamber of Commerce breathed a tremendous sigh of relief. (For the sake of accuracy it is admitted that no person, living or dead, actually heard this corporate exhalation.)

For perhaps three or four months longer the press of the world was inclined to editorialize about the low mental level of the Pennsylvania Dutch. But at that time, the highly regarded English writer and spiritualist, Sir Arthur Conan Doyle, was giving respectability to a cause not far removed from the beliefs generally subscribed to in the hinterlands of the Keystone State. Doyle's prominence caused scoffers to think twice before chiding a man because of his reliance upon members of a world unseen. Besides, this was 1929, and on October 29 of that year problems even more serious than witchcraft would be available for journalistic pontification.

A few months after the trials, one of Curry's twelve peers, Lester Sell, the Hanover merchant, was stricken with a latent attack of conscience and called on Mr. VanBaman to report a statement made by a fellow juror shortly after the panel retired to decide the prisoner's fate. Then, according to Mr. Sell, Foreman Alex McClean told his colleagues he'd been tied up and robbed by a pair of bandits some years before and "had it in for every son of a bitch like that ever since."

Sell had little trouble convincing Curry's lawyer that such a vindictive attitude probably did not help either the foreman or his colleagues render impartial justice. Sell's statement was corroborated by several of his fellow jurors and a petition, signed by them, was drawn up. Then, at the insistence of some New York civil liberties group, whose exact name VanBaman no longer remembers, Hess's counsel filed an appeal for a new trial. This was the one rejected by the State Supreme Court on January 18, 1930.

Attorney Cohen recalled another incident, not too dissimilar from the one experienced by Counselor Van-Baman.

"Shortly after the Blymire jury retired," said Cohen, "a tipstaff came to me and reported one of the jurors had made a pre-trial comment that 'they ought to burn the son of a bitch,' meaning, of course, Blymire.

"I took this information to Judge Sherwood and asked him what I should do about it. I don't remember if Mr. Herrmann was present during our conference but I think it probable that he was. The Court advised me not to do anything.

"But I'd made up my mind if the jury gave Blymire the death penalty I'd use that remark as the basis for a new trial. However, the panel recommended mercy so I did nothing."

Mr. Cohen shook his head sadly.

"The People didn't want justice; they wanted blood."

Meanwhile, Blymire, Curry and Hess were becoming model prisoners bent on building up good records.

"Blymire was a 'loner,' " said Paul J. Gernert, Chairman of the Pennsylvania Board of Pardons. "But he had an unblemished record with no disciplinary action against him. He was, however, regarded as 'peculiar.' Our prison psychiatrists say he functioned with an I.Q. of seventy-two but he was not psychotic. I do think, though, his mentality was far too limited for him to feel remorse for what he'd done.

"As for the other pair, Curry and Hess, we've practically nothing on our files about them. This leads me to the belief that they behaved well, both of them."

Then Gernert, born and raised in the Keystone State's hex belt, talked about powwowing, *The Long Lost Friend* and *The Seven Books of Moses*, the last book admittedly not a part of Blymire's library.

"When I was a kid," Gernert recalled, "I got hold of a copy of *The Seven Books of Moses* and started to read it but my parents forbade me. You know why?

"Well, they said if I did, I'd 'read myself fast,' which is a good old Pennsylvania Dutch way of saying I'd get stuck on the belief. And that's not too far off. You read or hear about these miraculous 'cures,' or whatever they are, and it doesn't take too much more to convince you."

The Chairman paused for a moment, then went on with another childhood recollection.

"Up near Reading," he said, "where I lived, we had a

neighbor who had a terrible case of palsy; the medical doctors couldn't do a thing for him. Now our neck of the woods was filled with powwowers and one of them was an old lady named Nace.

"To make a long story short, Mrs. Nace tried for this neighbor a couple of times and he was cured; the palsy left him completely."

Gernert shrugged his shoulders, then chuckled.

"Try to explain that one away, will you?" he asked rhetorically.

In 1933, the first of several clemency appeals was filed in behalf of the three prisoners, but like a number of those which followed, it was rejected by the Pardon Board because Amos Herrmann's successors launched strong protests against the convicted men's release. On June 20, 1934, the Pardon Board offered hope to Curry by commuting his life sentence to a term of ten to twenty years. He was then nineteen and had spent the last five years in Philadelphia's maximum security prison.

Hess was paroled June 16, 1939, and Curry on June 29 of the same year. Both completed their paroles with no listed violations nine years and eleven months later and then, as Chairman Gernert phrased it, they were "out."

But for years Blymire's efforts, or rather those made in his behalf, were unsuccessful.

"Protests against commutation of the sentence of the last of the three men sent to prison in 1929 for the 'hex' murder in York County of Nelson Rehmeyer were heard today by the State Pardon Board," reported the Associated Press on October 27, 1940, under a Harrisburg, Pennsylvania, dateline.

"Edward Buchen, Assistant District Attorney of York, told the board he has received 'protests from a number of persons,' including the daughter of the slain man, against release of John Blymire.

" 'They have a fear of residing in the same community with this man,' Buchen asserted."

On November 26, 1943, Governor Edward Martin, upon the recommendation of the Pardon Board, signed three pardons and granted twenty-two commutations but rejected another one hundred eight requests, including that of John Blymire.

"Commutation of Blymire's sentence was opposed at the October hearing by the York County District Attorney's office," reported the United Press. "Assistant District Attorney Edwin M. Buchen told the board that Rehmeyer's daughter was among the many in York County against release of the prisoner. . . ."

In 1952, the late Herbert B. Maris, an unusual member of the Philadelphia Bar, became interested in Blymire's case, Maris, a brilliant lawyer, spent much of his time, talents and money in behalf of men and women whom he believed were victims of court injustices.

After perusing trial records and conferring with Blymire several times at Eastern State Penitentiary, Maris filed an appeal in the prisoner's behalf and made a strong plea before the Parole Board for his client's release. On February 9, 1953, Governor John S. Fine, upon recommendation of the Board, commuted Blymire's sentence. The following day, Blymire, aged fifty-six or thereabouts, stepped out of the prison where he had spent twenty-three years and five months. He was free now except for a ten-year period of parole.

Through the efforts of Colonel F.D. Shaw (retired), a Philadelphia engineer, a home with an understanding family and a job as janitor in an apartment house were found for Blymire. Only occasional minor illnesses kept Blymire from performing his duties faithfully until 1965 when he retired. He lived simply and, with the money he saved, bought his own house. Lately his health has been poor and except for infrequent trips to York where he visits cousins, he stays at home.

Wilbert Granville Hess, upon his release from prison, went back home to live. "I'm not bitter anymore," he once told Arthur W. Geiselman, Jr., of the *Baltimore Evening Sun.* "I know I was a sucker. But I got married and made a man out of myself even though there were times when people around here made it tough for me."

Today, Hess is a solid, well-respected citizen, his past forgotten by all except a few diehards.

John Curry, by far the most intelligent member of the

trio, was only twenty-four years old when he "made" parole. One of his cellmates was Claude d'Arras, an elderly forger whose avocation was painting and who, under another name (or so he told Curry), had shown his canvases in a number of important American galleries including the Pennsylvania Academy of Fine Arts, where he claimed to have been a full-time instructor.

D'Arras was delighted to learn of his new cellmate's interest in art and determined to help him. Although there was then no occupational therapy at Eastern Penitentiary, the forger was able to obtain a few simple art supplies through Warden William Smith—tablets, drawing pencils, boxes of inexpensive watercolors and a number of "five and ten" brushes.

For nearly thirty years d'Arras had restricted his talents to the imitation of signatures (easily detectable fakes at that), but as Curry said, he must have been a fine artist in his day and he turned out to be an excellent teacher. Much of the great quantities of time the cellmates had was spent not only in developing Curry's latent ability to paint but also in turning this uncultured country boy into a somewhat polished young man.

D'Arras obviously had had considerable formal education, just how much Curry never did find out. The older man's English was that of a cultured gentleman; his French was fluent. He had traveled widely, knew history and was well enough informed in the social sciences to impart to his young cellmate far more than a smattering of knowledge.

A comparison between the relationship of John Curry and Claude d'Arras and that of Edmond Dantès and the Abbé Faria is inevitable. There were many major differences between these two friendships, of course. The forger was no intellectual giant; he had no vast wealth concealed in the outside world and revenge never became the *raison d'être* of Curry's life beyond prison walls.

When he was released from the penitentiary, Curry moved back to York County and lived with a private family in Thomasville, a small town not far from Rehmeyer's Hollow. While John was in prison his mother had divorced MacLean and married an Ohioan who ran a riding stable in suburban York. Curry's new stepfather was sympathetic; he taught the youth horsemanship, then employed him as a riding master.

One of Curry's pupils was the recreation and health director of the York Y.M.C.A. She and her teacher fell in love, received the blessings of the bride-to-be's parents and permission to marry from John's parole officer, and were wed in 1940.

Curry continued to paint and spent many spare hours studying with private tutors in Harrisburg, York and Lancaster. In 1943 he was drafted and after basic training was sent to Europe, where he served with distinction in the Army of the United States. In 1945 he was awarded the Bronze Star.

After the war ended he applied for and won a scholarship at *l'École des Beaux Arts* in Paris. Had he been able to attend, his wife would have joined him there. But because he had not yet completed his parole, the State Department refused to grant him a passport and so he was unable to remain abroad for study.

Curry came back to York after his army discharge in October of 1946. He bought a sixty-acre dairy farm a few miles south of Shrewsbury. Before long he had become a well-liked, well-respected member of the community. Most of the men and women in his area were aware of Curry's past. If he was bitter about the events that had damaged his life, he never said so to anyone.

After his return from the war, Curry spent a great deal of time in York's excellent Martin Memorial Library, with its fine collection of books on art, where for several years a "circulating" art gallery was run. Here Curry sometimes displayed his work. Miss Romaine Spangler, a library employee, remembers John Curry well.

"He used to come in often and once in a while brought his two children with him. I knew who he was but naturally I never mentioned the hex case to him. He was an avid reader, mostly in his own field, and he could discuss art works most intelligently.

"He was always very well dressed and polite, and appeared to be deeply attached to his two little girls and was extremely patient with them. I thought he was rather good-looking, too, strong and rugged."

Curry kept up his art studies, and in the early 1950s he began to paint portraits on commission. One of the friends he developed about this time was Herbert Lee, an artist and a well-known restorer of paintings, who, with his wife Louise, operates an art gallery in the City of York.

"I met John Curry for the first time late in the forties," Lee recalled. "He was a healthy-looking guy; weighed about one hundred seventy-five pounds or so with good coloring, the kind farmers have, a complexion you get from working a lot in the sun. He'd come into our store to buy supplies and we got to talking.

"John was one of the most interesting fellows I've met. He'd read considerably about art and it was obvious he'd spent many hours in European galleries, or at least ones in France. At first meeting I thought he was a typical outgoing guy but when I got to know him better I realized he had many depths which were hard to plumb.

"You can sense these in his work and when you see some of his portraits you realize John Curry kept much of himself below the surface. *Nobody* really knew him."

Lee stood in front of a portrait painted in the early 1960s when Curry had acquired considerable local fame as an artist. This was a study of an aged tinsmith whose picture had been commissioned by the subject's daughter.

"Note John's use of colors, particularly his purples," Lee pointed out. "There's an unrestrained wildness in them. His work was sure and his brush strong; you look at that old man up there and you've a feeling you knew him.

"Curry didn't charge a lot for his work, about one hundred fifty or two hundred dollars a portrait, and I think they're worth far more than that. You'll find them all over the county. He was a good artist, not great, and under other circumstances and with more and better training he certainly could have been a fine one."

Not until he'd known Curry for five or six years did Lee learn about the hex murder and his friend's participation in it.

"I'm from New England, myself (we once dealt with a couple of witches up there, if you'll remember), and I didn't get to York until 1940 so I didn't know a thing about the case. Louise is from this neck of the woods— her maiden name is an old Pennsylvania Dutch one, Partymiller—but she was too young when it happened to recall the details. It was all very vague in her mind.

"Well, one day John told me his story, without bitterness and without anger. He'd had a bad break, he said. 'One of those things, Herb,' and he shrugged his shoulders. 'The only part I resented was the fact that I was tried in the newspapers, and not in court.' That was the only time he ever talked about the murder. He never mentioned it again and neither did Louise or I.

"We saw each other only in the shop, never in each other's homes, but I knew he was happily married. He had enormous respect and affection for his wife and wanted to do the best he could for her and their children.

"People told me he was well liked in Thomasville, where they elected him treasurer of the Lions Club. I suppose some of the old-timers knew about John's involvement in the hex murder, but they were kind and willing to forget it. Besides, they must have been quite fond of John. He lived a good, useful life and left a heritage his family can be proud of."

This last statement appeared to end the reminiscences but then Lee, a tall, handsome, gray-haired man in his early fifties, pondered for a moment, nodded his head as though he'd made up his mind about something, and went on.

"I'll tell you a story," he said, "one I haven't told anyone, even Louise, but I think I ought to because it reveals a curious trait in John's character and one I think ought to be known to understand the whole man.

"One morning—this must have been in 1962, shortly before John died of a heart attack—he came into the store a few minutes after we opened up. 'Let's go out and get some coffee, Herb,' he said. I was a little surprised—we'd never done this before—but I said O.K. and we left Louise inside and drove up in his car to a donut place a couple of blocks away.

171

"I could see he was anxious to talk but we were on our third cup of coffee before he got started.

" 'You know, Herb,' he began, 'near the end of the war I was sent to Germany with the Army of Occupation.'

"I didn't know he'd been to Germany. In fact, I didn't know a thing about his war services; he'd barely mentioned them to me and then only in passing. But I nodded my head and he went on.

" 'One of the spots our company was billeted in was an old Rhine castle that must have belonged to some very wealthy Germans. The G.I.'s were going through the huge palace, exploring all the rooms, and a hell of a lot of valuable stuff was getting wrecked through careless handling because these guys simply didn't understand the delicacy of what they were tossing around.' "

Lee, who'd seen war service himself, said he could easily understand what Curry meant by rough handling of *objets d'art*.

" 'In one of the bedrooms,' Curry continued, 'way high up in the castle, there were four pictures on the wall— family portraits, I'd guess. They were in pretty bad shape but although I didn't recognize the artist's name I could see he must have been a very fine painter.

" 'I stood there for a while looking, then dusted them off so I could see them better. I don't know what impulse seized me, but I took them down from the wall and wrapped them up carefully. I carried them with me all through the rest of the war wherever I was sent.' "

Lee said he asked Curry what he'd done finally with the four portraits and Curry paused a minute or two before answering.

" 'They're in the trunk of my car, Herb,' he said. 'I'd like you to see them.'

"So we walked out to John's car; he opened the trunk and unwrapped them from a roll of canvas and spread them out for me. They were in very bad shape but even so I could see they were the work of some master though I didn't recognize his name either. I asked John what he wanted me to do about them.

" 'I'd like you to find out, if you can, who I stole them

172

from and return them before it's too late. I don't want them on my conscience.'

"I had a feeling then that John had a premonition of his death and wanted this matter squared away before anything happened to him. He told me I was the only person who knew about the theft and that included his wife. And it wasn't very long before he did die."

Lee said that as soon as he could spare the time he restored the pictures.

"I spent a good many hours on them but I think it was worth it. They turned out beautifully. I wrote a letter to some government agency in Washington, told them the whole story as John had told it to me and asked them to investigate. Soon after I got a reply saying someone would check into it. I waited a couple months; didn't hear anything further, so I wrote again.

"It's three years or more now and I still haven't heard. I have the pictures; they're in excellent condition and for John's sake I'd like to close out the affair and send them back to their rightful owners. I think I owe that much to John. Could be we owe him even more."

More than forty years have passed since that night Blymire led his two companions into Rehmeyer's Hollow to get the book and the lock. By now most citizens of York County have long since forgotten the famous hex murder and the subsequent trials in Courtroom Number Two.

A recapitulation of the Blymire affair furnishes some interesting statistics. Of the eight major participants in the crime—the trio of killers, the three attorneys for the defense, the prosecutor and the judge—all but two are still alive and functioning far beyond normal actuarial expectations.

If York, which once tried to conceal the hex murder from a prying world, would not resent a suggestion offered in all good faith by one who loathes physical exercise in every conceivable form, it might yet catch on as a muscle-flexers mecca. Signs at entrances to the city advertise the fact that York is the "Barbell Capital of America."

21

NELSON D. REHMEYER WAS BY NO MEANS THE last Pennsylvania witch murdered by the victim of his sorcery. There have been numerous other fatalities, as well as some where witchcraft was suspected but never proved. However, with few exceptions, all of these had overtones not heard in Rehmeyer's Hollow. It may be that the murder site was different—a city apartment or a home in the suburbs and not a lonely farmhouse. The participants may have been of cultures other than Pennsylvania Dutch, or perhaps the killer was neither caught nor suspected of his crime.

There was one murder, however, that bears a striking resemblance to the 1928 York County slaying. This, the shotgun death of Suzy Mummey, the "Witch of Ringtown Valley," contains many of the elements found in the savage death of Nelson Rehmeyer.

Ringtown Valley, settled in the mid-eighteenth century by the Pennsylvania Dutch, is a lovely oasis of rich farmland between the hard-coal towns of Shenandoah and Mahanoy City, where abandoned collieries, filthy culm banks and deep surface mining gashes blight the countryside.

Mrs. Mummey, a sixty-four-year-old widow whose husband, Henry, had died a violent death in a powder-mill explosion several years before, was known throughout the region as a powwow lady. Her clientele came from as far as Pottsville, the county seat, twenty miles away. As a matter of fact, Mrs. Mummey was trying for a gentleman's warts when two slugs from a twelve-gauge shotgun, fired from a distance of ten feet, put an end to the treatment and to the practitioner as well.

The murderer was a former neighbor, client and employee (as a part-time potato picker), twenty-four-year-old Albert Yashinsky, who had been hexed for nine years by some hitherto unknown witch. It was only after a long and weary search, including consultations with a dozen or more expensive necromancers, that the name of Albert's witch was finally revealed to him.

"Suddenly," Yashinsky said, "a voice cried out from the sky, 'Susan Mummey is in cahoots with the devil. Kill her!' And I did. I'm happy now. The spell is gone."

Yashinsky never was tried for his crime. Instead, a lunacy commission appointed by the Court adjudged him insane. He was committed to the Farview State Hospital at Waymart up in the Pocono Mountains where he has been ever since. Now fifty-eight, Yashinsky has been a model prisoner these past thirty-four years, always hoping some day to be released.

Until recently Albert's chance of getting out of Farview appeared slight. A few months ago, however, a Shenandoah attorney, William J. Krencewicz, became interested in the case and with help from Thomas Barratt, editor of the Shenandoah *Evening Herald*, is making an effort to have the prisoner reexamined by psychiatrists who he hopes will declare his client sane.

"I know if this happens," Albert told me a few weeks ago, "I'll have to stand trial for killing Mrs. Mummey, an act I deeply regret. But I'm willing to take that gamble. I was a stupid, foolish, superstitious young man when I did it. God knows I've been sorry ever since. But I do think I've been punished enough."

From time to time Pennsylvania legislators have attempted to declare hexerei and other branches of that discipline illegal. But except for a broad law that makes it a crime to practice medicine without a license, there is little except common sense to prevent witches from continuing to thrive in the hex belt of the Keystone State.

Hexerei still plays an important role in the lives of thousands of men, women and children who live in York, Lancaster, Berks, Dauphin, Lebanon and Schuylkill Counties and in others where the Pennsylvania Dutch have roots. One needn't be a detective to locate powwowers. None of them are inclined to conceal their talents or seem the least bit reluctant to discuss their *modus operandi*.

Without exception these ladies and gentlemen I interviewed, who ranged from fifteen to ninety-three years of age, had full confidence in their own power to heal, sure that if the patient himself had equal faith, regardless of the severity of his disease, the cure was literally at hand.

The majority of these witches—a name they, themselves, use only in describing a rival—made no offers to put the hex sign on anyone I did not like. It may well be that my acquaintance with these powwowers was too tenuous for an offer of such broad dimensions. However, I did receive assurances that if I ever happened to come under an evil spell cast by some known or unknown enemy I could have it removed forthwith.

Probably the best-known practicing powwower in eastern Pennsylvania is Mr. Clair M. Frank, a Lancaster County gunsmith. What is most impressive about Mr. Frank is his complete self-assurance.

"My gift comes from Jesus," Mr. Frank says, "and I use it only for good and to praise His name."

Mr. Frank lives in a pleasant, well-kept, two-story white frame house at the edge of Willow Street, a village on Route 272, six miles south of Lancaster, site of Franklin and Marshall College. The gunsmith was "recommended" to me by a school employee who has used Mr. Frank's services for years with unqualified success.

A large sign advertising ammunition and various types of hunting weapons for sale or repair stretches across a shop contiguous to the house. There is nothing either on the freshly painted picket fence surrounding his garden or upon the front door of his home to indicate the gunsmith's true calling.

This lack of a professional shingle might appear to make the task of an inquiring historian difficult. With Mr. Frank, nothing could be farther from the truth. Proud of his work, convinced of its value in a witch-ridden social order, this gentleman is delighted to list his many cures, interpret his philosophy and explain as much methodology as a nonpractitioner is likely to comprehend.

At first, however, Mr. Frank's ingenuousness was an unknown quantity. So I hesitated while I awaited a chance to insert hexerei into a conversation I had with this large, powerfully built gunsmith who was talking about hunting, fishing and the Red Sox's chances to win the World Series.

"Do you expect to go to the Series?" I asked.

"It all depends," he countered.

"On what, Mr. Frank?"

"On my five Indian guides."

"Your five Indian guides, Mr. Frank?" My voice rose in a question and I looked around. There was nobody in that parlor but Mr. Frank and me.

My hosts broad, sunburned face broke into a cheerful smile but his answer set my hackles in motion.

"You won't see them around here or anyplace. They're invisible."

And with this, we were off.

"Ever since I was born," Mr. Frank said, "I've had the power to heal and the power to fight the devil. And make no mistake about the devil's presence; he's everywhere. He puts his strength into witches; they're all around us."

I nodded nervously.

"Do you realize that in this tiny bit of Pennsylvania, right near Willow Street, there are eighteen witches doing the devil's dirty work?" my host asked. I assumed this was to be a purely rhetorical question, so I did not answer.

Admittedly I had not given much previous thought to the presence of that many witches. I shuddered slightly, glanced about the parlor and then out through the windows. My eyes returned to the comforting presence of my

177

host, all two hundred pounds of him. Mr. Frank took note of my apprehensions.

"Don't worry," he reassured me. "Between 'Big Chief' and the rest of the boys, we can lick 'em all."

I nodded again and Mr. Frank went on.

"For a good many years I powwowed for just my own family—wife, son, aunts, uncles and cousins. I tried for them all when they was sick or their cows wasn't givin' no milk or the hens wasn't layin', or I got rid of their warts or I'd take a hex off'n them that some enemy put on. Now I oney had a ninth-grade education but I didn't need no more. For what I was doin' you don't need much schoolin'.

"Well, after a while other people heard how good I was and wanted me to try for 'em. But I never wanted to do it until thirteen years ago when I was thirty-eight years old. Then I decided I'd help out everybody who needed me. I knew, though, I needed more power than I already had."

For Mr. Frank there was only one person in the entire world who could add to his source of hidden strength.

"She was a very old lady by the name of 'Amy.' Lived all by herself in a shack back of Garrett Mountain, up near Carlisle. Well, sir, I packed my bag, said good-bye to my family and off I went. I didn't ask beforehand if Amy'd help me out. I know'd in my heart she would.

"I stayed in that shack repentin' my sins day after day, hardly eatin' or drinkin' anythin' at all. This wasn't like attendin' a revival. This time I *really* searched my soul. Then, on the twenty-first day a miracle happened and I know'd I hadn't wasted those three weeks spent in prayer with that old lady.

"Suddenly I had a vision. I was in Heaven at a table where the settin's were all in gold and everythin' was very beautiful. St. Peter was sittin' at the head of the table. He spoke to me and invited me to set down with him and all the others."

My host's voice fell to a whisper; his bright blue eyes stared into space and tears streamed down his cheeks. He was completely oblivious to my presence.

"I did what St. Peter asked me and I set down with

'em all for a little while. Then he motioned me to get up and I did. I turned around and there, in front of me, was a long, long flight of golden steps. I know'd I was supposed to walk up 'em and so I did.

"At the top of the stairs was five Indians waitin' for me. They have been constant companions and guides through my life ever since.

"Once in a while, though, I'll send them off by themselves to help out some poor soul who's got a hex on him or is sick or somethin'. And once in a while, they'll go off on a mission of their own without tellin' me where they're goin'. But they always come back soon, every one of 'em.

"There they are now! There's Blue Cloud on his horse; there's Big Chief, there's one I call Guardian Angel. . . ."

I glanced around the parlor half expecting, half hoping, to see my host's quintet of Indians. But for me, at any rate, not a single redskin was within sight. I looked at my host. He was breathing heavily and his face had turned white. He was silent for a few moments, then gradually his respiration became normal and his eyes lost their faraway look. He smiled at me weakly and lit a cigarette.

"I smoke too damned much," he said. "I sure wish I could kick the habit."

A number of suggestions came to mind but I suppressed them and instead reminded Mr. Frank that he had named only three guides.

"Oh," he confided a bit apologetically, "that's all the names I know. The fourth one is just a little child—boy or girl, I've never been sure which. And the last one's really not an Indian, he's Hindu."

"I imagine," I told my host, "that with all this help from somewhere outside you're able to cure practically anything and solve every possible problem resulting from a spell."

He regarded me thoughtfully.

"Well, I guess you're pretty near right. But there are times when even these ain't quite enough."

"What happens then, Mr. Frank?"

"Well, then I have a consultation with my son, Clair. He's got fifteen Indian guides. It's really somethin' to see! Between us and the twenty Indians [nineteen by actual count plus one Hindu], don't you think we could beat anythin' the devil puts out?"

My answer to this was a limp "Oh."

"Would it be possible, Mr. Frank, for anyone to learn powwowing if he worked at it hard?" I managed to ask.

My host shook his head sadly. "I'm sorry. You have to be *born* with the power and even then you first have to win your own private war with the devil just like I did. My son's got the power but he don't use it. Don't want to have nothin' to do with powwowin' except times when I ask for his help.

"Lucky I don't have to ask for it too often. I'm the seventh son of a seventh son and that really gives me extra strength. And believe me, there are lots of times when I need all my strength. The witches 'round here are very powerful."

Mr. Frank paused to light a cigarette, and shook his head at this display of human weakness. "Ought to try hypnosis. Maybe that'd cure me of the habit. Thought about it often." He took several deep puffs, then continued.

"The two strongest witches in this part of the county, ones I had to fight with most, are both dead now. Passed on within the last five years. They were really strong; gave me lots of trouble. One was named 'Billy Be Damned,' and the other was called 'Nigger Wilson.' He was a colored gentleman. Things is a whole lot easier for me and my people with 'em gone.

"But I shouldn't let myself get too confident. Plenty others comin' from where 'Billy Be Damned' and 'Nigger Wilson' come from. And the new crop is gettin' more and more intelligent all the time. 'Round here I'm the only one who'll touch witchcraft. The rest are all afraid."

He smiled modestly.

"I do have another advantage over 'em, though. I got the power to tell right off if anybody's practicin' witchcraft against a person. And I can describe 'em perfectly. So I know right off who's the witch; then I can get at him.

"Tell you about a case happened only recently. There

was a farmer lived here in the county and three times in oney one year he had to sell his cattle to a 'Shinny Hoss'—that's what we call a man who buys dead cattle.

"Well, this here farmer had to keep restockin' his cattle. Finally, he realized, they'd been hexed and he come to me. It didn't take me no time to find who the witch was. It was a lady who wanted to buy his farm. She put a spell on his cows. I know'd right away it was her but I had to prove it. I'll tell you how I done that.

"Late the next night I went out by myself to the man's farm. Warned him and his family to stay in the house and not turn on any lights. Then I walked over to the barn and started to circle it. First two times I got 'round the barn lights flashed on and off. The third time it stayed dark but just as I got in back of the barn somebody brushed by me. My hair stood up. It was the lady, all right. Soon as I proved it I took off the hex."

I was about to ask my host how this was accomplished but he anticipated the question.

"Sorry," he said. "I'm really sorry," and he sounded genuinely regretful. "Wouldn't do you no good anyways to tell you. Has to be a secret."

He sought to assuage any injured feelings I might have developed because of this refusal.

"It's all too scary even for me. Sometimes I get frightened of the things I know—things that go on in my head."

To demonstrate the fearful consequences of his knowledge and power, Mr. Frank offered another recent success story.

"Short time back a farmer over in York County's hogs was ailin'. Fellow called in a couple vets but they didn't do him no good so he know'd the animals was hexed. Called on me and asked me to help him out.

"So I went down to his place at 5 A.M. on a cold winter mornin'. That's when I felt inside me was the right time. Well, when I got to the sty I looked at the hogs and started to rub 'em down. Just as I was doin' that I had a vision. I could see it was the farmer's sister-in-law's mother who put the hex on.

"Soon as I know'd who it was that did it I took off the spell. But the old lady dropped dead that mornin'."

I asked Mr. Frank how the hogs fared.

"Oh, they got better right away," he answered.

It would be a serious error to conclude that Mr. Frank's powers and those of his five guides are restricted to the removal of hexes or the destruction of witches. Actually, most of this powwower's practice consists of treating men, women and children who come to Willow Street from as far off as Youngstown, Ohio, suffering with all types of physical ailments. These illnesses, real or imaginary, range from "liver grow'd" to the wasting away. Almost everyone who has sufficient faith in Mr. Frank returns home cured after only a few treatments. In some instances a single visit will do it.

Any payment for Mr. Frank's services, as with many other members of his profession, is on a voluntary basis. After a treatment, most grateful clients insist on slipping a bill or some silver into the powwower's palm or placing it on his living room table beside a large family Bible. But Mr. Frank has never refused to help those who cannot or will not give a "freewill offering."

This Willow Street powwower is as busy as most city or county general practitioners.

"I got so many people comin' in to see me I 'empty' my waiting room three, four times a night. They come from hundreds of miles around. Lots of people from 'round here, too, most of 'em, I guess. Sheriff of the county, him and his wife are good patients of mine.

"Tell you somethin' else, though. Even if they won't admit it, there's many a doctor in this area gets stuck and can't cure a patient. So what does he do? He says after he gives up, 'Go 'round and see Franky—he'll take care of you.' Happens all the time. Not long ago there was a patient of a medical doctor, young fellow, the patient, I mean, who had that disease where all the blood cells turn white—leukemia, they call it. I cured him all right. Livin' in good health this very minute."

While Mr. Frank does not have an accident ward, he is called upon frequently to render emergency service, particularly for neighborhood farmers and laborers who have been badly burned.

"Many a man I've 'blowed fire' from," Frank says. "Happens all the time. Not long ago fellow was rushed in here for third-degree burns of the arm. I 'blowed' his fire and by night he was cured."

Confirmation of Mr. Frank's antiphlogistic victories is readily available from patients for whom he's "blowed fire." The only curative equipment visible in the Willow Street waiting room *cum* office consists of Mr. Frank's large hands, seven Himmels-briefs and a family Bible opened at Colossians with a circle penciled around Chapter 2:19: "And not holding the Head, from which all the body by joints and bands having ministered, and knit together, increaseth with the increase of God."

Unlike some colleagues who try for with crudely whittled crosses or other devices, Mr. Frank does not believe in the use of artifacts. He's familiar with Homan's *The Long Lost Friend* but shrugs off its much-heralded value.

"Who needs it? What cures," he avers, "is the layin' on of hands and faith. You *must* have faith."

Mr. Frank sighed deeply. "It's very exhaustin'. I get tireder after an evenin' tryin' for than I do after ten hours of hard physical labor."

During the day, when he's not fishing or hunting, sports in which he excels, Mr. Frank is at work in his gunshop. Office hours for the practice of necromancy are from 6 P.M. "right after supper, until I'm done. That's past midnight."

But often, patients suffering with sudden, serious indispositions requiring fast diagnosis and treatment resort to the telephone for help. Twice, during our conversation, Mr. Frank was interrupted by the ringing of his phone, which he answered promptly.

The first conversation was entirely in Pennsylvania Dutch, and since I do not understand that tongue and did not ask my host to translate for me, I am unable to report on what was said. The second time, however, both parties, or Mr. Frank at any rate, spoke in English.

I gathered that the caller's small child was suffering

183

from some troublesome disease and wanted immediate help. Mr. Frank confirmed this.

"Two-year-old boy," he said. "Got a bad case of diarrhea; temperature's up to 102. Told his mother I'd take care of it right away."

"And did you?" I asked.

Franky smiled knowingly. "Sure did. That kid'll be completely better by 3 A.M., no sooner and no later."

Despite my confidence in Franky's prognosis, I still would have liked to verify the patient's recovery time, but under the circumstances this was impossible. However, in the light of what so many of the truly faithful report, I don't doubt that exactly at 3 A.M. the little boy's body heat became 98.6 and his intestines began functioning normally once again.

What distresses Mr. Frank most is the fact that as yet he has been unable to try for cancer successfully.

"Workin' on it, though," he said reflectively. "Last year heard about a feller down in Florida knew how to cure it so I went down there to see him. Wasn't a real powwower; used a salve. Before he died he gave me a sample.

"But I'm pretty careful so I gave it to a druggist friend of mine to analyze. Came back with a report that the stuff contains three deadly poisons. I locked it up fast in my safe to make sure nobody gets holt of it before I can make it safe. Don't know how many years that'll take or if I'll live long enough. But I'm sure gonna try."

Erysipelas, "St. Anthony's fire," a frequently disfiguring and often painful ailment whose cure continues to baffle medical science, recently came under Mr. Frank's close scrutiny.

"Can't get rid of it altogether," he admits, "but I can reduce it to tiny pinpoints that hardly itch at all and they're almost invisible. Do it all the time."

If Mr. Frank has one official complaint he'd like to register, it would be against the Pennsylvania State Police.

"Never the medical men 'round here—one of my best friends' a doctor. It's the troopers; they watch me like a hawk all the time."

For a few moments the powwower's usually good-natured face clouded with suppressed anger. A second or two later he smiled broadly.

"Tell you some dealin's I had with the state cops; it's a joke and it was on me. Couple, three years ago, tobacco farmer out in the country come to see me and said somebody stole his tobacco lathe and cart.

"I listened to him and had a vision right away. I tole him exactly where the stolen goods was, in a barn at New Holland, and he could recover them right away.

"Well, this damn fool went to the State Police and tole 'em what I said. My vision was so perfect, even to what spot in the New Holland barn they'd be, that the cops accused me of being one of the thieves that took the lathe and the cart. They wouldn't *believe* it was a vision and give me a lot of trouble."

Franky shook his head indignantly at this recollection.

"But I have a damned good reputation everywhere. Everybody knows I'm an honest man; wouldn't touch nothin' belongin' to nobody. Then they finally was convinced and apologized for botherin' me.

"But that guy who asked me to get his stuff back that was stolen, I tole him to go to hell and the next time somebody takes anythin' from him go right to the State Police and don't bother me."

The telephone rang once more but this time it was someone inquiring about gun repairs. However, I'd had as much necromancy as I could digest in a single afternoon, so as soon as my host hung up the receiver, I said good-bye.

"Come back again whenever you're in the neighborhood," Mr. Frank sang out in the friendliest of fashions, "and we'll talk some more."

On my way to Spring Grove in lower York County where I'd heard there was a very powerful necromancer, I wondered why the story of Mr. Frank and his sets of fifteen and five Indians had such a familiar ring. Then it occurred to me there was a remote chance (later disproved) that the Willow Street powwower and I had shared the same fourth-grade physiology teacher, Miss Marguarete Entwistle. This elderly Pennsylvania Dutch

185

instructor gave us a romantic version of white corpuscular functions.

"These," she told her class of nine-year-olds, "are armored knights bearing crosses, lances tilted, riding white horses, traveling along the many paths in your bodies, their mission to destroy diseases planted there by enemies."

I saw Mr. Frank once more some eight or nine days after my first session with him. He was as gracious and friendly as before, but this time he was angry at something. When we were seated again in his waiting room, with the same open Bible to my left and the large oil painting of Christ hanging on the wall directly ahead, Franky told me what was irking him.

"It's these goddamned fakers," he said, the Dutch accent a bit heavier than usual as his blood stirred in wrath. "They're 'round here now, tryin' to take the people's money, pretendin' to powwow and cure for them, to get rid of spells, but not doin' a damned thing. I just told a quack off, fortune teller or such.

"Heard about one of them, a lady up in Lancaster, so I went to see her. She didn't know who I was and the power I have in me and at first I didn't tell her. I asked how much would she charge for a readin'.

" 'Three bucks,' she says, and I figure it might be worth it. Some of these fortune tellers are pretty good, they have visions and all, particularly real Gypsies.

" 'Go ahead,' I says. 'Give me a readin' ' "

Franky said he took three singles from his wallet and handed them to the lady.

"She started out all right and was goin' along pretty good, tellin' me things that was true, and if she hadn't got greedy and tried to con me, I wouldn't have nothin' to complain about. But right in the middle, just when it was gettin' interestin', she stops.

" 'That's all for your three bucks,' she tells me. 'If you want more you'll have to fork over for the five-dollar treatment.'

"That's when I got mad; I know'd what she was up to and what was comin' next. She'd ask me did I want the ten-dollar readin' and after that she'd ask if I wanted her to light candles. The job could run as high as two hundred bucks, which is what she'd been takin' from a couple of farmers out my way."

Franky lit another cigarette before continuing.

" 'Listen, you,' I says. 'Don't give me none of your crap. And don't try it on nobody else. If I hear about it I've a good mind to tell the state cops on you.'

"That *really* shook her up. But it's the oney way you can handle these kind of people. Scare the hell out of 'em."

My second visit to Mr. Frank terminated sooner than the first, not because my host wasn't willing to talk but because I had an appointment with a witch elsewhere in the county.

As I was about to leave, Franky, who by then had regained his normally equable disposition, stopped me.

"Remember what I tole you about cancer the last time you was here and how I was workin' on it?"

"Of course," I answered.

"Well," he went on, "I think maybe I'm gettin' someplace. Pretty soon I believe I might be able to cure it, in the early stages at least. That's without usin' the salve I tole you about."

Nothing Mr. Frank could say or do would surprise me so I said, "Let me know, will you, when you get it perfected?"

"I sure will," he promised.

22

ROGER ANGLE, WHO USED TO WORK FOR THE *Witchita* (Kansas) *Beacon* and is currently on the staff of the *York Gazette and Daily*, takes an extremely dim view of powwowers in general and "Professor" Howard C. Resh, a Hanover "faith healer," in particular.

The Professor is an eighty-two-year-old hexer whose

office is 434 Carlisle Street, Hanover's main business thoroughfare. The city, famous for making shoes and breeding harness race horses, has a population of almost 20,000, of which a large percentage is of Pennsylvania Dutch extraction.

"I'd never heard of powwowing and all that junk until we moved East last summer," Angle said. "Couple nights after we were installed in our new house I'd just mixed myself a tall one when Fontelle, my wife, sang out, 'Hold it, Roger! Before you do anything, I've got a job for you.'

"She was four months pregnant at the time and I'd been humoring her.

" 'Can't it wait 'till I finish this?'

" 'Nope,' she says. 'You'll have to do it right away, Roger, unless you want the baby to have six fingers.'

" 'On each hand?' I asked, 'Or is that the total?' I thought she'd flipped. 'What do you want me to do?'

" 'You know that closet in the cellar where we store all our winter clothes?'

"I nodded.

" 'Well,' she goes on, 'I want you to go down there right away and take out every camphor ball in the coats and suits, put them in a pile and rush them out of the house as fast as you can.'

"I stared at her. Now I was sure she *really* had flipped. But then she burst out laughing."

As Angle explained, a Pennsylvania Dutch neighbor had dropped in to pay a social call on his wife that morning, learned she was pregnant and elaborated upon the dangers of having camphor in a house where the mistress was "expecting."

"Naturally I never removed the camphor," Angle said, "and thank God, when the baby was born, it had the proper number of digits. But it occurred to me when I put on my topcoat last October, it didn't reek of mothballs the way it usually does. I never said anything to Fontelle, but sometimes I look at her and wonder. . . ."

Angle's second exposure to the mysteries of hexerei came soon after the first.

"I've a habit of rubbing some warts on my right hand

188

against my jaw," the reporter said. "Walter Partymiller, our cartoonist, saw me doing it one day and he says, 'Had 'em long, Roger?'

"I looked at Walter. I've always felt my three warts were rather personal, not conversation pieces. I answered, maybe a bit brusquely, 'Yeh. Quite a while.'

" 'Would you like to get rid of them?' he asked. I'd already tried just about everything and given up a long time ago, when I was still a kid.

" 'No, Walter,' I answered. 'Thank you kindly but I've grown rather fond of them. But what did you have in mind, anyway?'

"Walter grinned. 'Ever hear of powwowing?'

" 'It so happens, Walter,' I said, 'one of your compatriots [Walter's a Pennsylvania Dutchman] called on my wife the other morning and stuffed her ears full of that nonsense.'

" 'Well,' answers Walter, 'maybe it is nonsense and maybe it isn't. Anyway, what have you got to lose?'

" 'All right,' I answered, thinking there might be a feature in it for me. 'Who's your favorite witch?'

" 'Fellow named Resh, down in Hanover.' Walter grinned again. 'Never used him myself but I've heard plenty of people say he's the greatest. . . .' "

Late the following evening Angle paid a call on the Professor.

"I hit him at a good time, I guess. The office must have been filled but when I got there the last patients were leaving, a couple women and a little boy around seven years old.

"I rang the bell and an elderly man wearing an old cotton work shirt and dark cotton work pants held up with a pair of 'firemen's' suspenders came to the door.

" 'Are you the Professor?' I asked, and he nodded and told me to come in. I got right to the point and asked if he could get rid of my warts for me.

" 'How many?' he asks, and I told him three, then held up my thumbs—one wart on each and one on the index finger of my right hand.

" 'Hold your thumbs together,' he told me and I did. He stuck one of his index fingers in his mouth, wet it and drew a circle around one of the warts with the saliva. His wet finger then passed from my right thumb to my left, crossing above the wart on my left thumb.

"Then he took that finger away from my left thumb and put his middle finger of the same hand into his mouth, wet it and made a circle with it around the wart on my left hand, starting where he had left off with the other finger."

At this point. Angle paused for a moment to examine his finger.

"That spit all over my hand! It was not what I considered a hygienic experiment. The whole time the Professor was making circles with saliva he was muttering incantations in such a low voice that I couldn't understand a thing he said.

"He wound up making the sign of the cross three times.

" 'All right,' the Professor says, 'in three or four weeks the warts on your thumbs will be gone.'

"I lifted up my index finger. 'What about this one?'

" 'Just let that one go. You know what I mean,' he answers. 'If you want to come back in three or four weeks I'll look at it then, if it's still there.'

"Then he asked me where I was from and I told him York.

" 'You come all the way down here just for this?' and I said, 'Yes.'

"I asked him how much he wanted and he said, 'I get a two-dollar donation for "healing" but since all you got was a couple warts, I won't ask you to pay nothin'.' I didn't insist."

Six weeks later Angle's warts still embellished his thumbs and right index finger.

"I went back to the Professor to register a complaint. This time I think he suspected something and wouldn't let me enter the house; told me to stay at the door. He went inside, came back a couple minutes later and handed me a little bottle, about the size of the kind they put iodine in. It smelled like cough medicine.

" 'Put this stuff on every day and if it's warts you got, it'll make 'em go away.'

"Then he took a look at my hands.

" 'Maybe it ain't warts you got; maybe it's sumpin' else.'

"They sure looked like warts to me but I didn't want to argue with the Professor. 'How much is it?' I asked, and he says, 'Twenty-five cents is all. Costs me more'n that. Can't buy the stuff anywhere 'round here. Very powerful.'

"That was six months ago and I followed the Professor's instructions faithfully until I used up all the junk I bought from him. I still got the warts. But sometimes Fontelle will look at them and tell me she thinks the one on my index finger is drying up. Well, all it cost me was two bits and I'll get a feature story out of it yet."

Despite occasional failures such as the removal of Roger Angle's warts (and the reporter, admittedly, is a man of little faith), and despite perennial opposition from area M.D.'s, Resh continues to try for believers who come to his office six days a week, fifty-two weeks a year. If the Professor is to be believed, many of his patients are leaders in their own communities whether they hail from nearby Baltimore, Maryland, far-off Scranton, Pennsylvania, or Hanover itself.

"They all come to see me when their family doctors give up," claims Resh with no false modesty. "Pretty near none of 'em that ain't been in to see the Professor some time or other."

While a qualitative verification of Mr. Resh's clientele might prove difficult, a quantitative analysis is simple. You merely stand outside the Professor's home during his office hours (2–4 and 6–8 P.M. every weekday and Sunday; there are no Saturday hours) and count heads.

A dozen cracked stone steps wind up from the pavement to a crumbling front porch, faded and gray and adorned with imitation latticework that leads into the house, a hideous relic of mid-Victorian turreted ugliness.

The Professor, himself, is a fat, wheezy little man whose looks do not belie his age. His large waiting room is cluttered, chairs and tables are covered with dust and the uncarpeted floor is littered with old newspapers that remain wherever they happen to fall. Brightly colored lithographs of Christ and a half-dozen framed Himmels-briefs adorn the walls and several family-sized Bibles rest on rickety tables elsewhere in the room.

With my host's permission I made space for myself by shoving a number of books and miscellaneous manuscripts from an aged couch to the floor while the Professor sank into a large swivel chair facing me. He needed no prompting to discuss his career, his pet hates and his sexual prowess.

"I was chust seventeen when I got started," Mr. Resh said, his Pennsylvania Dutch accent so thick that the words were nearly unintelligible. "I've been goin' good and gettin' better ever since. But I gained my most power in 1948. That's when I got a vision and from then on I ain't raised, et, or touched no pork.

"I can cure pretty near everythin' now and the people 'round here know it. The liver grow'd, opnema, warts, heart trouble, whatever they got I can handle. It really ain't me, it's Chesus. You got to let Chesus straighten you out. You got to give Him a chanct."

Mr. Resh's bright blue eyes left me and he stared, almost transfixed, at a picture of Christ on Calvary. After what seemed like several minutes, he shook his head sharply as though to clear away a distant vision and looked in my direction once more. "Yes, yes," he repeated, "you must give Chesus a chanct."

In passing, Mr. Resh ticked off a number of his more remarkable cures including the bloodless, reparation of defective gall bladders, malfunctioning stomachs and inefficient prostate glands. However, the Professor appears to take more pride in orthopedic successes than in his treatment of pathological or organic ailments.

"Fellow from town had a bad stroke wunst not long ago," Mr. Resh recalled. "Went to old Doc ——— who couldn't do nothin' for him oney take his money. Fellow couldn't walk and couldn't hardly talk. After a while he got disgusted with the medical doctors and come to me.

"In three days I got him better. Now you wouldn't think to look at him anything was ever the matter with this fellow. And all the doctors in town are sore at me because I could cure him and they couldn't."

One of Mr. Resh's pet hates is the medical profession, and he has no hesitation about expressing his opinion of it.

"Greedy! That's what they are and they don't know what they're doin' half the time. And they don't have no faith in Chesus. Now I got nothin' against hospitals, understand. If a man's got a broken leg or his arm's busted or somethin' like that, there's where he should be. But he oney ought to stay there until the leg or the arm's set and then get out fast.

"What they got to make sure when they go into a hospital is not to take none of them drugs. That's what the doctors want them to take and that's where the sin comes in."

The temperature in Mr. Resh's waiting room was even higher than it was outside in the streets of Hanover, where the thermometer reading had been in the mid-nineties earlier that day. As my host grew more and more excited, increasingly large streams of perspiration kept rolling down his wrinkled cheeks and into a dirty wet handkerchief he used for mopping up.

"Lady from Ephrata way come to town couple years ago," the Professor continued. "Had to get her little girl fitted for braces—kid had polio and couldn't walk around or play. Doctors from town said she couldn't never walk no more without braces.

"Well, somebody tole her to come to me. It was a tough case but I said I'd try for her and I did. Tole her afterward I got done to throw way the braces. She done what I tole her and walks perfect."

Local physicians, Resh claims, are incensed over his ability to heal when they fail and, at times, have threatened to take legal action against him.

"They sicked the County Health Officer on me when I put up my sign. He tole me to take it down but I said, 'No, I won't.' "

Resh nodded his head and seemed to smile inwardly at that recollection.

"I fixed that County Officer all right; made him let me alone," he added, but did not elaborate.

"One of them doctors," Resh continued, this time with

a touch of pride, "is jealous over me because when I go to the skating rink I can 'play around' with any woman I want to and he can't."

The Professor nudged me. "You're a man and I'm a man so you know what I mean."

The Professor's meaning did not escape me.

Then he opened a drawer in his rolltop desk and extracted a yellowed newspaper clipping which he handed to me. I glanced at a three-column cut showing the powwower gliding along a skating rink with apparent ease.

"Never had a pair of 'em on me 'til I was seventy-five," he said. "But I sure learned fast."

The Professor is a practicing Christian, although he belongs to no particular denomination.

"Used to know some Seventh Day Adwentists and I liked some of the things they done and believed in like observin' Saturday as the Sabbath, which it is. But I left the Adwentists when I found they let women preach. That's no good.

"If Chesus wanted women to learn he woulda taught them. They oney was twelve Apostles and they was all men, remember. No, what women must do is stay at home and be ready for their husbands' demands. Know what I mean?"

The old man winked.

The greatest blow the Professor suffered, he will tell you, came when he discovered his wife *flagrante delicto*.

"She was twelve years younger'n me and we was married thirty-five years but I diworced her right away."

Completely convinced of his inner powers, there is nothing of the charlatan or deliberate faker in Resh.

"Chesus learned me how to heal and that's how I do it," he repeats constantly. Nor does there appear to be avarice in Resh's make-up, professionally speaking at any rate.

"If my patients like to leave a dollar or two with me as a 'goodwill' offerin', I accept. But if they ain't got no money, I try for 'em anyways."

While two female clients of the Professor were willing

194

neither to discuss their ailments nor talk about the treatments they'd both just undergone, each seemed pleased to comment on the powwower's beneficence.

"If you don't have nothin'," the younger of the pair, a pretty red-cheeked woman in her late twenties, said, "he don't want nothin'. And he don't never ask for no money. You gotta leave it there for him by the Bible."

The older patient, whose age must have approached that of the Professor, nodded her head in approval. "Right," she added. "Right every time. He's a good man."

As we parted—it was nearly 6 P.M. and already clients were standing on the front porch I'd vacated two hours before—I experienced an example of the Professor's generosity.

"Here," he said, handing me a Himmels-brief he removed from a desk drawer, "keep it with you always and you don't never need to fear nothin'."

The "freewill" offering I attempted to leave beside the family Bible was refused with a pleasant smile.

"Didn't do nothin' for you," the Professor said. "Come back to see me sometime case you get troubles."

I replied that I would. However, if I continue to be diligent about the Professor's "Home and Protection Letter" and keep it on my person at all times, there really should be little reason for a return trip to Hanover.

The Himmels-brief declares that its bearer "shall be safe from the enemy's weapons of destruction. God will preserve him from robbers and murderers; it shall make him imprevious [sic] to all deadly weapons that may be brought to bear upon him, by command of our most gracious master, Jesus Christ.

"God is with him who carries this heavenly letter in war and in peace; he will be protected from all danger— in the distress of visitation of fire or water, it shall protect him. . . ."

Proof is offered in the text.

"Whosoever doubts the truth of this may attach a copy of this letter to the neck of a dog and then fire upon him, and he will be convinced of its truthfulness."

I must confess that so far, at least, I am singularly lacking in any desire to run a scientific test of the Himmels-brief's potency. So be it.

23

EXCEPT FOR TWO DAYS A MONTH, THE ROHR-baugh Convalescent Home in rural Spring Grove (pop. 55), York County, Pennsylvania, is about as quiet a spot as you're likely to find anywhere in the Keystone State. But on the first and sixteenth, it becomes a mecca for scores of ailing men, women and children who flock to this tiny village, there to be powwowed back to health by Mrs. Leah Frank.

Mistakenly, I assumed there was some significance in the choice of the two days on which Mrs. Frank practices her profession.

"When I reached ninety, and that was four years ago," Mrs. Frank explained, "I thought maybe I'd better quit altogether; it's so hard on a body. But my people wouldn't let me, tole me they needed me. So, instead of workin' every day, I tole 'em I'd 'try for' two days a month and I picked the first and the sixteenth. Then people will know when to come and not be disappointed in between. That's all there is to it."

Through the windows of the second-floor bedroom she seldom leaves, Mrs. Frank can view the soft hills of York County where she has lived all her years. As a matter of fact, the aged powwower spends most of her daylight hours in an old-fashioned Morris chair facing the east. "I'd rather see the sun come up than go down," she says gently.

Except for a slight diminution in hearing and arthritis, only lately beginning to cripple the long, tapered fingers she needs for "laying on" ill or otherwise troubled patients, Mrs. Frank remains in excellent health. Her cheeks, though wrinkled, have a healthy glow; her teeth are her own, and her sharp blue eyes still regard with abiding interest that small portion of the world she sees.

"Prettiest part of the world, though I wouldn't know much about the rest of it," Mrs. Frank said in a clear voice with a strong Pennsylvania Dutch inflection. "Born and raised ten miles from here and never been no further away than forty. But you don't have to travel to learn things and how to take care of 'em that needs you, do you?"

She smiled and went on.

"I've been tryin' for people for a long, long time. I always know'd I had the power but I learned how to use it from a veterinarian who practiced powwowin' too. That was back in 1904; I've been doin' it ever since.

"Course that's not all I ever done. I just used to try for people on the side like most us faith healers do. From the time I was a little girl 'till I was seventy-seven years I worked in a mill and I worked hard, too. Anymore I don't work so hard. Now I'm so old I oney powwow."

What troubles Mrs. Frank is the current shortage of apprentices willing to undergo the rigors of training in order to become worthy practitioners.

"I don't mean those that don't have the power inside 'em 'cause they'll never learn no matter how much they want to. Some of 'em try but I always say to 'em, 'If you can't stop blood, you'll never be a powwower, so don't waste your time.'

"What I'm referrin' to is those that got the power but don't want to use it. It ain't easy; you have to work hard and it makes you mighty tired to try for people."

Mrs. Frank did not elaborate upon the curriculum required before the neophyte can become a full-fledged practitioner. She did say, however, that after "blood stopping," which, incidentally, she claims can never be taught and must be known congenitally, the next training step is wart removal. After that come the many other branches of the discipline concluding with cures for the opnema, St. Anthony's fire and finally tumors.

Mrs. Frank also holds to the orthodox belief, one shared by the majority of her colleagues, that an instructor in powwowism or witchcraft may impart his knowledge only to members of the opposite sex.

"A man shouldn't teach another man or boy and a woman can't teach another woman or girl," claims this nonagenarian necromancer. "I'm helpin' train a young man who lives 'round here and he's doin' all right. But I sure wish I could teach my granddaughter. She was born with the power but she don't know how to use it. She could do wonderful good."

I asked Mrs. Frank what would happen if she attempted to teach the profession to her granddaughter. She shuddered.

"Oh, my goodness! That would be terrible. I'd suffer for it the rest of my days and maybe lose my own power if I tried."

Like the Willow Street powwower, to whom she is not related, Mrs. Frank is aware of the presence of evil area witches. However, she does not subscribe to Clair Frank's depressing theory that practitioners of the black art are getting smarter as well as increasingly numerous.

"Not many of 'em 'round as there used to be," Mrs. Frank said cheerfully. "And they're gettin' dumber and dumber all the time. But when *I* was a girl!"

She paused, shaking her head at some unpleasant recollection, then continued.

"Tell you what happened to me a long, long while ago. Didn't know what it was to me but I started to fade away and get listless like I didn't have no energy at all. It got worse and worse every day and I was gettin' weaker and weaker all the time. I couldn't do nothin' at all for myself.

"I know'd I was gonna die soon if I didn't get help. Well, I heard of some man 'round our way who knew how to handle the devil so I went to him to see what he could do. He tole me right off somebody put a hex on me which was what I figured all along. But he didn't know who done it.

"Then he said there was more than one person who cast the spell and he'd help me find 'em and fix 'em so they wouldn't trouble me. Tole me to keep lookin' in the palm of my hand until I could see their faces.

"Didn't take me very long. There were three of 'em and one after another I seen 'em clearly right there in the palm of my left hand. I know'd every one of 'em. They all lived near me.

"Well, the man advised me to talk to each of the witches and said he'd 'see' 'em first and I know'd exactly what he meant. I done what he said and a couple hours after I talked to the last one I started to feel better. Before long I was myself again. Nobody ever put a hex on me after that and I've been fine since. But I wouldn't want to got through it *ever* again."

Unlike most of her fellow practitioners, Mrs. Frank modestly refused to chronicle any of her more miraculous cures.

"I treat 'em for whatever ails 'em—liver grow'd, the opnema, wildfire and so on. I'm grateful to Chesus for givin' me the power. I'm glad to use it to ease the sufferin'."

But Mrs. Claude Rohrbaugh, operator of the nursing home, doesn't hesitate to discuss Mrs. Frank's many successes.

"She's the best powwower in the county, maybe the state," Mrs. Rohrbaugh avers. "Tell you one that happened two, three years ago. An old friend of my husband and me was very sick. He was ailing for a while and finally went down to Johns Hopkins Hospital in Baltimore to see what was giving him bad headaches and dizziness.

"The staff down there tole him, after they diagnosed his case, X rays and everything else, that he had a tumor of the brain and that they'd have to operate at once. Admitted him and said they'd do the operation in two or three days, after they prepared him.

"My friend got scared; tole 'em at the hospital he had some business to take care of up home before he was operated on and would they give him permission to go for just a day."

The patient returned to York County that same morning and immediately sought the Rohrbaughs.

"He was worried sick," Mrs. Rohrbaugh recalled. "Asked me what he ought to do. I didn't want to interfere oney I felt it was my duty to tell him about the old lady upstairs even though he'd been to what's supposed to be the best hospital in the United States.

"But he wanted to see the old lady anyway and I fixed it up. Well, she tried for him and got rid of his tumor. It's gone completely; he don't have no headaches no more and the dizziness left. Today he's a fine healthy man due to Mrs. Leah Frank's powers."

Mrs. Rohrbaugh paused for a moment or two, then went on.

"Tell you how she tried for me. I was getting bad pains in my backside; it went on for a long time but instead of going to Mrs. Frank like I shoulda, I went to see a doctor. He examined me; said I had fissures of the rectum and that I needed to get operated on right away. Made a reservation at the hospital; that was Johns Hopkins, too.

"Well, I come to my senses, canceled my reservation at Johns Hopkins and went upstairs to the old lady. She tried for me; the fissures got healed and the pain went away. I ain't never had 'em since, not once.

"I could tell you hundreds of other cases but all you have to do is come 'round here and talk to any of the people who line the steps outside on the first and sixteenth waitin' to be tried for. Baltimore, York, Harrisburg and even Philadelphia. Just talk to any one of 'em."

I followed Mrs. Rohrbaugh's suggestion and the first day of the following month I pulled up my car on the side of the road by the Home. Despite the fact that I'd arrived early, a few automobiles and one horse-drawn buggy were already parked in the driveway and a couple of patients were seated on the back stoop waiting until Mrs. Frank was ready to receive them.

I looked like the "furriner" I was and had no desire to scare off any of Mrs. Frank's patients, so I appraised the task ahead with considerable trepidation. As it turned out, my fears were not entirely justified. Although two of Mrs. Frank's clients—an elderly gentleman dressed in plain black clothing and sporting a neat, white beard, and a fat, middle-aged woman—were not as communicative as they might have been, they did, nevertheless, lend considerable support to Mrs. Rohrbaugh's claims for her favorite powwower's prowess.

The gentleman had a large wen on his left cheek.

"I had two of 'em. Mrs. Frank tried for the one on my right cheek and got rid of it last month. Now she's gonna try for this one," he said, placing an index finger on the remaining unsightly protuberance. At least this was my interpretation of the patient's testimonial, since his English was only slightly more fluent than my Pennsylvania Dutch.

With a strong assist from the middle-aged woman, who spoke some English, I gathered that the gentleman was a retired tobacco farmer and had been Mrs. Frank's patient for more than twenty years. He'd been cured of a variety of ailments including lung disease, the *de*cline and some serious functional disorder which I inferred from my interpreter's gestures was a double hernia.

The lady, who had only recently transferred her allegiance to Mrs. Frank after a disillusioning experience with a male witch (upon which she would not elaborate), was suffering from a mysterious female complaint.

"It's like the liver grow'd, oney worse," she said. "Gets me here," she added, pointing to that section of her anatomy known regionally as "the privates." "But Mrs. Frank'll try for me like she done for lots of others all the time. I know she can help."

I hesitated before asking the lady what would be considered a reasonable fee for powwowing an ailment of such a personal nature.

"Why nuthin', 'cept what I leave for a freewill offerin'," she answered, apparently annoyed that a question which might impugn Mrs. Frank's motives had been raised.

"If I had my way they'd take it out of Blue Cross. She does more for people than them doctors does and Blue Cross pays them," the lady stated angrily.

24

MRS. HELEN BECHTEL, WHO PRACTICES POW-wowing at Jim Thorpe (formerly Mauch Chunk), Pennsylvania, is one of the few members of the profession who has engaged Lucifer, himself, in hand-to-hand combat and survived to tell the tale.

"Happened couple years ago," Mrs. Bechtel recalled. "It was a terrible, terrible experience and I hope I won't never haf to go through it again."

Mrs. Bechtel, a pleasant-looking blonde in her mid-fifties, shuddered deeply; shook her head; wiped her brow with the back of her right hand and went on.

"Tell you how it was. Feller named Walter Miller who runs a hardware store in Mauch Chunk [Mrs. B., like many other natives of this mining community, frequently forgets the new name of the town] had a hex put on him years before. Couldn't eat, couldn't sleep and was wastin' away, like the opnema.

"D'yex know what I mean?" she asked, turning her bright blue eyes in the direction of Mrs. Helen Dougherty, widow of a local physician, and Mrs. Gertrude Apfelbaum, publisher of the daily Jim Thorpe *Times-Herald*, who sat with me in our hostess' neat, clean parlor. All three of us nodded in agreement, Mrs. Dougherty and Mrs. Apfelbaum adding that, of course, they knew Walter Miller well. Mrs. Bechtel continued.

"Yez know how sick Walter was. He went to one powwower after another and paid out his good money and din get no relief. Most of 'em, and I hate to say it, is quacks and don't do nuthin' for nobody. But that's besides the point. Finally, Walter come to me and tole me his troubles.

"I know'd he was hexed and so did he but what he din know was who put the hex on him. Well, I listened to his story; it was pretty late by the time he got done, but by then I was sure it was somebody in his own house.

"Well, that night I had a dream. In it I seen someone with three fingers off'n her hand and right away I know'd that had to be the witch that put the spell on Walter.

"Next night I went over to Walter's house and tole him. I could feel somethin' pullin' at me the minute I walked in. I wasn't afraid; I had my holy water along.

"I took Walter with me and together we went through every room in that big ole house. Walter lives alone since his mother died. [The asides were for my benefit; both Mrs. Dougherty and Mrs. Apfelbaum were familiar with the hardware dealer's biography and current way of life.]

"Finally we climb up the attic steps and all the while that feelin' I had is gettin' stronger and stronger."

Even now, some two or three years after the episode, Mrs. Bechtel's blue eyes lit up as she recalled the frightening experience she had undergone.

"I led the way up that dark flight of steps, Walter right behind me. I pushed open the attic door. It was pitch black and I don't mind tellin' you the feelin's I was gettin' then was strong. Walter was really scared.

"I pushed him back of me and I tole him, 'Walter,' I says, 'don't be afraid. I'll protect you no matter *who* or *what's* in this room.' I pulled the stopper out of my holy water bottle and got it ready.

"Just then the feelin' I had grow'd unbearably strong. The light of the moon shined through a window covered with cobwebs but you could see somethin' anyway; the rays shined down on the center of the attic and rested on a floorboard. Somethin' was pullin' and pullin' at me, makin' me move there.

"It was terrible powerful on one spot and I whispered to Walter, 'Lift up that floorboard. Whatever it is or whoever it is put the hex on you is under there.' "

At this point I must say Mrs. Bechtel and her three guests were all gasping with excitement.

"I stood aside," our hostess went on, "and he tugged and tugged at the board and finally raised it up. Underneath it right in the middle was an old doll.

" 'My God! Helen,' he says, 'it's a doll I used to play with when I was a little boy. I ain't seen it for fifty years. How'd it get here?'

"Walter was afraid to pick it up but I wasn't. I held it up to the moonlight so's I could get a good look at the thing. Even though it was hid for fifty years or longer it was in good condition, a little dusty maybe but otherwise perfect. Then I looked at the thing's left hand. So help me there was three fingers missin'!

"Right at that moment there was a weird howl that sent the blood curdlin' through my veins. I could feel somethin' tryin' to get at Walter. He was shakin' all over. I stepped in front of him to protect him. I could see what I thought was a beast ready to leap. But it wasn't no beast; it was the Devil hisself."

Mrs. Bechtel, who appeared to be almost in a trance, paused to catch her breath before concluding the story of her encounter with Satan.

"The Devil grabbed holt of me and pinched my behind so hard I screamed with pain—squeezed me so tight the marks was there for days. Kept tryin' to shove me aside and reach Walter but I wouldn't let him; I kept pushin' him back.

"Then I got my right arm free and sprinkled holy water all over the Devil. At the same time I called out, 'Stop in the name of the Father, the Son and the Holy Ghost!' and the Devil rushed out of the room through the window as fast as he could. His power over Walter was destroyed and he was free of the hex."

In gratitude Mr. Miller offered his tutelary benefactor a large sum of money which she refused. As a matter of fact, this powwower never accepts anything, including so-called "freewill" offerings, from clients.

How does Mrs. Bechtel, a devout Roman Catholic, justify the practice of necromancy?

"I talked to our priest about my powers and how I made use of them," Mrs. Bechtel said. "And his answer was, 'If a man has faith it must help.' He didn't tell me to stop."

Mrs. Bechtel offered to give us a demonstration and Mrs. Dougherty, a retired registered nurse, accepted with alacrity.

"My ankles are awfully swollen, Helen," she said. "They've been that way for years. Jim [Mrs. Dougherty's late spouse] couldn't do a thing. Do you want to try for them?"

Our hostess nodded. "Take off your shoes," she said, and Mrs. Dougherty removed a heavy pair of specially built oxfords. Mrs. Bechtel carefully examined the patient's ankles; then she walked into the kitchen and returned a few minutes later with a bottle.

"Holy water," she explained, and proceeded to spray Mrs. Dougherty's feet and ankles with generous splashes. We sat in complete silence as the powwower touched both of Mrs. Dougherty's bare ankles lightly with her fingertips. Gradually she moved her hands upward all over the patient's legs and body, stopping at the top of the head, where her fingers rested for several moments.

Mrs. Bechtel bent down on her knees in front of Mrs. Dougherty and whispered softly for at least ten minutes. Next she made the sign of the cross, arose, sprinkled the patient with holy water again and magnanimously tossed some my way, before she put the stopper back.

"You'll be all better soon, Mrs. D.," she said. "And you can throw away those health shoes you're wearin'."

On our way to Slatington for a visit with another member of the profession, who had offered to try for several warts on Mrs. Dougherty's right hand, we talked about Mrs. Bechtel's treatment.

"I had a very strange feeling," the retired nurse confessed. "When Helen was touching my ankles and working her fingers up to my head it was almost as though she was drawing the pain from my feet and moving it through my body and out through the top.

"Actually, my feet do feel a lot better now; best they've felt in years. One thing about Helen Bechtel. I've known her for a long time, and she's absolutely sincere. And we've all heard of her remarkable cures."

Our next port of call was the home of Milton Schoch, an aged gentleman who practiced powwowing in rural Carbon County for sixty-five or seventy years. His specialty was warts but he also cured trench mouth and "blow'd" fire.

While Mr. Schoch said his grandfather had taught him hexerei, there was a consensus—at least Mrs. Dougherty, Mrs. Apfelbaum and I were in accord—that much of this aged gentleman's necromantic knowledge came straight out of the *Sixth and Seventh Books of Moses*. However, when Mrs. Schoch asked her husband to show us this infamous volume, the powwower rather testily issued a prompt disclaimer.

"Gave the books away years ago," he said. "You ought to know that, Mother."

However, Mr. Schoch graciously offered to try for Mrs. Dougherty's warts.

"I'll need your baptismal name first," he told her and our voluntary guinea pig replied, "Helen Louise Very."

The powwower then placed the patient's hand in his own; blew three breaths on each of the four small growths; touched them lightly with his fingertips; made the sign of the cross and assured Mrs. Dougherty the warts would be gone in no time.

Several months later I checked with Mrs. Dougherty for a medical progress report.

"I think my ankles are down a little; they do feel slightly better," she said. "But I still wear the health shoes."

"How about the warts?" I asked.

"Oh, I have them yet," she answered. "But that poor Mr. Schoch, he died since."

25

YOU DON'T HAVE TO BE PENNSYLVANIA DUTCH to practice powwowing in the hex belt of the Keystone State as long as your clients are. Mrs. Anne Fauzio of Nesquehoning, Carbon County, a second-generation American of Italian extraction, is an excellent example of this necromantic tolerance.

Mrs. Fauzio differs from most of her colleagues in at least two respects—she will accept neither money nor gifts from grateful patients, and she limits her curative powers to the relief of migraine headaches, hives and shingles.

Mrs. Fauzio is a short, attractive, olive-skinned woman in her early forties. Her hair is jet black and glistening and her large, dark eyes radiate warmth. In the well-furnished parlor of her spacious stone house, Mrs. Fauzio explained her *modus operandi* to her friends, Mrs. Dougherty and Mrs. Apfelbaum, and to me.

"Tell you how I cure for the hives," she said. "First of all I need silver. A quarter used to be all right but the new ones aren't any good; you need the old kind.

"Well, then, I take the quarter with the silver in it and touch it to every hive on a person's body. At the same time I make the sign of the cross three times, say three 'Our Fathers' and three 'Hail Marys' in a 3-6-9 sequence. The patient repeats after me what I say. Sometimes the hives go right away; sometimes it needs three, four treatments, but I positively can get rid of them.

"Use the same treatment for shingles, but for migraines I don't need silver. Just say the prayers and so on, and, of course, touch the top of the person's head with my hands."

Mrs. Dougherty was happy to vouch for Mrs. Fauzio's remarkable cures.

"Everybody with hives or shingles from all 'round here come to Anne," the physician's widow testified. "And as far as I understand, she cures 'em. I know for a fact she won't take a penny. I didn't know about the headaches until today but if Anne says she can get rid of migraines. I believe her. She never lies."

Mrs. Fauzio looks like the "easy touch" she is; neighbors and friends say she never turns away an itinerant beggar from either her home or the highly successful restaurant she and her husband operate on Route 44, a few miles east of Jim Thorpe. Because of her very special psychic gifts, Mrs. Fauzio frequently gets a "hit" on the numbers which she plays from time to time, donating every cent of the winnings either to local charities or to her church, St. Mary's Roman Catholic of Summit Hill.

On our way to East Mauch Chunk where we were scheduled for a session with another non-Germanic powwower ("Positively the greatest in the state," claimed Mrs. Fauzio ecstatically), the lady told us about her biggest "hit" and the simplicity with which it was accomplished. We had been discussing Mr. Clair Frank, his five Indian guides and how he acquired them. I was anxious to hear Mrs. Fauzio's professional opinion of the meeting between the Willow Street practitioner and St. Peter and whether this kind of upperechelon confrontation was rare.

"Happened during a vision?" she asked, and I nodded. "Happened to me, too," Mrs. Fauzio said. "Never met St. Peter or got any Indians," she added regretfully, "but I did see and talk with Jesus. He gave me the right number to play and I hit for over $2,000. I'll tell you about it.

"Not long ago I needed some extra money for a couple of very poor miners' families and I didn't exactly know how I was going to get it. Well, I prayed and prayed and one night I had a vision. I went to Heaven and there was Sweet Jesus on the cross. He looked just like you see Him in His pictures."

Mrs. Fauzio's dark eyes stared ahead with a faraway look which I sincerely hoped would not interfere with her driving; the mountain road we were traveling on at a fair rate of speed was narrow and winding with only scattered guard rails between us and a deep ravine. But after a few competently maneuvered hairpin turns I was able to sit back, relax and listen. Mrs. Fauzio went on.

"I said, 'Sweet Jesus, what number shall I play?' He could hardly speak and had trouble turning His head in my direction. He could only move it a little to one side. He didn't answer and I said, 'Sweet Jesus, I'm going to give away all the money I win. *Please* tell me what I should play.'

"Then Jesus turned His head toward me and answered in a very strange voice, 'Play 6-4-3.' I thanked Him and the vision ended."

"You played the number right away, didn't you?" I asked Mrs. Fauzio.

She shook her head. "Didn't play it at all, in that sequence anyways."

I must admit I was baffled and probably looked it. I simply could not understand how *anyone* would pass up such a seemingly direct tip. Mrs. Fauzio smiled at my bewilderment.

"Tell you what happened," she went on. "It was stranger than you can imagine. The next morning I'm about to pick up the telephone to call a number writer I know in Philly and tell him to put five bucks on 6-4-3. But just at that moment the phone rings. I answer; it's the number writer himself. He hardly ever calls me.

" 'Annie,' he says, 'I called you this time because I had a vision last night.' When he told me that I almost collapsed. 'What was it?' I asked.

" 'Well, Annie,' he goes on, 'I saw Sweet Jesus. He come to me and said, "Call Annie Fauzio right away and tell her the number she's to play is not 6-4-3 but 3-4-6." ' What shall I do?'

" 'Why, play 3-4-6,' I said. 'Of course that's what Sweet Jesus wants. Somehow He made a slight mistake and set it right by getting in touch with you.' "

Needless to say it was 3-4-6 that hit the day Mrs. Fauzio played. At the going odds—slightly better than three hundred to one—the winner was able to distribute a sizable largess. Unfortunately, Mrs. Fauzio's visions are rare.

"My mother had 'em all the time," she said. "It was Mom who taught me how to powwow. I don't have her full power, though. The only time she could have given me that was either on Christmas Eve or on her deathbed."

Mrs. Fauzio sighed. "I missed out both times and it's too late now. Mom died a couple of years ago."

26

DESPITE HIS LARGE AND UNQUESTIONABLY PROFitable clientele, Adam J. Romanchik, M.O. (Mayan Order), lives rather modestly in a three-story frame house furnished in what the trade calls "genuine borax." No outside shingle announces the occupant's profession; like many general practitioners these days he is so busy with old patients he has little time and less inclination to try for new ones.

Mr. R. is a slightly tubby, balding gentleman just under five feet, six inches in height. Although he was born, raised and educated in the United States, his diction affirms his Russian ancestry. As a matter of fact, Mr. Romanchik was a third-grade parochial school classmate of Mrs. Apfelbaum.

Mr. Romanchik's afternoon guests, in addition to Mrs. Fauzio, Mrs. Apfelbaum and me, included the peripatetic

Mrs. Dougherty, still hoping to find a powwower who would reduce the swelling of her ankles and banish the warts from her hand.

Our host ushered the four of us into his tiny, tile-paneled, second-floor study and shut the door firmly. Even before any of us sat down the Professor pointed to a small brown silk bag fastened to the wall above the door.

"Do youse see that?" he asked. We nodded. "O.K., then. Very special bag; very high-powered stuff inside. Whatever diseases any of youse have, whatever curses, hexes or spells any enemy put on any of youse, youse'r free from as long as youse'r here and that bag's there."

After this comforting statement he paused; watched our reactions carefully (they were all favorable, of course), then added, "This room is soundproof."

I thought this last was a kind of *non sequitur* but my companions took it in stride and happily nodded their heads in unison.

"Which of youse'd like a readin' first?" the Professor asked as soon as the ladies were seated. Because of the limited number of chairs and space to put them in, I stood in a corner, my back against the door, a vantage point from which I could overlook the entire proceedings.

To the Professor's gracious offer, Mrs. Fauzio replied promptly, "Me." Our host shifted the lady's chair to the side of a small table directly below two golden wall plaques. Upon one was etched the Twenty-third Psalm and upon the other, the Lord's Prayer.

From the Professor's controlled attitude, there was no way to tell whether or not he was aware of Mrs. Fauzio's concealed forces. However, I do not think it unreasonable to assume he must have been conscious of the fact that another set of potent thought waves were swirling about the cubicle, bouncing against the paneled walls and ricocheting into his own psychic undulations. Besides, this was not Mrs. Fauzio's initial visit with the East Mauch Chunk powwower.

For several moments our host gazed silently into her dark eyes. Then suddenly he turned around and from a lowboy, over which was hung a highly colored lithograph of Jesus, Mr. R. extracted a heavy object about the size of a grapefruit and covered with thick blue velvet cloth.

Still wordless, he carefully placed this mysterious package on the table directly in front of him, seated himself and slowly removed the velvet wrappings. Now clearly visible was a shiny crystal ball.

"Very, very rare," Mr. R. confided, almost in a whisper. "Costs a lot of dough, too. Only one other like it in the whole world."

He glanced around the room, noting his guests' reactions. Apparently pleased by our expressions of awe, he confided further. "The other one's in Brooklyn."

Mrs. Fauzio, completely relaxed on a chair to the Professor's right, waited as did the rest of us for the reading to begin. But Mr. Romanchik was not quite ready. From a drawer in a corner cabinet he pulled out a bright yellow cloth headdress similar to the kind sported by Hollywood sheiks during the Valentino era. He adjusted this so that the material, fringed with baby blue tassels, fell upon the nape of his neck. From where I stood only a large bald spot, in the center of the Professor's remaining gray hair, was visible.

Mr. R. sighed deeply, looked into Mrs. Fauzio's eyes once more, then turned about and gazed into the crystal ball.

"I see a tall, dark man . . . ," he said and at this point, I must admit, my attention began to wander, catching only an occasional phrase—"Youse is too kind and warm-hearted. Your friends often take advantage of you. Youse'll have to go through a bad period before the sun shines for youse onct more."

The subject of this venture into the occult nodded her head vigorously in violent approval of nearly everything Mr. Romanchik said, with the exception of a predicted pregnancy. That drew a look of shocked surprise from Mrs. Fauzio.

Our host continued in this vein for perhaps fifteen minutes, then suddenly began to pray in four different languages—Hebrew, Latin, Russian and English—all, including his mother tongue, more or less on the fractured side.

Then he rose, picked up a thin paperback book with a torn cover, faced Jesus and, after the fashion known in Orthodox synagogues as "dovening," began to hum passages from the text. At the same time he bent his shoulders rhythmically back and forth at a slight angle while his head moved up and down. I noted that the selected readings were from the *Sixth and Seventh Books of Moses*.

When a half-hour of this gibberish was over, Mr. Romanchik made the sign of the cross three times and stood erect, a beatific smile on his lips.

"Youse'll never believe it," he said, as if to test our credulity, "but I don't remember a single thing I tole Annie." Then, waving his hand in the general direction of outer space, he added, "It come from way out there."

The Professor's four guests registered appropriate astonishment.

"Took me a long time to learn the stuff. Very hard on the mind. Tires youse a lot; big, big strain."

The Professor frowned deeply. He shook his head from side to side as if to emphasize the fact that even now he still suffered from the effects of the great intellectual battle he had fought some years past.

"Look!" he said, pointing with pride to a framed diploma that hung on the wall to the right of and slightly below Jesus' portrait. "MAYAN ORDER" headed the sheepskin in bold black letters. The script that followed announced that Adam J. Romanchik had passed every required subject with high honors and was, therefore, entitled to all the rites and privileges of the organization as attested by the signatory, "Rose Dawn, Leader."

I fully expected that the Leader's headquarters would be in Los Angeles; I was mildly surprised to find that Miss (or possibly Mrs.) Dawn's mailing address and that of the Order was San Antonio, Texas. As we learned a moment later, academic achievements *per se* were not enough to earn prized membership in the Mayans.

"Youse gotta perform at least three miracles before they'll let youse in," Mr. Romanchik said.

I was about to ask our host what his three qualifying feats were but the Professor anticipated me.

"I done so many I lost count," he said, shrugging his shoulders modestly.

"I get lots of help from these here bottles, too," he added, showing us a dozen or more small flasks arranged neatly on the lowboy.

"This here one's for when you're sad," he said, selecting a vial filled with red liquid, "and that one's for special power. And this here one's called 'love oil,' if youse understand what I mean," he added, glancing knowingly at the ladies out of the corner of his eyes.

I asked the Professor how these potions were dispensed—internally or externally.

"Oh," he replied, "youse gotta rub a couple drops on your hands; that's all. Just like youse use dove's blood, youse know."

I nodded sagely.

Mrs. Fauzio, who had to return to her restaurant to serve a group of special guests, stood up. She thanked Mr. Romanchik profusely and complimented him upon his great vision. "Best reading I've had in years," she added. Before closing the door she turned to the ladies.

"Helen," she advised, "let the Professor powwow your swollen ankles; Gertrude, let him do your neck."

With alacrity, Mrs. Dougherty acquiesced and the Professor turned his attention to the retired R.N. But first he carefully re-wrapped the crystal ball and returned it to the cabinet. Then he placed Mrs. Dougherty on the chair vacated by Mrs. Fauzio and began the process of trying for.

Except that his treatments lasted considerably longer and that he prayed in at least four languages (five, if I counted the occasional use of a phrase which sounded to me very much like "Oi Vey!"), Mr. R.'s methodology differed little from that used by his Pennsylvania Dutch colleagues in the hex belt.

In fairness to the Professor I suppose I should add that his laying on of hands was considerably more violent than others I'd witnessed performing the same act, and that he gritted his teeth with passion as he dramatically swept away the pain from Helen's ankles and Gertrude's neck.

At the conclusion of their individual treatments, each

lasting almost an hour, Helen, rubbing her ankles vigorously, and Gertrude, twisting her neck from side to side, admitted that their pains had been lessened considerably.

The Professor beamed.

"Youse'r both positively cured completely right now," he said. Then he added, "If youse ain't, come back again."

Mr. R. thought for a moment.

"Youse wasn't too bad to cure. Tell youse about a feller, a blind man, I powwowed for couple months ago."

We listened.

"Well, a guy from Catasaqua couldn't see nuthin'. Stone blind. Kept goin' from doctor to doctor and all they done was take his money and didn't do nuthin' for him. So somebody recommended me. Well, I powwowed for the man and in three days I got his full sight for him in both eyes.

"Now he's back at work; a welder and that takes good eyesight. Feller was so grateful he give me $8,000."

This was the first time mention was made of any monetary award for the Professor's humanitarian efforts. Mr. Romanchik continued.

"Course I give 'em much more than regular powwowing. That feller and all the rest think it's worth it. What I'm givin' these days is. . . ." For a moment the Professor stumbled over a multisyllabic word but he continued bravely with what sounded like "sickoloremia."

The Mesdames Dougherty and Apfelbaum accepted this confidence with ease but I was puzzled. Our host noted my perplexity.

"I'll show youse," he said, lifting a book from the shelf and handing it to me. "This here's what I mean."

I had time for only a cursory glance at *Cyclomancy, The Secret of Psychic Power,* but that was sufficient to reveal that the Professor had indeed mastered another and even more difficult discipline than he had yet demonstrated.

"How To Move Objects Without Touching Them," "How To Materialize Objects Out of Thin Air," and "How To Acquire X-Ray Vision" were a few of the intriguing chapter headings in Mr. Frank Rudolph Young's text.

"I can do even more than what's writ in that there book," Mr. R. said, and we all registered amazement.

"I can talk to trees and order 'em what to do."

Obviously bewildered, the two ladies and I waited for confirmation of this incredible achievement. The Professor smiled, knowing full well he had ample proof on hand even for the most skeptical.

"Tell you what I mean," he said. "Did any of youse see that pear tree in my yard?"

We shook our heads.

"Well," the Professor went on, "two years ago it wasn't bearin' no fruit and I got upset. So I went over and talked to it very nice, said some prayers and tole it I wasn't satisfied with the way it was actin'.

"The next year it give seven bushel; they was fallin' all over the yard and me and me wife din know what to do with all them there pears. So I had another talk with the tree; tole it that was too much and that we din need more than a bushel or so. I done some more prayin'. Well, this past year what we got was a bushel and a little more. Just the right amount.

"On your way out take a look at the tree and youse'll see what I mean."

Mrs. Dougherty, who had had similar trouble with a couple of her own fruit trees, congratulated the Professor on his crop control.

"Oh, that's nuthin' at all. D'yer know what else I kin do?"

We waited, prepared for almost any revelation except, perhaps, what we heard next. The Professor clenched his teeth and took a deep breath, then exhaled slowly, emphasizing every word.

"I can destroy any man in the world by sayin' oney two words!"

Now we all gasped for breath and clenched *our* teeth. Mr. R. smiled.

"Don't worry," he said comfortingly. "I believe in the Golden Rule. If I done that to somebody, somebody could do it to me."

216

I asked our host if there was any explanation for his remarkable powers.

"Oh yes," he answered. "I'm the seventh son of a seventh son and I was born with a 'veil.' Not oney that, but I got two antennas grow'n out of my forehead. You can't see 'em but they look like those rabbit ears they put on TV sets.

"These here antennas [he touched his forehead] bring in lots of stuff nobody else can see or hear. Give youse a f'rinstance. Couple weeks ago lady from Mahanoy City come to me; wanted to know what number to play. I turned on the antennas and it come back fast—'9-2-7.' That's what I tole the lady to play. Dunno if she played, but it won. Checked on it myself."

The Professor paused before revealing his knowledge of still another discipline.

"Lot depends on what month youse was born in," he explained, "and how good youse know what the stars is sayin'. Now I was born under Jup'ter and Venice and so was me twin brother."

I don't know if I was the only one of the Professor's guests to shudder inwardly at the thought of another Romanchik possessing such great mystic powers. As though he'd read my mind, the Professor added reassuringly, "Me brother hain't got none of the powers I got even though he bees me twin."

This last statement of fraternal duality brought to my mind a number of questions (e.g., order of birth, distribution of antenna, width and breadth of caul, etc.) which I admit I failed to ask. Now, too late, I wonder what the Professor's answers would have been.

There was a timid knock (presumably unastral). The Professor rose, opened the door and whispered something.

"Sorry," he said, turning to us, "but I got some people waitin' for me downstairs."

Mrs. Dougherty, more sophisticated in these matters than either Mrs. Apfelbaum or I, stood up and opened her purse.

"How much do I owe you, Professor?" she asked.

"Whatever youse want to give," he answered promptly. "I usually get at least two bucks."

Mrs. D. handed the Professor a couple of singles and Mrs. A. followed suit. I didn't know what was expected of me but apparently my visit was on the house. Mr. Romanchik shook his head when I reached for my wallet. "Don't pay me nuthin'," he said affably. "I din do nuthin' for youse."

As we were about to depart from the study, the two ladies and I glanced upward wistfully at the small bag hanging over the door, aware that its protective umbrella soon would cover us no longer.

"Do you have any more like it?" Mrs. Dougherty asked with some hesitation. The Professor shook his head sadly, but then brightened considerably. "I could order one if any of youse want one. Cost ten, fifteen dollars. Very rare stuff inside. But I got an even stronger one than that."

We turned around as Mr. R. held up a yellow sac similar in color, it seemed to me, to the headdress worn during the crystal gazing.

"This one's fifty dollars but it's very, very, very special and terrible powerful. Do any of youse want me to order one of these for youse?"

Mrs. A. and I both shook our heads; Mrs. D. appeared lost in thought.

"I don't want the fifty-dollar one," she said after a moment. "But order one of the ten-, fifteen-dollar ones for me."

Our host smiled. "O.K. But you won't get it for a while. Leeme your phone number and I'll call youse soon's it comes in."

When we got downstairs I noted that three of the overstuffed chairs in the Romanchik parlor were occupied by two overstuffed elderly gentlemen and one rather pleasantly overstuffed young lady, all of whom must have been waiting patiently quite a while for their turns.

"I'll be wid youse in a minute," the Professor told them as he escorted us to the door.

"Chust dake your time, Professor," one of the gentlemen sang out. "We ain't goin' no blace."

We thanked our host, who graciously told Mrs. A. and me to come back any time we wished. Then he whispered something in Mrs. D.'s ears. The lady blushed.

As soon as the door was shut, Mrs. D. turned to me.

"Do you know what the Professor just said?"

I shook my head.

"He told me I'd soon be having a romance with a tall, dark man who looked exactly like you."

Right before we rounded the corner on our way to Jim Thorpe I couldn't help glancing at that pear tree in the Romanchik garden. Stripped of fruit and foliage, it did have a frustrated, hangdog look. Of course, this might have only been my imagination.

27

THE BEST-KNOWN POWWOWER IN THE CITY OF York is Mr. Ervin B. Emig of 1198 Prospect Street, an eight- or ten-minute ride from the courthouse and even less from the residences of retired Judge Ray P. Sherwood, Walter VanBaman, Esq., and the old "Bulldog," Harvey A. Gross.

Prospect is a quiet, tree-lined street in a strictly residential neighborhood. Mr. Emig's house, a modest, one-story frame dwelling with a small, well-kept front lawn, occupies a corner lot. Unlike Professor Resh, whose well-lit sign boldly announces that Hanover practitioner's puissance, his York colleague seems content with an unilluminated shingle not more than ten inches long and a couple of inches wide upon which are painted only his initials and surname. But over the years this small nameplate has proven big enough for the hundreds of men, women and children, second and third generations, in some instances, who have been flocking there every day in the week.

The Professor, a dumpy, gray-haired old man, answered our ring. "Chust zit dahn," he said, and Mrs. Anna Snelbecker, a "stringer" for the *York Dispatch* and other newspapers, and I found a couple of unoccupied chairs in the Professor's crowded waiting room.

At the moment the *braucher* was in the act of dismissing a young mother and her four- or five-year-old daughter, who had just been tried for.

"Bad bellyache and Doris ain't et nuthin' last few days," the mother said to no one in particular as she took a couple of bills from her pocketbook and handed them to Emig; he pocketed them without seeming to be aware of their existence.

"She'll be all right wunst she goes home," he said consolingly. "If'n she don't stop shittin' and start eatin', come back tomorrow. But I think she's good now."

Doris, a meek little girl with long black braids, a child who looked as though she'd have to be carried wherever she was going, clung to her mother's skirt and stopped whimpering. The *braucher* smiled, patted Doris' head gently and her mother's behind with considerably more élan, pushed the pair out the front door and began to try for his next patient.

This was a tall, dark, flat-chested, painfully thin woman aged anywhere between sixty and seventy. "What's the matter?" the Professor asked. "Can't stop menstratin'," she answered, and the *braucher* nodded his head sagely.

"We'll take care of that right away," he said. "Come over to me here wunst. What's your name?"

"Agnes," she answered, dragging herself across the room with a conscious effort. For a moment or two Mrs. Snelbecker and I thought she mightn't make it. Emig led the patient to a corner and seated himself on a straight-backed chair opposite me. He then turned on a table lamp, and stood the woman directly in front of him.

From a shelf, he took a small brown stone about the size and shape of a pullet egg, and with it began to outline Agnes' figure, beginning with her high-button shoes and ending with her little Amish cap. During the ten minutes this took he kept mumbling, or perhaps praying; he then made the sign of the cross over the patient's breasts and turned her around so that she now had her back to him and her face toward me. In this position he repeated the process, concluding by making the sign of the cross over the woman's neck.

The powwower then stood up and whispered something into Agnes' ear. After a moment of silence, he looked at her questioningly. Apparently she wasn't quite sure what to say; she raised her eyebrows, a troubled expression creeping over her deeply lined face.

"Chust rebeat what I chust said," Emig told her and the patient obeyed promptly. He wound up with another sign of the cross.

"How do you feel now?"

She shook her head sadly. "Don't feel no better at all."

"You *will*," he promised, a slight hint of anger creeping into his voice. "Soon as the moon wanes. Chust have faith."

And with that, he edged his patient toward the front of the room, where the pair paused long enough for the woman to transfer a bill and some change from her hands to his. Then she opened the door and stepped out into the warm summer night. The Professor, a look of exhaustion on his round face, shook his head dolefully.

"Still ministeratin'," he said. "Shoulda stopped long ago. She's fifty-two awreddy."

He cast his eyes over the remaining patients.

"All right," he called out, "whose turn's next?"

A fat young woman in her late twenties stepped forward. "Me," she said, and pointed to an ugly growth on her left leg.

"Oh, yes, Petty," the Professor said, "I remember. Feelin' any better?"

"Lots," she answered. "I think the sore's smaller, don't you?"

With a professional air, the *braucher* carefully examined the growth, which ran from Betty's knee almost to her midriff.

"Much, much better," he replied. "Chust a couple more dreatments and it'll be all gone like I said."

The patient looked pleased and so did the Professor.

"Ready, wunst?" he asked. Betty nodded and stood with her back to Emig just as the previous patient had done. At the conclusion of his regular treatment the Professor lightly brushed the tumor, or whatever it was, with an upward stroke of the stone, moving his pudgy hand gracefully into the air as if, in that way, he was banishing some small segment of the growth. Then he made the sign of the cross.

Betty adjusted her skirt, grinned cheerfully, opened her purse and extracted a five-dollar bill which she handed to the Professor. He added this to a fat roll and smiled.

"You chust wait 'til the moon wanes wunst, Petty. You'll see it'll be even better then. Come here after."

There was a temporary cessation of patients. The Professor turned to me.

"You wanted to know how I heal?" he asked, and I nodded. "Well, you seen for yourself how I done it. It ain't easy, though, and I been tryin' for folks since I was twenty-one. I was seventy-six on my last birthday, April 23. Born on a farm in 'ninety down York County.

"Always know'd I had the power—God give it to me—but what I didn't know was how to use it. Went to a powwow doctor in Chambersburg and he learned me good. That wasn't enough. So for ten years I studied the human body and believe me I know what goes on inside a man and woman better'n most people."

The Professor seemed rather pleased with himself. He continued.

"Could tell you hundreds of my cures. People come from all over the world to see me. Last week was a Hytollian lady come all the way over from Italy, and 'fore that I tried for a California lady. That one I done by mail.

"Got a book explains you how to do it. Cost me four hundred dollars but it was worth it. Here, I show you."

Emig walked to a shelf filled with carnival bric-a-brac and extracted a thin volume with a torn brown jacket. I fully expected to see a copy of either *The Long Lost Friend* or the *Sixth and Seventh Books of Moses*.

Instead, the Professor handed me a 1902 edition of *Osteopathic Practice and Psychic Research*, published in Chicago. Inside the flyleaf was the figure "ten" encircled in red, which led me to believe that the powwower either was considerably exaggerating the price he paid for it or had been taken by some astute dealer in secondhand literature. After spending a bit more time in Mr. Emig's company, I prefer the former theory.

"It's not all chust tryin' for," the Professor continued. "Zum people got a spell put on 'em and they need zumbody to take it off'n 'em. Or they might be afraid zumbody's gonna put one on 'em and they need protection fast. That's when I help 'em. Wanna zee how I do it?"

I nodded and he turned around to open a desk drawer. He removed from it a small, unlined pad about three by four inches, costing no more than a nickel even in these days.

"Very expensive paper," Emig said, shaking his head sadly. "Everything's gone up sky high."

I sat waiting for him to continue but he was silent. He studied me carefully from over the top of his rimless glasses.

"Hmmmm," he said after a while. "You got somebody hates you by the name beginning with 'U'? I see somebody don't mean well by you."

I shook my head.

" 'J' mebbe?" Emig questioned hopefully.

I pondered. There was my wife, of course, and an ex-editor of mine; any number of others came to mind, all of whose Christian names began with that letter. I didn't even consider family names.

"Offhand, Professor," I answered, "I can think of quite a few."

"Well, one of 'ems got it in for you and he'll get you if'n you don't watch out. What you need is one of these here 'protection' papers."

"O.K., Professor," I said without pausing. "You never can tell. Better give me one."

"Oh, it ain't that easy," he admonished. "First you got to sit very quiet while I work it out."

I grew silent. After a bit the Professor tore a sheet from the pad, scribbled a few words of fractured Latin and turned it over to me.

"Now," he continued, "write your whole name on the side of the protection paper and hand it back."

"Full name?" I asked.

"Full name," the Professor answered. "Don't use no initials."

I followed instructions. The *braucher* touched his lips to the paper, made the sign of the cross and gave me the paper.

"That'll cost you a dollar," he said promptly, and happily annexed my "freewill" offering.

"Sent six thousand of 'em to the soldiers over in the war," the Professor added. "Not one of 'em got so much as a scratch let alone gettin' their heads blow'd off like the way their buddies standin' right beside 'em was killed."

Emig's front door opened to admit two more patients, both poorly dressed women well into middle age. The Professor told them to "zet don." He turned to me.

"Had enough?" I nodded. Mrs. Snelbecker, who had been taking notes surreptitiously from her corner of the room, thanked the *braucher* and said, "Good night."

He shook our hands; his palms were moist.

"Remember," he said, "any Chee Ice you know in the war or any of your friends need help, chust call on the Professor. All his par comes from Cheesus."

Not everyone in York appreciates the Professor's humanitarianism. Only recently I spoke to a young mechanic who believes that his wife's mental illness, diagnosed as paranoia, is due at least in part to the combined necromantic efforts of Emig and the mechanic's mother-in-law.

"It wasn't only my wife he worked on," reported Edward Fenstermacher angrily, "but that damned old faker told my son, who's only ten, that his mother put a hex on him and he shouldn't even trust her.

"My big problem now is to get Ceil [Mrs. Fenstermacher] out of a Philly mental hospital and keep her and my boy away from Emig and my mother-in-law, who thinks that she's a witch. She rides around the house on a broomstick. The pair of them, Emig and her, were working in cahoots."

Fenstermacher shook his head sadly.

"It's this damned hexerei business; it's ruined our lives and a hell of a lot of other people's lives. You'll find that out if you dig deep enough in York County where they have faith in all that witchcraft crap.

"You got no idea how many powwowers like Emig there are in this part of the state. Just get involved like I did once and you'll see. You can't imagine it unless you get to be a part of the thing. Tell you how it started as far as I was concerned, and went on for a hell of a while before I found out."

Fenstermacher settled back in a chair in my York motel room, lit a cigarette and began.

"Ever since Ceil and I was married, and that was back in 1954, we had mother-in-law trouble. Not the kind you read about in the funnies, although maybe that's where it belongs. No, the kind of trouble we had was different.

"I thought we was doin' all right, Ceil and me. I had a good job at the mill, we made a down payment on a house and things looked pretty good. When we was ready and had some cash put away we figured we'd start raisin' a family. We belonged to the Lutheran church and we went regular.

"But Mrs. Gross—that's my mother-in-law—she wasn't satisfied. Used to come over to our house pretty near every night and tell Ceil and me we wasn't livin' right; wasn't followin' the old customs. I'm a Dutchman myself, and I knew exactly what she meant. I didn't want no part of it and I tole her so."

The mechanic paused for a few moments in deep thought.

"Like once when Ceil was sick I called a doctor, a medical doctor, I mean, to see her. But her mother wouldn't have none of him and when she saw Ceil, tole her she'd never get better unless they called a powwower. She got my wife so upset she really *was* sick. Whether or not they called in a hexer when I was at work I'll never know.

"But that's the way it was all along; me fightin' against superstitions, sometimes winnin' and sometimes losin' and never really knowin'. By this time Eddie was born. His eyes was crossed from birth and, of course, my mother-in-law was sure it was because we was hexed and we wouldn't do nothin' about it. This was tearin' my wife and me apart.

"Well, I took Eddie to an eye doctor and he tole me that when the right time came and Eddie was old enough they'd be able to do somethin'. I was satisfied. I wasn't sure Ceil was but I tried to persuade her this was the only sensible thing to do. All the while her mother's tellin' her the opposite and that we ought to take the boy to Emig."

Fenstermacher lit another cigarette with the butt of the one he was smoking and went on.

"In December of 1965, after all these years of tryin' to keep hexerei out of our house, things sort of come to a head. Ceil had been gettin' worse and worse, torn between her mother and the way she was raised, and me. When Mrs. Gross was in the house she'd side with her, and when she wasn't, she believed me. But that month, right before Christmas, she began to sit around the house, not sayin' nothin', not doin' nothin', hardly movin'.

"It was very bad for Eddie; the poor kid didn't know what the hell it was all about. Try to explain to a nine-year-old boy what was goin' on. You just couldn't; he didn't make no heads or tails of it at all. I didn't know it at the time but he didn't want to understand what I was tellin' him. Unbeknownst to me his grandmother had been workin' on him secretly and so was Emig.

"One night, after my mother-in-law went home, my wife wasn't feelin' too good. She kept beggin' and beggin' me to take her to Emig to prove that I was wrong and her mother was right, and that we did have a hex on us. And oney the Professor could take it off but I had to believe.

"Well, she kept pleadin' so hard that finally, to keep her quiet, I said, 'O.K., Ceil, get your coat on and we'll go.' That's when I found out what had been goin' on for years and where a hell of a lot of my money was spent."

Fenstermacher stood up and paced the floor in anger. Then he continued.

"The minute I walked in I know'd the man was a quack but my wife was so upset I says to myself I'll try anythin' she wants. He was givin' me some crazy line about our bein' hexed and her needin' lots of treatments just like she'd been gettin', naturally without my knowledge.

"Then he lets out he's been tryin' for Eddie's cross eyes and I nearly blew my top. I didn't know Ceil and her mother'd been takin' the boy to Emig for years. I was mad as hell but I didn't say nothin'.

"Well, to make a long story short, I found Ceil had been payin' the Professor four bucks every time she saw him and that was a couple times a week.

"I was so damned mad at Emig, then, I didn't know what the hell to do. But you couldn't say anythin' against him to Ceil or her mother. I don't know how much money he was takin' from us but that wasn't the worst part; he was ruinin' our lives.

"Ceil says I wasn't givin' Emig a fair chance. So I said, 'All right, I'll give him a chance and prove to you he's a faker.' I was hurt in an auto accident back in 1951 and my left leg got a little stiff after it. It never got no better and the doctors tole me it never would.

"Well, I went to Emig without my wife one night and this was oney to please her. The office was filled and I waited my turn; then I asked him to take care of me. He gets out a little stone and starts movin' it over my leg and the rest of my body."

From what he said, Fenstermacher apparently was given Emig's usual treatment.

"When it was over he asks me if I felt the pain bein' pulled away from my leg and I tole him the truth—I didn't feel a damned thing. He shakes his head. 'I think somebody put a hex on you,' he says. 'I'll find out right away.'

"Then he opens up a desk drawer and pulls out a piece of fancy string and tells me to kneel down in front of him. 'What for?' I asks, and he says, 'I'll hold it over your head; if'n it moves, you got a spell on.'

"I done what he tole me and when I stood up he's shakin' his head harder. 'The string moved,' he says, 'you got a spell on you, all right. We'll have to take it off 'fore I can cure for your leg.' I asked him how much he wants and he says, 'Nothin' this time. Come back next week and you give me four dollars then.' "

227

Fenstermacher returned to Prospect Street the following week, went through the same procedures, paid the requisite fee and was told he'd have to keep coming back because "your spell is still workin' against you." But Fenstermacher never went back. His wife, son and mother-in-law, however, kept visiting the Professor.

"By April of 1967," Fenstermacher continued, "Ceil was in very bad shape. She believed every single thing Emig was tellin' her and was sure witches were livin' in the house with us. Well, *I* knew the oney witch that was really there. Finally I got hold of a psychiatrist; he examined Ceil and a couple days later he had her committed to a mental hospital.

"After she was gone I discovered Emig wasn't the only powwower she'd been goin' to. There was a woman named Riggs and one named Betty Smith and an old man named Druck. The whole damned county's crawlin' with witches and it's time somebody did somethin' about them."

Apparently no one, least of all the elected or appointed officials, has the slightest intention of disturbing the necromantic *status quo*. This, witches, *brauchers* and powwowers continue to practice their arts, both white and black, in the hex belt of the Keystone State, giving aid to the troubled, removing spells and "trying for" warts, the liver grow'd, the opnema, the wasting away and mankind's other ailments. Of course, only those who have faith will be benefited or cured. They, like John Blymire, must follow the devil's spoor to its end so that they, too, may cry out in exquisite relief, "Thank God, the witch is dead!"